LAN TROUBLESHOOTING HANDBOOK

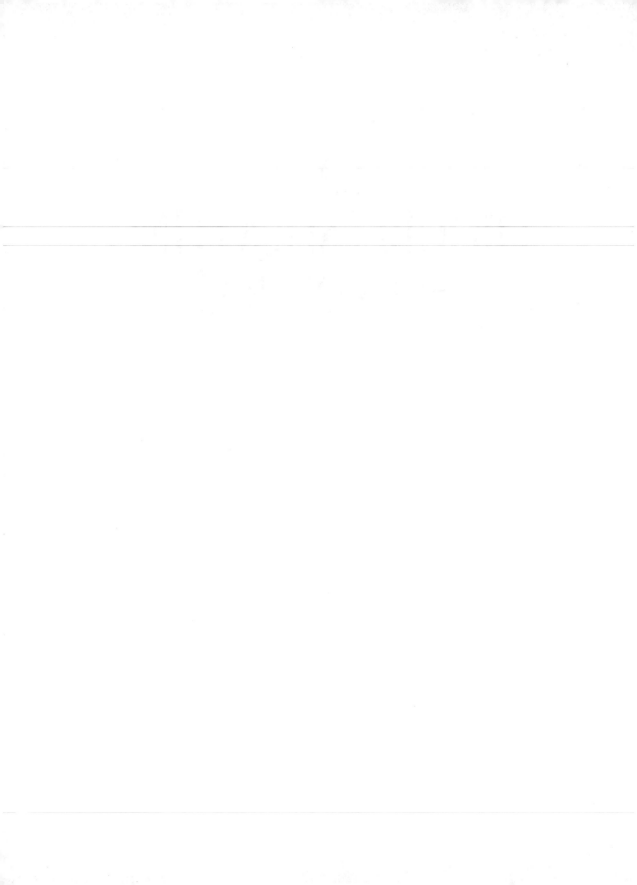

LAN TROUBLESHOOTING HANDBOOK

Second Edition

The definitive guide to installing and maintaining ARCNET, Token Ring,
Ethernet, StarLAN, and FDDI networks

Mark A. Miller, P.E.

M&T Books
A division of MIS:Press
A subsidiary of Henry Holt and Company, Inc.
115 West 18th Street
New York, New York 10011

© 1993 by M&T Books

Printed in the United States of America

Limits of Liability and Disclaimer of Warranty
The Author and Publisher of this book have used their best efforts in preparing the book and the programs contained in it. These efforts include the development, research, and testing of the theories and programs to determine their effectiveness.

The Author and Publisher make no warranty of any kind, expressed or implied, with regard to these programs or the documentation contained in this book. The Author and Publisher shall not be liable in any event for incidental or consequential damages in connection with, or arising out of, the furnishing, performance, or use of these programs.

All brand names, trademarks, and registered trademarks are the property of their respective holders.

Library of Congress Cataloging-in-Publication Data

Miller, Mark, 1955–
    LAN troubleshooting handbook / Mark A. Miller. — 2nd ed.
        p. cm. — (The Network troubleshooting library)
    Includes bibliographical references and index.
    ISBN 1-55851-301-9 : $34.95
    1. Local area networks (Computer networks)—Maintenance and repair. I. Title. II. Series
TK5105.7.M55 1993   93-13289
621.39'81—dc20   CIP

96   95   94   93   4 3 2 1

Copy Editor: Barbara Conway
Cover Design: Lauren Smith Design
Developmental Editor: Cheryl Goldberg
Production: Charlene M. Carpentier

Contents

Preface

It is exciting to be involved in a profession as dynamic as today's computer and communications industries. Since the first edition of this book was written in late 1988, new technologies, such as 16 Mpbs token ring, 20 Mpbs ARCNETPLUS, and 100 Mbps Fiber Distributed Data Interface (FDDI) networks have revolutionized the LAN market. It was, therefore, appropriate to update the information in this handbook to provide details on these new technologies.

A number of vendors assisted with product information and photographs. In alphabetical order, these are: Pantelis Athanasiou, Bob Berger, Ron Bredehoeft, Steve Dawson, Bill Franklin, Andy Friedland, Jon Haase, Christine Jones, Wayne Kaikko, Brenda Kennedy, Gina Kilker, Jeff Lewis, Carl Liebold, Jackie Lustig, Steve McCasland, Mark Mullins, Ken Pimental, Karen Richardson, Jan Shanahan, Carl Siemon, Dick Spingler, Barry Trent, Jayshree Ullal, and Sarah Ushler.

I was also fortunate to be assisted by network administrators and technical experts who provided answers to difficult questions. These included: Juancho Forlanda, Jim Hayes, David Heck, Bob O'Hara, Lori Harmon, Robert Hollingsworth, Bahaa Moukadam, and Bruce Watson.

My editors, Brenda McLaughlin and Cheryl Goldberg, did their usual superb job of keeping the project on schedule. Thanks to the following M&T Books staff members as well: Charlene Carpentier, Meredith Ittner, and Laura Moorhead.

Holly, Nathan, and Nicholas provided their patience once again during the long hours, and Boomer and Brutus were quiet during most of the important times. Support of this magnitude is indeed hard to find.

MARK A. MILLER
April 1993

Preface to First Edition

This book has a very fundamental thesis: how to keep your local area network (LAN) alive. There are three parts to that goal. First, you must understand how the LAN *should* operate if you are to properly define when it is *not* operating. Second, you must have the proper hardware and software tools readily available to troubleshoot problems. Third, you must take preventative measures to keep those failures from recurring in the future.

To accomplish this goal, the book is divided into network generic and network-specific chapters. Chapters 1, 2, 3, and 4 address the generic issues of LAN standards, documentation, test equipment, and cabling. Chapters 5, 6, 7, and 8 address specific issues associated with popular LAN architectures: ARCNET, token ring, Ethernet, and StarLAN, respectively. Also included in the network-specific chapters are examples of protocol analysis of Novell's NetWare, IBM's NetBIOS, DEC's DECnet, and TCP/IP. Chapter 9 concludes with a dose of preventative medicine. Each topic is relatively self-contained to your network.

Today's technology is changing too rapidly for any one person to have intimate knowledge of all available LAN hardware and software products. As a result, I relied on the following experts on specific networks to provide comments on the manuscript. In alphabetical order, they are Bill Aranguren, James Baker, Ernesto Bautista, Dan Beougher, David Bolles, Linda Collins-Hedegard, Billy Cox, Charles Dillon, Michael Fischer, Rich Geasey, Mike Harrison, Kathy Hoswell, Geof Karlin, Gary Kessler, Mark Kulper, Ike Mustafa, Maraget Rimmler, Bob Ryan, Carl Shinn, Jr., Mike Willett, and Scott Zumbahlen.

Recognition is due the companies that provided LAN test equipment for evaluation. Those productions are mentioned throughout the book, but principally in Chapter 3.

No consulting engineer could exist without an expert secretary. Krystal Valdez took many manuscript pages (most of which were written on airplanes) and made them readable. Thank you, Krys, for all the hard work.

The staff at M&T Books worked very diligently (despite an earthquake!) to make this book a reality. Special thanks are due to Ellen Ablow, Brenda McLaughlin, Michelle Hudun, David Rosenthal, and Kurt Rosenthal.

Finally, I owe a great deal to my family. Holly, Nicholas, and Nathan have provided much encouragement and support. Your love makes it all worthwhile.

MARK A. MILLER
December 1988

Why This Book Is for You

The many comments from readers of the *LAN Troubleshooting Handbook*'s first edition have helped me identify the three types of readers who benefit most from this book. I think of them as the scouts, front-line fighters, and field generals.

- If you're a scout, local area networks are a new interest or job responsibility for you and you wish to learn more about them. Although you may find this book somewhat advanced, the tips in it will help you begin to become more proficient.
- If you're a front-line fighter, or LAN administrator, you probably spend a good part of your day fighting for improved LAN performance. This book offers you a thorough understanding of the technologies involved in maintaining your network.
- If you're a field general, or data processing manager, you may be responsible for strategic issues rather than daily operations. The details provided here will help you make those decisions, such as when to choose Ethernet, token ring, or FDDI.

Do you fit into one of the above three categories? Do you need a thorough understanding of LAN cabling systems, ARCNET, Ethernet, token ring, or FDDI technologies? Is your network documentation completed? Do you anticipate the need to install or troubleshoot a LAN in the future? If the answer to any of the above questions is a Yes, then this book belongs in your technical library.

Introduction

When operating properly, local area networks (LANs) are marvels of space age technology, increasing workplace efficiency and productivity. But when they fail, well, you know the scenario. Hundreds of users are without their spreadsheets, documents, or databases. Letters go unprinted, electronic messages go unsent. In short, commerce grinds to a halt.

The cost of even one hour of downtime can be enormous. For example, what if your firm was a specialty mail-order retailer, and you were unable to take orders for one hour? Or one day? How much business would you lose as a result?

This, the first volume in the *Network Troubleshooting Library*, addresses the bottom-line need of LAN reliability. It examines how a LAN should work, the tools required to keep it working, and what to do if it stops working. In particular, the *LAN Troubleshooting Handbook* primarily addresses hardware issues. Other titles in the *Network Troubleshooting Library* address software and network management. In short, this edition serves as the foundation of your network infrastructure on which you can build applications and internetworking capabilities.

This second edition includes information on new technologies that have emerged in the four years since the first edition was published. These include ARCNETPLUS, IEEE 802.3 10BASE-T, FDDI, and much more.

How This Book Is Structured

This book takes a modular approach to addressing network troubleshooting. The first four chapters discuss issues common to all LANs, such as LAN standards, documentation, test equipment, and cabling systems.

Chapter 1 describes the ISO/OSI model and how you can use it to help with LAN troubleshooting and maintenance.

Chapter 2 offers resources that you can use to document your network. With documentation that lists all available human and technical resources, you'll have all the information on hand to troubleshoot your LAN quickly should disaster strike.

Chapter 3 describes the various types of equipment you can use to test copper and fiber-optic transmission media and power lines, and gives advice on how to assemble your LAN troubleshooting toolkit.

Chapter 4 gives all the basic information you need to troubleshoot your cabling system. For example, it talks about the types of cabling available and the differences between copper and fiber-optic cabling, the effects of crosstalk and noise, and various tests you can use to locate sources of failure.

The next five chapters are devoted to the details of specific networks, including ARCNET, token ring, coaxial Ethernet, StarLAN, twisted-pair Ethernet, and FDDI. Each of these chapters describes the various components of these networks, including network architecture, topology, cabling, hardware components, and the structures of the data transmission frames. Each chapter also gives lots of practical tips on troubleshooting hardware and on using a protocol analyzer to track down data transmission errors.

The final chapter summarizes the information presented into a series of practical tips that you can use to keep any network up and running.

Whether you're brand new to LANs, a veteran administrator, or interested in strategic design issues, the combination of theoretical information and practical tips gives you a great deal of insight into your LAN's operation.

CHAPTER 1

LAN Standards and the OSI Model

In the countless networking seminars I've attended as both a student and a teacher, I've noticed one common thread. The International Organization for Standardization Open Systems Interconnection (ISO/OSI) model is always present, regardless of the seminar subject, title, or duration. The ISO/OSI model is important because it provides a framework for interoperability between networking products. Let's take a brief tour of the ISO/OSI model and apply it to troubleshooting and maintaining local area networks (LANs) (see Reference 1-1).

1.1. A Historical Perspective

In the 1970s manufacturers designed computer networks to take advantage of specific mainframe features. IBM first published its System Network Architecture (SNA) in 1974. In 1976 Digital Equipment Corporation unveiled its Digital Network Architecture (DNA). Other major vendors soon followed, and before long, Burroughs' Burroughs Network Architecture (BNA), Honeywell's Distributed Systems Architecture (DSA), and others were all vying for their portion of the market. These networks, however, shared several characteristics: a proprietary architecture, different protocols, and a variety of interfaces. Some network specifications adhered to industry standards, such as EIA-232, while others were completely proprietary.

A variety of standards organizations have emerged to get these proprietary architectures to interoperate. These organizations include the International Telecommunication Union (ITU), the International Organization for Standardization (ISO), the Institute of Electrical and Electronics Engineers (IEEE) 802 committee, and various other standards committees. These organizations address the computer network and/or communications arena from various perspectives.

The ITU is a United Nations agency that coordinates various international communication standards, including radio, telephone, and computer communication. One ITU committee is the Comité Consultatif Internationale de Télégraphie et Téléphonie (CCITT), whose United States representative is the State Department. CCITT work has led to standards such as V.32, a recommendation for dial-up, full-duplex, synchronous or asynchronous communication at 9.6 Kbps over the public switched telephone network (PSTN); X.25, the interface standard to packet switched public data networks (PSPDNs); and I.431, 441, and 451 for access to an Integrated Services Digital Network (ISDN).

The ISO, which is represented in the United States by the American National Standards Institute (ANSI), defines international standards in a variety of areas. ISO's most notable contribution in the data communication world is the ISO/OSI model.

The IEEE 802 committee has been the principle force in setting LAN standards. I address those standards specifically in Section 1.4.

Finally, a variety of other organizations, both private and government, address specific areas. Examples are the Electronic Industries Association (EIA), European Computer Manufacturers Association (ECMA), United States Department of Defense Military Standards (MIL-STD), Federal Information Processing Standards (FIPS), and common carriers such as AT&T. Appendix A lists the mailing addresses of these standards organizations.

1.2. The ISO/OSI Reference Model

In response to the proprietary network environment that existed during the mid-1970s, in 1978 the ISO began developing a model for computer communication protocols that would allow networks to interoperate. The results of their work were published as the ISO/OSI model in 1984 (see References 1-2 and 1-3). The ISO/OSI model remains the only widely accepted framework for multivendor connectivity. I will consider each of the model's seven layers separately (see Figure 1-1).

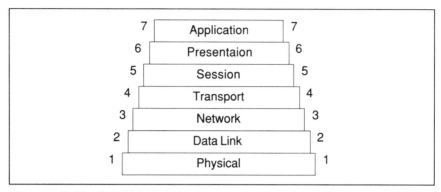

Figure 1-1. The ISO/OSI model

1.2.1. Physical layer

The physical layer describes the physical, electrical, and procedural specifications required to transmit data across the physical medium or cables. In addition, it defines connectors, pinouts, and voltage or current levels. The physical layer deals in units of bits.

1.2.2. Data-link layer

The data-link layer maintains a reliable connection between adjacent nodes, particularly for an error-prone (or noisy) physical channel. Thus, it must package the bits into frames, provide a mechanism for addressing multiple nodes or workstations, and provide error-free, node-to-node connections. The data-link layer deals in units of frames.

1.2.3. Network layer

The network layer is responsible for routing, switching, and controlling the flow of information between hosts. Little network-layer responsibility exists for LANs if there is only one transmission path (that is, only one route). But the network layer is quite important for wide area networks (WANS) or internetworks. Layers 1 through 3, taken collectively, make up the communications subnetwork or subnet, a collection of switching nodes that provide a path for the data packet. The network layer deals in units of packets.

1.2.4. Transport layer

The transport layer guarantees an error-free, host-to-host connection. In other words, it assures source-to-destination (or end-to-end) reliability. In many cases, the communications subnet requires data units smaller than the length of the transport layer message. Thus, another transport layer task is to break up the arbitrary-length message into smaller units, manage their transmission through the communications subnet, and assure their correct reassembly at the distant end. The transport layer and higher layers deal in units of messages.

1.2.5. Session layer

The session layer establishes and terminates communication sessions between host processes. It also manages the session, performing synchronization and translation between name and address databases.

1.2.6. Presentation layer

The presentation layer translates the data format of the sender to the data format of the receiver. Rather than offering communication functions, the presentation layer provides user services, such as code conversion, data compression, or file encryption.

1.2.7. Application layer

The application layer provides protocols for common end-user functions or applications, such as file transfer, electronic mail, network management, or remote database access.

1.2.8. Wide area networks

When a WAN connects two hosts, the ISO/OSI model must include WAN components, as shown in Figure 1-2. Note that only the communication subnet nodes implement Layers 1 through 3, while hosts implement Layers 1 through 7. The transport layer is the first end-to-end layer, assuring reliable host-to-host message delivery.

As noted earlier, a great deal of literature is available about the ISO/OSI model, all based on the ISO standard (Reference 1-2) and the identical CCITT standard (Reference 1-3). Excellent reference texts include Andrew Tanenbaum's *Computer Networks* (Reference 1-4) and William Stallings' *Local Networks* (Reference 1-5).

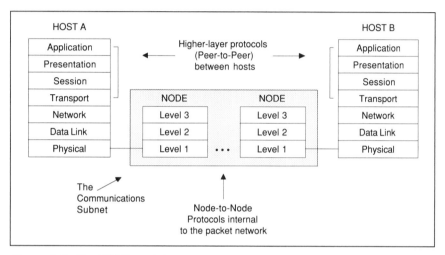

Figure 1-2. The WAN model

1.3. Applying the OSI Model to LANs

Network architecture theory is interesting, but only to the extent that you can use it in practice. To make the theory more practical, you first need to know which layers are implemented in software and which in hardware. In Figure 1-3 you can see that the physical layer (cables, connectors, and so on) is clearly hardware. The end-user layers (transport through application) are clearly software. The data-link layer can be a combination of hardware and firmware, such as protocol handler and memory ICs, that implement software functions, or some other combination of hardware and software. The network layer, when required for WANs, is usually implemented in software; one exception, however, is older electro-mechanical switching systems, which are generally being replaced with all-electronic devices within the PSTN.

Another important question is, Where on the LAN (or the LAN components) can you find these functions? In Figure 1-4, you can see that the cables, connectors, transceivers, and so on, define the physical and data-link layers. The Network Interface Card (NIC) or network adapter resides in the host or workstation. The network and transport layers consist of software drivers specific to the network, such as Novell's SPX/IPX or TCP/IP (more on these in Chapters 5 and 8, respectively). The Network Basic Input/Output System (NetBIOS) is a software interface resident at the session layer (see Chapter 6). Presentation and application layer functions fall to the combination of DOS, the Network Operating System (such as NetWare, OS/2 LAN Manager, Banyan VINES) and the application protocols for file transfer, electronic mail, and so on.

Finally, you might ask, Why should I care? That's easy. Troubleshooting involves making your best educated guess as to the cause of the network failure, and then analyzing that failure. By understanding the functional layers of the ISO/OSI model and its hardware/software implementation, you're in a better position to make your first troubleshooting attempt effective.

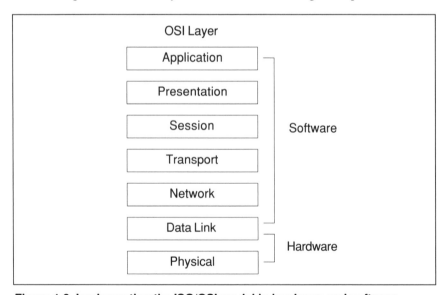

Figure 1-3. Implementing the ISO/OSI model in hardware and software

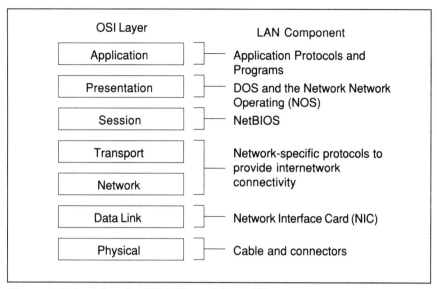

Figure 1-4. Applying the ISO/OSI model to LANs

1.4. IEEE 802 Standards

In February 1980 the IEEE responded to the challenges of the single-vendor, closed-architecture networking environment by starting Project 802. It published its first standard in 1985. The fundamental standard, 802 (Reference 1-6), provides an overview of the architecture. The other standards, such as 802.3, describe specific network topologies. The IEEE family of LAN standards includes the following:

- 802   Overview and Architecture
- 802.1   Higher Layers and Internetworking
- 802.2   Logical Link Control (LLC)
- 802.3   Carrier Sense Multiple Access with Collision Detection (CSMA/CD)
- 802.4   Token Passing Bus
- 802.5   Token Passing Ring

- 802.6   Metropolitan Area Network (MAN)
- 802.7   Broadband Technology Advisory Group
- 802.8   Optical Fiber Technology Advisory Group
- 802.9   Voice/Data Integration on LANs
- 802.10   Standard for Interoperable LAN Security
- 802.11   Wireless LANs

In my discussion of baseband (digital transmission without modulation) LANs, I'll concentrate on 802.3 and 802.5. However, I'll also consider the 802.4 architecture and the 802.2 protocol.

1.4.1. IEEE 802 versus OSI

The IEEE and OSI networking models were developed for different purposes. The IEEE model was developed specifically for LANs; the OSI reference model for computer networks in general. Nonetheless, it's possible to compare the two models (see Figures 1-5 and 1-6). Note that 802.1 is more comprehensive, while the other standards address only the physical and data-link layers. As I discussed previously, these layers handle the reliable transmission of data between adjacent network nodes.

The IEEE 802 standard implements the ISO/OSI model's physical and data-link layer functions in three layers: the physical layer, the media access control (MAC) layer, and the logical link control (LLC) layer (see Figure 1-5). The physical and MAC layers are further specified by 802.3, 802.4, 802.5, and so on; the LLC protocol is global across all 802 networks. The following section summarizes the functions of each layer.

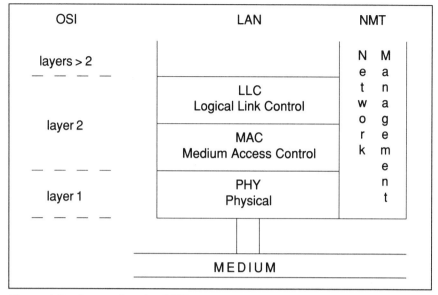

Figure 1-5. Comparing the IEEE 802 Model with OSI

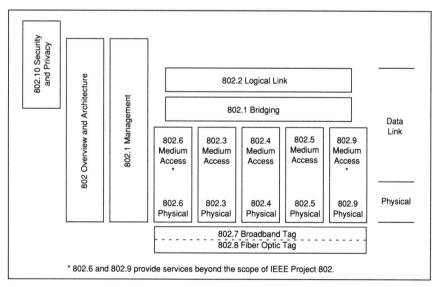

Figure 1-6. The IEEE 802 model

1.4.1.1. Physical layer. The IEEE 802 physical layer is analogous to the physical layer of the ISO/OSI model. Its functions include

- Physical topology
- Cable and connector types
- Transmission rate(s)
- Signal encoding
- Synchronization

1.4.1.2. The media access control layer. The IEEE MAC layer corresponds to the lower portion of the ISO/OSI model's data-link layer. Its functions, which relate primarily to hardware, include

- Logical topology
- Access to the transmission media
- Frame format definition
- Node addressing
- Reliability or frame check sequence

1.4.1.3. The logical link control layer. The IEEE LLC layer is analogous to the upper portion of the ISO/OSI model's data-link layer. Recall from Figure 1-3 that the upper portion of the ISO/OSI model's data-link layer is implemented in software. The LLC layer performs these functions:

- Managing the data-link communication
- Link addressing
- Defining Service Access Points (SAPs), logical interfaces between the LLC and higher layers
- Sequencing (as required)

DSAP Address	SSAP Address	Control	Information
8 bits	8 bits	y bits	8*M* bits

y = 8 or 16
M = number of octets of higher-layer information

Figure 1-7a. The Logical Link Control Protocol Data Unit

1.4.2. IEEE 802.2 logical link control

Since LLC is common to all of the MAC implementations, I will consider it first. The LLC provides a way for the upper layers to deal with any type of MAC layer. The data field of the MAC frames transmits the LLC Protocol Data Unit (PDU), as shown in Figure 1-7a (see Reference 1-7).

The Destination and Source Service Access Point Addresses (DSAP and SSAP, respectively), each 1 octet (8 bits) in length, provide a way to identify a higher-layer protocol destined to receive the PDU. In this way, LLC provides multiplexing over the data link.

The Control field, 1 or 2 octets in length, defines three types of PDUs: Information (I), for the transmission of user data; Supervisory (S), for acknowledgments and flow control of the I frames; and Unnumbered (U) frames that control the data link and permit the exchange of unsequenced data (see Figure 1-7b).

	1	2	3	4	5	6	7	8	9	10-16
Information Transfer command/response (I - format PDU)	0			N(S)					P/F	N(R)
Supervisory command/responses (S - format PDUs)	1	0	S	S	X	X	X	X	P/F	N(R)
Unnumbered command/response (U - format PDUs)	1	1	M	M	P/F	M	M	M		

where:

N(S)	=	Transmitter send sequence number (Bit 2 = low-order bit)
N(R)	=	Transmitter receive sequence number (Bit 10 = low-order bit)
S	=	Supervisory function bit
M	=	Modifier function bit
X	=	Reserved and set to zero
P/F	=	Poll bit - command LLC PDU transmissions Final Bit - response LLC PDU transmissions (1 = Poll/Final)

Figure 1-7b. The LLC PDU control field bits

LLC is modeled after the ISO High-Level Data-Link Control (HDLC) protocol and allows three types of operation: Type 1 (unacknowledged connectionless), a datagram service with no acknowledgments, flow control, or error control; Type 2 (connection-oriented), a virtual circuit service; and Type 3 (acknowledged connectionless), a datagram service with acknowledgments.

The Information field contains the higher-layer information that the software driver downloads to the NIC. Any user information, such as a file being transferred, resides in this field.

1.4.3. IEEE 802.3 Carrier Sense Multiple Access Bus with Collision Detection (CSMA/CD)

The CSMA/CD standard for bus topology networks (see Reference 1-8) is modeled after the original Ethernet network standard developed by

DEC, Intel, and Xerox (see Figure 1-8a). It offers a variety of physical layer options. The nomenclature used in the network designation specifies the transmission rate in Mbps, whether it uses baseband or broadband signaling, and the length of a segment in hundreds of meters. These options include

- *10BASE5*. 10 Mbps transmission, baseband signaling, 500 meters per coax segment
- *10BASE2*. 10 Mbps transmission, baseband signaling, 185 meters per thin (RG-58A/U) coax segment
- *10BASE-T*. 10 Mbps transmission over twisted pairs
- *1BASE5*. 1 Mbps transmission, baseband signaling, 500 meters per twisted-pair segment
- *10BROAD36*. 10 Mbps broadband transmission, 3600 meters per coax segment
- *10BASE-F*. 10 Mbps transmission over fiber-optic segments

Figure 1-8b shows the MAC frame format for 802.3. Chapters 7 and 8 discuss the IEEE 802.3 framing and topology.

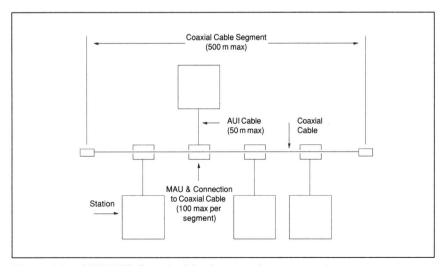

Figure 1-8a. CSMA/CD Standard for bus topology networks

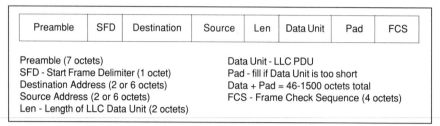

Preamble	SFD	Destination	Source	Len	Data Unit	Pad	FCS

Preamble (7 octets)
SFD - Start Frame Delimiter (1 octet)
Destination Address (2 or 6 octets)
Source Address (2 or 6 octets)
Len - Length of LLC Data Unit (2 octets)

Data Unit - LLC PDU
Pad - fill if Data Unit is too short
Data + Pad = 46-1500 octets total
FCS - Frame Check Sequence (4 octets)

Figure 1-8b. IEEE 802.3 MAC frame format

1.4.4. IEEE 802.4 token passing bus

The 802.4 token passing bus standard (see Reference 1-9), also a bus topology, provides a broadband, deterministic network for applications, such as factory automation, where a probabilistic (that is, CSMA/CD) bus architecture is unsuitable. The token passing bus configuration, shown in Figure 1-9a, results in a physical bus, but a logical ring. In other words, the permission to transmit the token follows a logical ring progression between workstations (designated A, B, C... in Figure 1-9a), regardless of their physical location on the bus cable.

The 802.4 MAC frame format is shown in Figure 1-9b. This physical layer standard includes both single and dual cable broadband systems; transmission rates of 1, 5, and 10 Mbps; and phase continuous or phase coherent

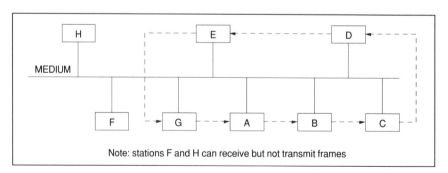

Note: stations F and H can receive but not transmit frames

Figure 1-9a. IEEE 802.4 token passing bus configuration

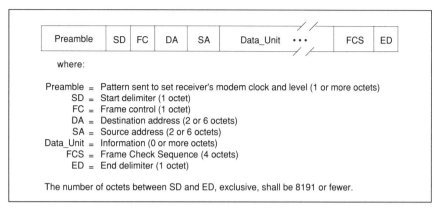

Figure 1-9b. IEEE 802.4 MAC frame format

Frequency Shift Keying (FSK), or multilevel duobinary amplitude modulated Phase Shift Keying (PSK) signaling schemes. The MAC frame format is similar to other 802.X LANs using 2 or 6 octet addresses for consistency. Other elements of the frame formats, such as preambles and delimiters, address specific requirements of that topology.

1.4.5. IEEE 802.5 token passing ring

The 802.5 token passing ring standard (see Reference 1-10) provides for a ring topology, which consists of a closed set of active taps connected by point-to-point links. Workstations gain access to the ring when they receive a token, which is passed in a logical (and physical) ring sequence between workstations. The physical topology is electrically a ring but is wired as a star. Figure 1-10a shows that when a workstation is not active on the ring, it is in bypass mode, thereby maintaining the electrical continuity of the ring. Figure 1-10b shows the 802.5 MAC frame format. Chapter 6 will discuss other token-ring frame formats.

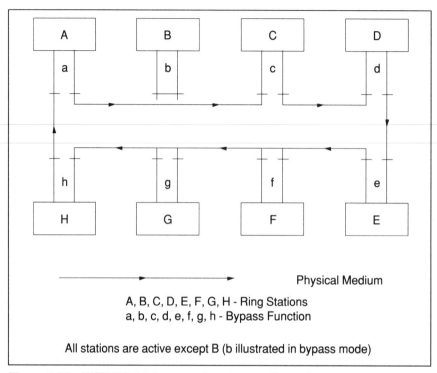

A, B, C, D, E, F, G, H - Ring Stations
a, b, c, d, e, f, g, h - Bypass Function

All stations are active except B (b illustrated in bypass mode)

Figure 1-10a. IEEE 802.5 token passing ring configuration

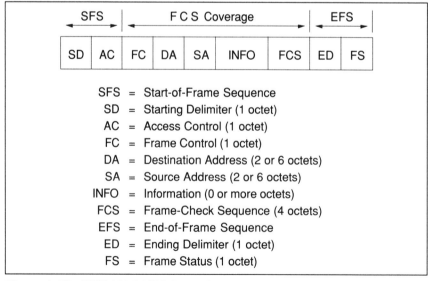

SFS = Start-of-Frame Sequence
SD = Starting Delimiter (1 octet)
AC = Access Control (1 octet)
FC = Frame Control (1 octet)
DA = Destination Address (2 or 6 octets)
SA = Source Address (2 or 6 octets)
INFO = Information (0 or more octets)
FCS = Frame-Check Sequence (4 octets)
EFS = End-of-Frame Sequence
ED = Ending Delimiter (1 octet)
FS = Frame Status (1 octet)

Figure 1-10b. IEEE 802.5 MAC frame format

1.5. ARCNET and ARCNETPLUS

Datapoint Corporation developed and released the Attached Resource Computer Network (ARCNET) in 1977 (see References 1-11 and 1-12). ARCNET, a proprietary architecture, does not adhere to the IEEE family of standards, although topologically it has many similarities to IEEE 802.4. Chapter 5 is devoted to ARCNET and the enhanced ARCNETPLUS.

1.6. LAN Software Standards

One could write volumes about the need for software standards for LANs. The IEEE LAN model considers this issue only within the 802.2 LLC standard, leaving the higher layers (3 through 7) open for specific user applications.

In the early days of LANs, two standards emerged that address Layer 5 and Layer 6: NetBIOS and MS-DOS, respectively. NetBIOS from IBM and Sytek, Inc., provides a way to establish communications links between workstations. The DOS standard from Microsoft includes functions required for multiuser file access. Most manufacturers adhere to these standards today. Other protocols, such as TCP/IP, have implemented Layers 3 and 4. Layer 7 is still very user-dependent. Standards for electronic mail (CCITT X.400) and File Transfer Access Management (FTAM, ISO 8571) are among the protocols defined for these user applications. References 1-13 through 1-16 are examples of recent journal articles discussing LAN operating system software and issues of performance and interoperability. Chapter 6 discusses the various NetBIOS functions, and Chapter 8 discusses TCP/IP.

1.7 References

1-1. Some of the material in this chapter first appeared in "Troubleshooting Local Area Networks with the OSI Model" by Mark A. Miller. *Micro/Systems Journal* (October 1988): 18–25.

1-2. International Organization for Standardization. *Information Processing Systems–Open Systems Interconnection*. Basic Reference Model, ISO 7498, 1984.

1-3. The International Telegraph and Telephone Consultative Committee. Recommendation X.200, *Blue Book,* vol. VIII.4, 1988.

1-4. Andrew S. Tanenbaum. *Computer Networks.* 2d ed., Prentice-Hall, 1988.

1-5. William Stallings. *Local Networks*, 3d ed., Macmillan, 1990.

1-6. Institute of Electrical and Electronics Engineers. *Local and Metropolitan Area Networks, Overview and Architecture.* IEEE Std 802, 1990.

1-7. Institute of Electrical and Electronics Engineers. *Logical Link Control.* ISO 8802-2, IEEE Std 802.2, 1989.

1-8. Institute of Electrical and Electronics Engineers. *Carrier Sense Multiple Access with Collision Detection (CSMA/CD) Access Method and Physical Layer Specifications.* ISO/IEC 8802-3, ANSI/IEEE Std 802.3., 1990.

1-9. Institute of Electrical and Electronics Engineers. *Token Passing Bus Access Method.* ISO/IEC 8802-4, ANSI/IEEE Std 802.4, 1990.

1-10. Institute of Electrical and Electronics Engineers. *Token Ring Access Method.* IEEE Std 802.5, 1989.

1-11. Datapoint Corporation. *ARCNET Designer's Handbook.* Document 61610, 2d ed., 1988.

1-12. Datapoint Corporation. *ARCNETPLUS Design Specification.* Document 51385, September 1992.

1-13. Ken Neff. "Three Hot Network Operating Systems." *LAN Times* (February 18, 1991): 53–73.

1-14. Irwin Greenstein. "Exploring Client/Server Operating Systems." *Network Management* (December 1991): 27–33.

1-15. *LAN Magazine* Staff. "Departmental LANs—Network Operating Systems." *LAN Magazine* (August 1992): 108–116.

1-16. Jim Cavanagh. "Cast Your Network OS Ballot." *LAN Technology* (October 1992): 35–50.

CHAPTER 2

Documenting Your Work

Project managers have a saying, "Once a project is 95 percent complete, it stays that way forever." That's certainly true when it comes to tying up the loose ends of network installation. It's very easy to put off documenting the network until later, which for most of us means never.

2.1. The Network Library

Networks always fail at the worst times, such as when the VP is coming for a visit, or when month-end reports are due. The speed with which you can define the problem, isolate the failure, and repair, replace, or reinitialize the faulty component depends on your knowledge of the network hardware and software. To keep up with this knowledge, you need a library that contains the following types of information: technical resource material specific to your network, a list of human resources (that is, people to call when a problem arises), drawings of the network topology and cable plant, and details of the individual workstations.

2.1.1. Technical Resources

All network hardware and software components come with installation guides. Most of these guides do a good job of guiding the reader through the installation, administration, and maintenance of the network, but some fall short on the technical details of network operation. For that reason, it's often useful to obtain the technical specifications that the engineers used when designing your network hardware and software.

Each NIC includes controller chips that implement the access protocol. Examples include the Texas Instruments' TMS380 token ring controller and the Intel 82586 LAN coprocessor, which is an Ethernet CSMA/CD or Star-LAN controller. The manufacturers of these protocol handler ICs can provide useful hardware specifics. The following is a partial list of firms to call for data sheets on their respective devices:

- *ARCNET.* Standard Microsystems Corp., 516-273-3100 or 800-992-4762; and NCR Microelectronics, Inc., 303-226-9500 or 800-334-5454.
- *Ethernet.* Intel Corp., 800-548-4725; and National Semiconductor Corp., 408-721-5000.
- *FDDI.* Advanced Micro Devices, Inc., 408-732-2400; Motorola, Inc., 602-952-3589 or 800-521-6274.
- *StarLAN and 10BASE-T.* AT&T Microelectronics 215-439-6011 or 800-372-2447; and NCR Microelectronics, Inc., 303-226-9500 or 800-334-5454; Intel Corp., 800-548-4725.
- *Token Ring.* Texas Instruments, Inc.,713-274-2380; and Standard Microsystems Corp., 516-273-3100 or 800-992-4762.

Chapters 5 through 9 provide references for specific devices and documents.

Software developers, including Microsoft Corp., Novell, Inc., Banyan Systems, and others also provide technical documentation on their protocols. Become familiar with these resources and add them to your technical library as well.

If your LAN is part of a WAN, you should consider other reference materials, such as EIA or CCITT standards or AT&T Publications (PUBs) on communication lines. See Appendix A for addresses of standards organizations.

2.1.2. Human resources

When you face a network failure, you can significantly reduce troubleshooting time by calling someone who has already solved a similar problem. Be sure to become acquainted with these resources before a network failure strikes.

Your first line of defense should be to maintain a telephone directory of everyone who has had direct responsibility for any previous installation and maintenance of the network. This list would include personnel from your own company as well as electrical contractors, hardware and software vendors, and network designers or consultants.

Also consider users of networks similar to yours. These people might include your counterparts managing networks in other company locations, or contacts from user groups, trade associations, and so on.

Technical resources are available from network vendors also. Most vendors have a free or low-cost technical support hotline. You can find a wealth of information about both hardware and software in the Computers and Technology section of the CompuServe Information Service. Banyan, IBM, Novell, and 3Com sponsor software forums. Apple, DEC, Hewlett-Packard, IBM, Standard Microsystems, and Texas Instruments sponsor hardware forums. Contact CompuServe at 800-848-8990 or (within Ohio) 614-457-8600 for further information.

Finally, you can obtain a wealth of information quickly by attending seminars, trade shows, and conferences that address the LAN and networking industries. Examples include the Communications Networks Conference (ComNet), sponsored by the World Expo Corp., 508-879-6700; and InterOp, sponsored by InterOp Co., 415-941-3399.

2.2. Cable System Documentation

When you suspect a cable fault, it's critical to have accurate documentation; a crisis is no time to be figuring out which wire pair goes to Nathan's workstation. Therefore, it's important to maintain accurate blueprints of your wiring plan.

For large buildings that use twisted-pair wiring, you should keep an as-built drawing of the cable layout, as shown in Figure 2-1. Because twisted-pair wiring was originally used by telephone companies, its labeling uses telephone industry nomenclature. Label the cables first by number, then by the pair count. Thus, the notation 1, 301–400 indicates cable number 1, pairs 301 through 400. Each unique feeder cable has its own number. Distribution cables that branch off the feeder cables have unique pair counts. Chapter 4 discusses the color codes for these pair counts. Be sure to note wiring closets, along with their room numbers, and any access restrictions, such as cipher locks on the doors. You also need specific documentation for each wire pair, as shown in Figure 2-2. You can document dial-up, intrabuilding, interbuilding, and LAN circuits in a similar manner.

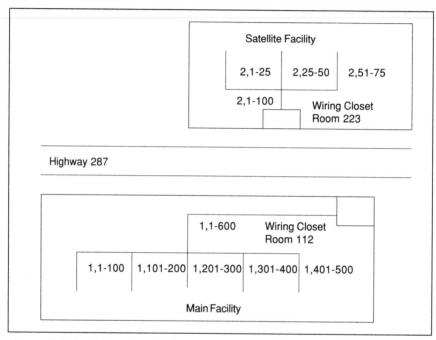

Figure 2-1. As-built twisted-pair cable layout

As with twisted-pair wiring, the easiest way to identify coaxial and fiber-optic cables is with a drawing similar to Figure 2-1 or with a separate notation on a copy of the building's blueprints. Because the cables are not coded and may reside in a common cable tray, however, you'll need additional doc-

Dial-up Circuits

Telephone Number	Station Location	Wire Closet	Wire Block	Cable Pair
555-1212	30K15	22	17	2,224

Intra-Building Circuits

Circuit Number	Modem Location	Pair	Origin			Destination		
			Wire Closet	Wire Block	Cable Pair	Wire Closet	Wire Block	Cable Pair
675-2233	2B07	TX	26	12	1,103	19	7	6,451
		RX	26	12	1,104	19	7	6,452

Inter-Building Circuits

Circuit Number	Modem Location	Pair	Origin			Destination
			Wire Closet	Wire Block	Cable Pair	
AEDG1255	AE13	TX	32	21	5,507	Colorado Springs
		RX	32	21	5,508	

LAN Circuits

Originating Node	Pair	Origin			Destination			Connecting Node
		Wire Closet	Wire Block	Cable Pair	Wire Closet	Wire Block	Cable Pair	
PC1	TX	26	12	1,103	26	7	2,201	Server1
	RX	26	12	1,104	26	7	2,202	

Figure 2-2. Twisted-pair wiring documentation

umentation. One convenient way to document these cables is to use Mini-Tags from Almetek Industries, Inc., in Hackettstown, N.J. (908-850-9700). As you can see in Figure 2-3, the tags come in two parts. The first part is a black polyethylene holder through which you can easily thread the cable. You can place letters and numbers into the holder to identify each cable uniquely. You should use the tags at both ends of the cable, and at any splices, junctions, or transceiver taps that may be accessed in the future. At minimum, identify the origin and destination ("to" and "from") for each cable, plus any additional information you require, such as workstation or server locations. These tags are far superior to adhesive tape labels, which tend to unwrap and fall off with age.

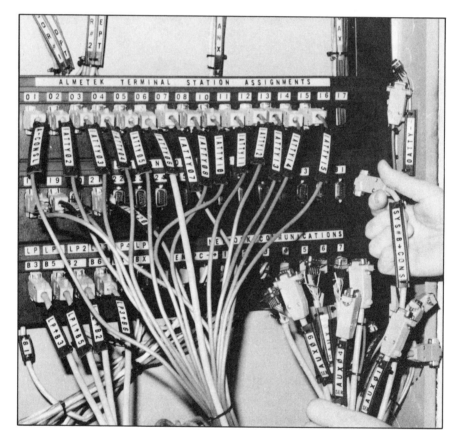

Figure 2-3. Minitags from Almetek Industries, Inc.
(Photo courtesy of Almetek Industries, Inc.)

2.3. Network Topology Documentation

Documentation for the network topology comes in two distinct parts: the physical topology and the logical topology. The physical topology refers to the location of workstations within the building, which cables go inside which walls, where the cross-connect fields or wire closets are located, and so on. Figure 2-4 shows a sample telephone and equipment room layout with a small Ethernet network in an adjacent room.

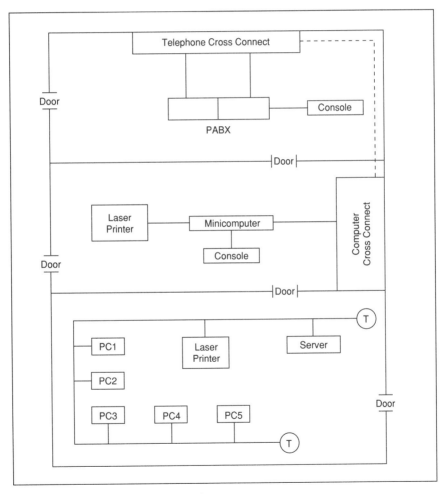

Figure 2-4. Physical network topology

The logical topology deals with which users are attached to which server, as well as the associated user group assignments. If Nicholas calls with a network problem, a drawing similar to Figure 2-5 will pinpoint the server to which he is attached.

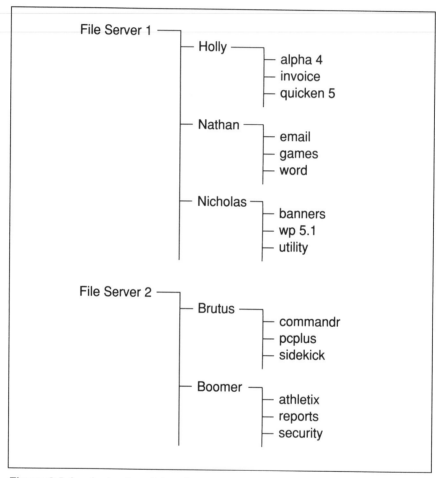

Figure 2-5. Logical network topology

Knowing both the physical and logical connections to the network are invaluable when a network user is unable to access the server. First, you must determine where the user is physically located, then which server the user is logically attached to. Having these details readily available can save a great deal of time

2.4. Workstation Documentation

Each user on the network has unique hardware and software requirements. The workstation documentation should, therefore, cover both hardware and software components.

The hardware section would discuss the workstation and all internal peripherals, such as communication ports or video adapters (see Figure 2-6). Pay special attention to the LAN adapter or NIC, noting the Interrupt Request (IRQ) line, RAM buffer memory location, I/O port address, and node address. For ARCNET networks, you must set the node address manually with DIP switches. For token ring, Ethernet, and StarLAN networks, the address is burned into a ROM on the board, and you use the diagnostic disk that accompanies the board or a protocol analyzer to read it. Reference 3 discusses the use of these two tools.

User Hardware						
Workstation Type	Peripherals	Port	IRQ	RAM Buffer	I/O Port Addr	Node ID
AST 386SX	Floppy (3.5)	A	6	–		–
	Fixed (80M)	C	14	–	1F8	–
	Serial	COM1	4	–	3F8	–
	Serial	COM2	3	–	2F8	–
	Parallel	LPT1	7	–	378	–
	Token Ring	–	2	E000	A20	000093123456

Figure 2-6. Workstation documentation

User Software

CONFIG.SYS
```
SHELL=C:\COMMAND.COM /P /E:512
DEVICE=C:\WINDOWS\HIMEM.SYS
DEVICEHIGH=C:\DOS\SETVER.EGA
DEVICEHIGH=C:\WINDOWS\EMM386.EXE RAM 512 FRAME=E000 I=B000-B7FF
   X=C000-C100
DOS=HIGH.UMB
FILES=40
BUFFERS=20
STACKS=9,256
DEVICE=C:\DOS\ANSI.SYS
```

AUTOEXEC.BAT
```
C:\WINDOWS\MOUSE.COM /Y
C:\WINDOWS\SMARTDRV.EXE
@ECHO OFF
PROMPT $p$g
SET PATH=C:\DOS;C:\XLN\BIN40;F:\LOGIN
SET TEMP=C:\DOS
SET DATAFILES=C:\MAGIC\DATA
REM SFT HPIGC_UTIL=C:\HPIGC\

:IPXODI
CD \NET
CALL C:\NET\LAN
CD \
GOTO TCPIP

:TCPIP
C:\XLN\BIN40\YESNO "Load the TCP/IP Protocol?"
IF ERRORLEVEL 1 GOTO NOTCPIP
SET NAME=KEVIN
SET EXCELAN=C:\XLN
C:\SLN\BIN40\TCPIP
C:\SLN\BIN40\TELAPI
```

LOGIN SCRIPT
```
MAP ROOT W:\SYS:APPS\WP51
MAP S4:=C:\WINDOWS
MAP S5:=C:\HPNET\NETPROG
MAP S6:=C:\
MAP S7:=C:\ALDUS
MAP S8:=C:\PM4
MAP S9:=E:GUPTA
MAP S10:=E:\PB
MAP S11:=E:\SQLBASE
MAP S12:=E:\EXCEL
```

Figure 2-6. *Continued*

```
MAP S13:=D:\TCWIN\BIN
MAP S14:=D:\PROTOGEN
#CAPTURE Q=PROGSI_Q I=1 TI=10 NFF NB NT

#CAPTURE Q=PROGLJ_Q L=2 TI=10 NFF NB NT
#CAPTURE Q=PROCPJ_Q L=3 TI=10 NFF NB NT
DOS SET ID=P_STATION
DOS SET US=LOGIN NAME
DOS SET US=LOGIN_NAME
DOS SET VRN=FULL_NAME
DOS SET SRV=FILE_SERVER
DOS SET USID=USER_ID
#COMMAND /S Y:\SYSTAG\CHECK

WRITE " "
WRITE "****************************************"
WRITE "ENTER [Y] TO LOAD WINDOWS WITH NETWORK"
WRITE " "
WRITE "                    OR "
WRITE " "
WRITE "ENTER [N] TO LOAD WINDOWS WITHOUT THE NETWORK"
WRITE "****************************************"
```

Figure 2-6. *Continued*

You can document user software, including any configuration (CON-FIG.SYS), batch (AUTOEXEC.BAT), or login script files on paper, back it up on a floppy disk, or store it in the user's subdirectory on the server.

2.5. Trouble Reports

Network problems tend to repeat themselves. Therefore, keeping a record of historical difficulties may be useful for solving future problems. You can use a network maintenance report like the one shown in Figure 2-7 for this type of documentation. Make entries for the problem, diagnosis, and any hardware or software components that require replacement. Keep these reports in a notebook for future reference or for use when a change in network administrators occurs.

Failure Date _____

Network User _____ Telephone _____

Network Address _____ Location _____

Briefly summarize the maintenance problem

_____

_____

_____

Hardware or software replaced

_____

Hardware or software updated

_____

Is the problem now completely resolved? _____

Is the network user satisfied? _____

Any other comments?

_____

_____

_____

Person completing this form _____

Date _____ Telephone _____

Figure 2-7. Network maintenance report

2.6. Documentation Tools

As LANs have grown in size and popularity, utility programs have become available to help document your LAN (see Reference 2-1).

One example is ARGUS/n, a LAN documentation and monitoring utility from Triticom (Eden Prairie, Minn., 612-937-0772.) ARGUS/n supports Novell NetWare-based LANs and internetworks, and it produces both hardcopy (Figure 2-8a) and on-screen reports (Figure 2-8b). The monitor screen details the active workstations on the network and the applications that they execute.

```
   --=<< ARGUS/n Hardware Configuration Report >>==--

Report Date: 01/29/93
Report Time: 11:19:01
Report Type: Station listing
Network Segment: 00002001 (Ether1)
Number of Stations: 1
Selection Criteria: None


NAME: BAT    NODE: 000000003B64    NET: 00002001
(Ether1)
MEM01:
MEM02:
MEM03:
MEM04:
DOS Version : 5.0                    Processor   : Intel
80486
Bios Date   : 06/06/91              Coprocessor :
Installed

Base Memory      :   640K              # of diskette
drives : 2
Extended Memory : 7168K        Available Extended
Memory : 0K
EXPANDed Memory : 0K at    0h    Available EXPANDed
Memory : 0K


Floppy Drive A: 3 1/2" 1.44 MB   Floppy Drive B: 5 1/4"
1.2 MB


          Type Cyln Heads Precomp  Ctrl   LandZ  Sect
Size
Hard Drive C:47  1024  10      0      8       0     17
89.13M
Hard Drive D:  No Drive or ESDI or SCSI

Primary Video Type    : VGA w/color display
Secondary Video Type : None
I/O Ports  : LPT1=378h LPT2=3BCh COM1=3F8h COM2=2F8h

IPX/SPX     : V3.10
LAN Driver : NetWare Ethernet NE2000 V1.02EC (890309)
LAN Config : IRQ = 3, I/O Base = 300h, no DMA or RAM
```

Figure 2-8a. ARGUS/n hardware configuration report

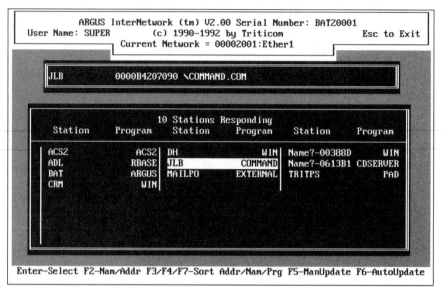

Figure 2-8b. ARGUS/n on-screen report
(Screen shot courtesy of Triticom)

Another tool is the LAN-D/S Lite Documentation Software from Cable Technology Group, Inc., of Newton, Mass. (617-969-8552). LAN-D/S Lite is an AutoCAD application that helps you document wiring and LAN topologies (see Figure 2-9). It produces physical network documentation that you can can store and modify easily later.

Many vendors also offer forms specific to their network product. For example, the forms shown in Appendixes B, C, and D were provided by IBM and AT&T for their customers' use (see References 2-2, 2-3, and 2-4). The vendor of your network hardware or cabling system may provide similar resources.

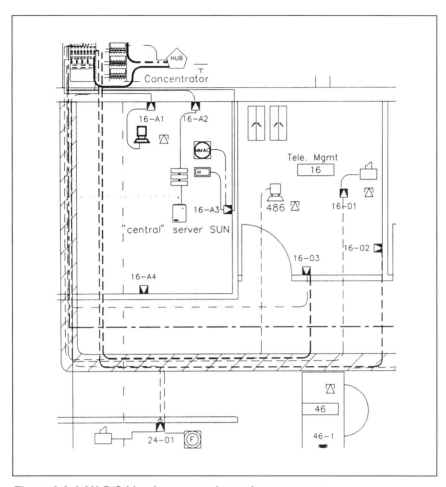

Figure 2-9. LAN-D/S Lite documentation software output

COMPUTERS/TERMINALS

- Micro Computer
- Workstation
- Mini Computer
- Server
- CPU
- PBX
- Terminal Server
- DTE
- Printer
- FAX
- Telephone

OUTLETS

- Standard Outlet
- Standard Outlet with Conduit
- Other Outlet
- Other Outlet with Conduit
- Phone Outlet

COMMUNICATION DEVICES

- Concentrator
- Bridge/Router
- Router/Gateway
- Gateway
- Microwave Bridge
- Media Access Unit
- Multi-Media Access Unit
- Fiberoptic Repeater
- Broadband Repeater
- Local Repeater
- Multi-Port Repeater
- Remote Repeater
- Modem
- Multiplexer

CABLING DEVICES

- Punch-Down Block
- Patch Panel
- Fiber Enclosure
- Component Board
- Equipment Rack
- Equipment Cabinet
- Local Distribution Frame
- Broadband Transceiver
- Broadband Headend
- Broadband Tap
- T-Connector

CABLING DEVICES

- Ground
- Cable Splice
- Cable Coil
- Terminator
- Riser Sleeve
- Plenum Label
- Thick Transceiver
- Thick Transceiver (future)
- Fiberoptic Repeater
- Multi-Port Transceiver
- Cable Changer

CABLE TYPES

- UTP Twisted Pair Cable
- STP Twisted Pair Cable
- Twisted Pair Bundle
- Telco
- IBM Type 9
- Coax
- Thin Ethernet Cable
- Fiberoptic Cable
- Other Cable
- Broadband Cable
- Thick Ethernet Cable
- Jumper Cable

SITE PLAN

- Manhole
- Pedestal
- Utility Pole

Notes:

(1) Eleven pre-drawn communication rack symbols not shown, consisting of combination of 6, 8, 12, 16, and 24 ports of modular, RS232, and IBM connectors.

(2) Four pre-drawn concentrator chassis with vertical cards not shown.

(3) Vertical and horizontal card builder to populate cards and panels as required. Eight connectors available -- mod, fiberoptic, BNC, AUI, DB50, DB25, DB9.

(4) Site plan symbols used only in LAN-D/S.

Figure 2-9. *Continued*

40

2.7. References

2-1. Hurwicz, Michael. "Taking Inventory of the LAN." *Network World* (October 14, 1991) 65-72.

2-2. *IBM Cabling System Planning and Installation Guide*. Document GA27-3361-07, October 1987.

2-3. *IBM Token Ring Network Introduction and Planning Guide*. Document GA27-3677-04, June 1992.

2-4. *AT&T StarLAN 10 Network Hardware Design Guide*. Document 999-120-002, 1989.

CHAPTER 3

Test Equipment for Your LAN

The tools in your troubleshooter's toolkit should include cable system testers, power line monitors, and analog and digital interface diagnostic equipment. While there's no way to offer a comprehensive list that will apply to every network, you can use this chapter as a starting point for assembling your own kit.

3.1. Cable Testing Tools

LANs employ both copper (twisted-pair and coaxial) and fiber-optic transmission media. Because of the vast difference in technologies, I will discuss the tools for testing these cable types separately, starting with copper-based transmission media. The products are listed in this section in order of price, beginning with the least expensive tone generators costing $150 to $200 and ending with the most expensive optical time domain reflectometers costing tens of thousands of dollars.

3.1.1. Tone generator and detector

Tone generators and inductive amplifiers are useful for verifying the continuity of a cable pair or identifying an individual cable pair. The telephone industry has used both of these instruments extensively to trace twisted-pair cabling between cross-connect fields (usually 66-type wiring blocks) in telephone equipment rooms. To identify a cable pair correctly, connect the tone generator to one end of a twisted pair. Use the inductive amplifier to find the other end of the pair. When the other end is located, the audible signal, or tone, can be heard. Figures 3-1 and 3-2 show the Model 77HP tone generator and Model 200EP inductive amplifier from Progressive Electronics, Inc. (Mesa, Ariz.).

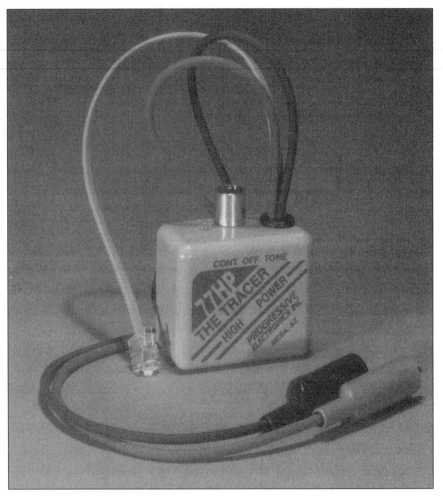

Figure 3-1. The Model 77HP tone generator
(Photo courtesy of Progressive Electronics, Inc.)

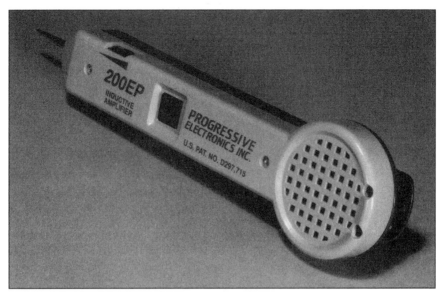

Figure 3-2. The Model 200EP inductive amplifier
(Photo courtesy of Progressive Electronics, Inc.)

3.1.2. Wire testing

In addition to LAN traffic, a building's cabling system may carry voice, burglar or fire alarm, audio or video signals. Thus, it can be useful to have a tool that can test these other systems as well. The Infotest from Leviton Manufacturing Co., Inc. (Kirkland, Wash.) is one such universal tool (see Figure 3-3). This device functions as a tone generator, inductive probe, telephone test set (without dialing capability), continuity meter, and telephone line monitor. When first connected, it scans the line to determine the line polarity, whether it is in use, and whether an AC signal, such as ringing current is present. LED indicators on the unit display these line conditions visually.

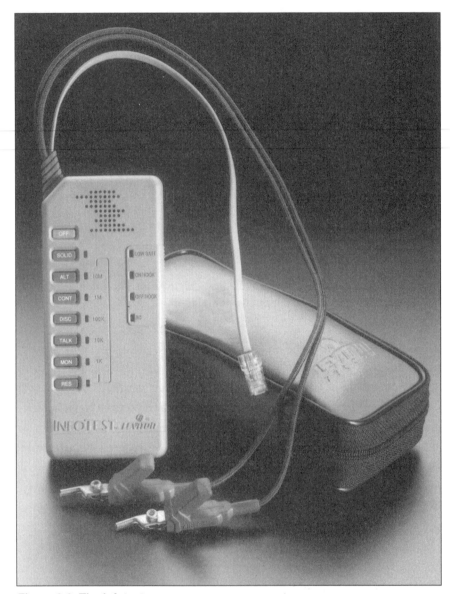

Figure 3-3. The Infotest
(Photo courtesy of Leviton Manufacturing Co.)

3.1.3. Modular cable tester

Modular cables (sometimes called RJ-11, RJ-14, or RJ-45 connectors) are becoming increasingly popular with LANs. International Data Sciences, Inc. (Warwick, R.I.) has designed the Model 84 LAN cable-pair tester specifically for testing modular cables (see Figure 3-4). The Model 84 steps through each pair and determines whether it is good, open, shorted, reversed, or miswired to another pair. Three different jacks on the front panel are wired for different configurations, thus eliminating the need for adapter cables.

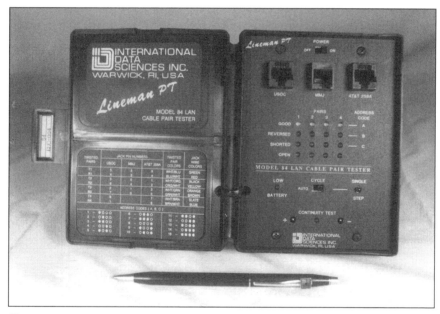

Figure 3-4. The Model 84 LAN cable-pair tester
(Photo courtesy of International Data Sciences, Inc.)

3.1.4. Time domain reflectometer (TDR)

A TDR tests for physical problems such as breaks or kinks in the cable. It operates by transmitting a short pulse of known amplitude and duration down a cable, then measuring the corresponding amplitude and time delay for any resultant signal reflection. Open and short circuits, impedance mismatches, crimps, kinks, and sharp bends in the cable all create unique reflections. Chapter 4 examines cable testing in more detail.

Figure 3-5 illustrates one example of a TDR, the MT350 scanner by MicroTest, Inc. (Phoenix, Ariz.). The MT350 certifies whether new or existing unshielded twisted pair (UTP), shielded twisted pair (STP), or coax will support ARCNET, Ethernet, IEEE 802.3 10BASE-T, or 4/16 Mbps token-ring transmission. The MT350 also tests for open and short cables, cable and terminator resistance, noise level or interference into the LAN cable, and near-end crosstalk (NEXT). It can provide output to an oscilloscope or to a printer.

Figure 3-6 shows a more complex TDR, the Tektronix, Inc., (Redmond, Ore.) Model 1503C. In addition to the standard TDR functions, this device provides a graphical display on the front panel and a strip chart recorder. The recorder allows you to take benchmark measurements of the cable plant when it is first installed; you can use these as a reference when network failures occur.

Figure 3-5. The MT350 scanner

(Photo courtesy of MicroTest, Inc.)

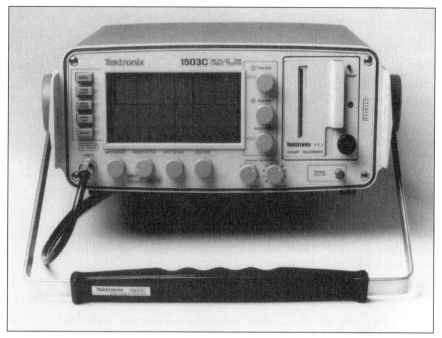

Figure 3-6. The Tektronix Model 1503C
(Photo courtesy of Tektronix, Inc.)

3.1.5. Optical power source and meter

Fiber-optic cables experience problems similar to those of copper media, but optical (rather than electrical) signaling requires more complex test equipment. For example, while there's some room for error with electrical signals, a speck of dust can disrupt optical transmission. Figure 3-7 shows a test kit containing an optical power source and optical power meter from Fotec, Inc. (Boston, Mass.). These tools operate somewhat like the tone generators and detectors discussed earlier; you connect the optical power source to one end of the cable and measure the optical power at the other end. Chapter 4 discusses fiber-optic testing in greater detail.

Figure 3-7. The Fotec fiber-optic test kit
(Photo courtesy of Fotec, Inc.)

3.1.6. Optical time domain reflectometer (OTDR)

OTDRs go a giant step beyond products such as the optical power source and power meter because they can help you pinpoint exactly where a problem in the fiber-optic cabling has occurred. On the other hand, OTDRs typically cost tens of thousands of dollars.

The Tektronix TFP2 FiberMaster OTDR, shown in Figure 3-8, provides dual-wavelength multimode plus dual-wavelength single-mode optical testing. With these two modules incorporated into the unit, you can analyze a variety of telecommunications systems, including LANs, WANs, cable television, and telephone. You can produce hard-copy output via an internal printer; an internal 3.5-inch floppy drive provides mass storage.

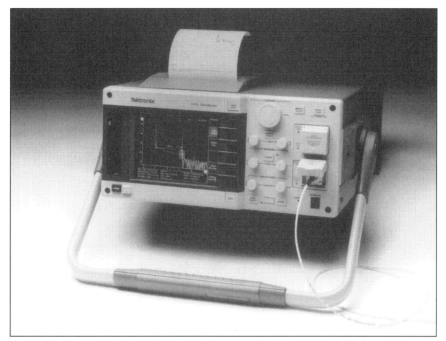

Figure 3-8. The Tektronix TFP2 FiberMaster OTDR
(Photo courtesy of Tektronix, Inc.)

3.2. Power Line Testing Tools

People have written entire books about the damage that electrical transients, surges, and improper grounding techniques can cause to sensitive computer equipment. Rather than detailing power protection per se, I will concentrate on equipment you can use to test for power malfunctions. If you discover a power problem, you may be able to use power conditioning equipment, or you may need to hire an electrical contractor to correct the building's power distribution.

Figure 3-9 shows an easy-to-use device for discovering power problems, the AC monitor from Tasco, Ltd. (Englewood, Colo.). When plugged into an electrical outlet, the AC Monitor indicates the magnitude of the AC line voltage and records spikes, high and low voltage conditions, and power failures. An audible alarm sounds any time a potentially damaging condition occurs.

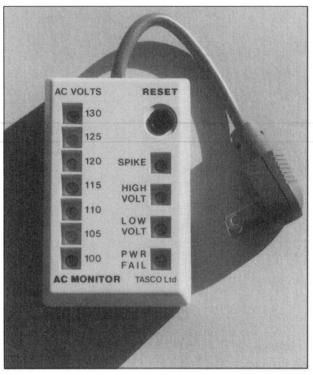

Figure 3-9. The AC monitor
(Photo courtesy of Tasco, Ltd.)

Figure 3-10 shows a more complex device, the Computer Power Monitor, also from Tasco, Ltd. The Computer Power Monitor tests for the magnitude of line to neutral and neutral to ground noise, and tests the electrical wiring at an outlet. Diagnostic LEDs indicate the corrective action you need to take.

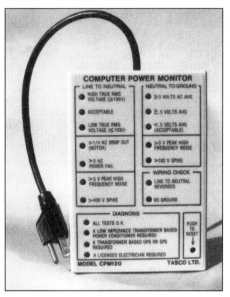

Figure 3-10. The Computer Power Monitor
(Photo courtesy of Tasco, Ltd.)

Tracking down the sources of electrical noise often requires an oscilloscope, which displays signal voltage as a function of time. The Oneac Corporation's (Libertyville, Ill.) OneView Line Noise Viewing Interface, shown in Figure 3-11, offers a convenient interface between the AC line and the oscilloscope. When connected to a two- or three-channel oscilloscope, the OneView displays both common mode (line or neutral conductor to ground) and normal mode (line to neutral) noise. You can identify the sources of electrical noise by selectively turning on and off various appliances, such as printers, coffee pots, light dimmers, radiant heaters, and so on. You can then add power conditioning equipment to protect the LAN equipment.

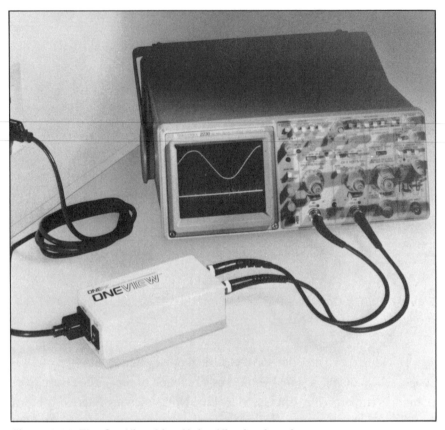

Figure 3-11. The OneView Line Noise Viewing Interface
(Photo courtesy of Oneac Corp.)

For long-term monitoring with tabulated results, you need a strip chart recorder. Figure 3-12 shows the Oneac OneGraph Evaluation Power Monitor. This device monitors both normal mode noise (line to neutral) and common mode noise (line to ground) over either an eight-hour or a six-day duration and produces a strip chart recording for further analysis.

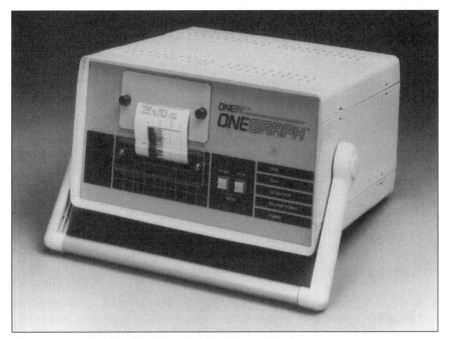

Figure 3-12. The OneGraph Evaluation Power Monitor
(Photo courtesy of Oneac Corp.)

3.3. Analog Interface Testing Tools

Because baseband LANs transmit digitally, it's easy to overlook the need for analog test equipment. For example, you may need to test telephone wiring for modem connections. Three analog testing devices are valuable additions to the tool kit: the volt-ohm-milliameter (VOM), the oscilloscope, and the transmission impairment measurement system (TIMS). Figure 3-13 shows the test points used by analog and power line test equipment.

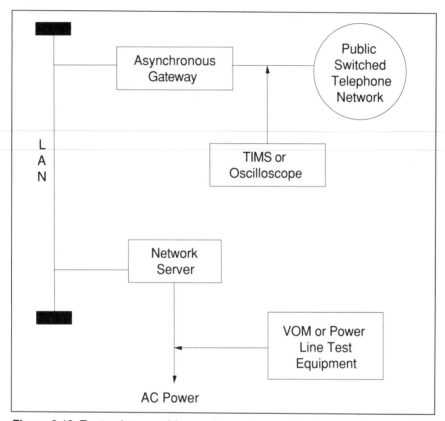

Figure 3-13. Test points used for analog and power line test equipment

3.3.1. Volt-ohm-millimeter (VOM)

As the name implies, the VOM measures potential (in volts), resistance (in ohms), and current (in milliamperes). Typically packaged in a calculator-sized box, the VOM has a liquid crystal display (LCD) and measures the following ranges:

- DC Voltage   200 millivolts to 1000 volts
- AC Voltage   2000 millivolts to 750 volts
- Resistance   0.1 ohms to 20 megohms
- DC Current   200 milliamps to 10 amps
- AC Current   200 milliamps to 10 amps

Figure 3-14 shows the Triplett Corporation's (Bluffton, Ohio) Model 4404 Digital Multimeter. The "digital" in the product's name refers to an LCD digital display on the front panel. Older devices have analog displays.

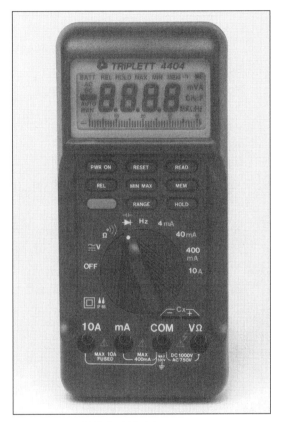

Figure 3-14. The Model 4404 Digital Multimeter
(Photo courtesy of Triplett Corp.)

3.3.2. Transmission impairment measurement system (TIMS)

The TIMS measures analog impairments that may disrupt data communication on telephone lines. TIMS looks at parameters, such as signal-to-noise ratios, line loss, impulse noise, envelope delay, phase jitter, and so on. As Figure 3-13 shows, the TIMS attaches to the output (telephone line) side of an asynchronous gateway or communications server in WAN configurations.

The Triplett Model 5 Loop Tester shown in Figure 3-15 is a portable unit featuring an LCD display.

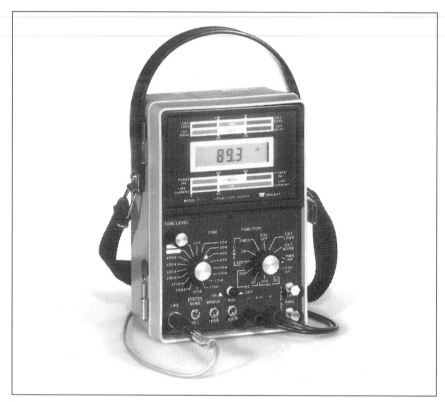

Figure 3-15. The Triplett Model 5 Loop Tester
(Photo courtesy of Triplett Corp.)

3.3.3. Oscilloscope

The oscilloscope is a graphic device that displays the signal voltage (vertical axis) per unit of time (horizontal axis), and as such, provides a true representation of analog or digital signals. You can use it to measure the voltage output of EIA-232 or EIA-422 interfaces and to analyze the noise of commercial power sources. Figure 3-16 shows the Tektronix, Inc. (Beaverton, Ore.) Model 2235 oscilloscope.

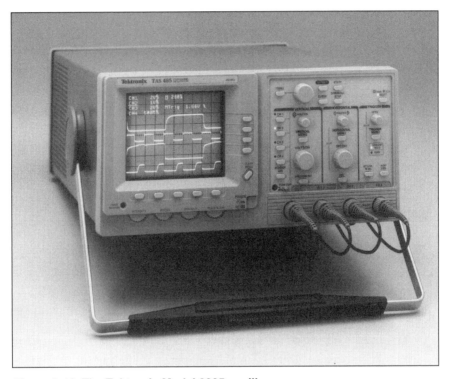

Figure 3-16. The Tektronix Model 2235 oscilloscope
(Photo courtesy of Tektronix, Inc.)

3.4. Digital Interface Testing Tools

The digital (or discrete) signal levels present at the LAN interfaces to PCs, printers, modems, and other peripherals are the test points most familiar to network managers. Figure 3-17 shows a variety of these points and where to connect the different tools. Appendix E shows pinouts for many of the interfaces commonly found on LAN peripherals.

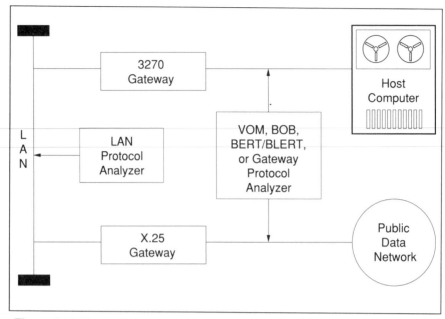

Figure 3-17. Test points for digital equipment

3.4.1. Breakout Box (BOB)

You can use a BOB to display and monitor the status of the EIA-232-D interface leads between Data Terminal Equipment (DTE) and Data Circuit-Terminating Equipment (DCE). A BOB is most useful for its ability to reconfigure the interface by opening a path between corresponding pins of the interface connectors and rearranging the path. In this manner you can use a BOB to configure a null modem cable quickly. The Datatran Corp. (Denver, Colo.) Datatracker Model DT-5, shown in Figure 3-18, is an example of a full-featured BOB that allows you to monitor and reconfigure all leads on the EIA-232-D interface.

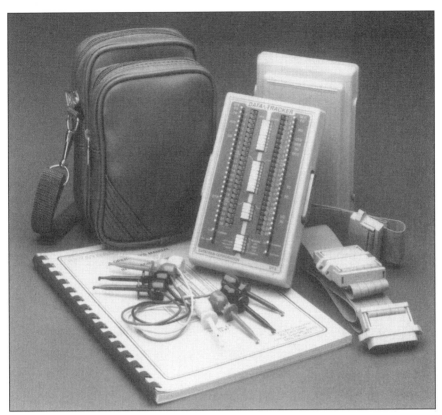

Figure 3-18. The Datatracker Model DT-5
(Photo courtesy of Datatran Corp.)

3.4.2. Serial and parallel interface testing

Some testing applications require extensive analysis of the data itself, not just the interface signals. When you transmit data over a serial connection, for example, you may want to test for data corruption. Datatran's AutoFox (see Figure 3-19) provides these advanced functions. The AutoFox can capture incoming data, analyze it, store it, edit it, then retransmit it. It also performs bit error rate tests (BERT) and block error rate tests (BLERT). The AutoFox includes interfaces for both serial (such as EIA-232) and parallel (such as Centronics and Dataproducts) interfaces, allowing for printer testing as well.

Figure 3-19. The AutoFox
(Photo courtesy of Datatran Corp.)

3.4.3. Smart Cable 821 Plus

IQ Technologies, Inc. (Bothell, Wash.), offers three products that can be real time savers for the network administrator: the Smart Cable 821 Plus, the Smart Data Meter 931, and the Macintosh Smart Cable.

If you've ever tried to wire, say, your workstation to the printer, you'll appreciate the Smart Cable 821 Plus (see Figure 3-20). This device will automatically do such configurations for you, configuring an EIA-232 connection between two asynchronous devices. You use LED indicators to configure three switches that control the internal connections of the SC821. The first switch selects the data leads for either straight through or crossover; the second switch configures the control lines, and the third switch sets the handshaking leads. An additional bank of DIP switches sets other leads required for specific applications. You can thus configure a null modem cable in less than a minute without using a soldering iron.

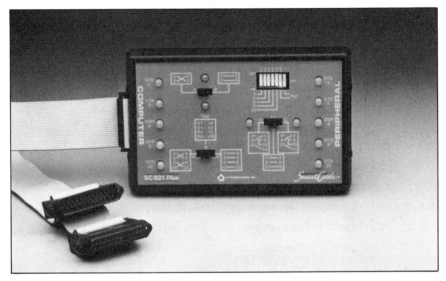

Figure 3-20. The Smart Cable 821 Plus
(Photo courtesy of IQ Technologies, Inc.)

3.4.4. Smart Data Meter 931

The IQ Technologies Smart Data Meter 931 (see Figure 3-21) offers a low-cost, easy way to determine your data transmission parameters. Hook the Smart Data Meter to any EIA-232 compatible device, then command the device to transmit data to the data meter. The data meter's display will provide the bit rate, number of data bits, parity, and number of stop bits. The device can also determine the proper transmission settings for a receive-only

Figure 3-21. The Smart Data Meter 931
(Photo courtesy of IQ Technologies, Inc.)

device, such as a printer, by sending all possible combinations of parameters until it finds the correct setting. This tool makes it relatively painless to determine the proper settings for a server-to-printer interface.

3.4.5. Macintosh Smart Cable

A third IQ Technologies device, the MC600 Macintosh Smart Cable, is the Macintosh version of the Smart Cable 821 Plus. It provides connections between the Macintosh serial port and another EIA-232 port (see Figure 3-22). The Macintosh end uses a DIN-8 connector, the other end has a standard DB-25 plug.

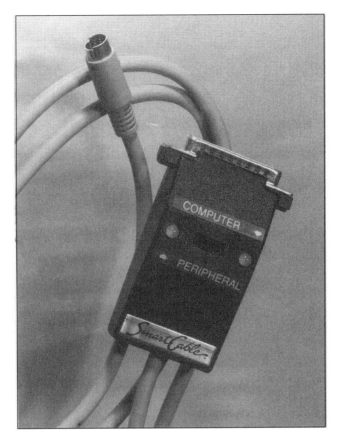

Figure 3-22. The MC600 Macintosh Smart Cable
(Photo courtesy of IQ Technologies, Inc.)

3.4.6. Datatran Micropatch

Figure 3-23 shows the Datatran Micropatch, a compact device that can be used to wire a custom null modem. Once you've used a BOB or a smart cable maker to verify the null modem configuration, you can wire the null modem inside the small (1-1/2" x 2-1/2" x 1/2") Micropatch for direct connection between DTE and DCE, using a minimum of space and clutter. You then close the unit to avoid any accidental disconnections.

Figure 3-23. The Datatran Micropatch
(Photo courtesy of Datatran Corp.)

3.4.7. Interface Converter

Similar in size to the Micropatch, the Interface Converter from B & B Electronics Manufacturing Co. (Ottawa, Ill.) is an economical product that lets you use a piece of test equipment, such as an EIA-232 BOB, to test other interfaces, such as EIA-422, EIA-485, or EIA-530. Figure 3-24 shows the EIA-232 to EIA-422 model converter.

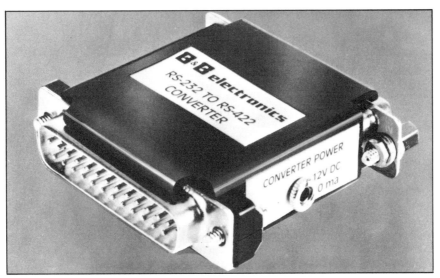

Figure 3-24. The EIA-232 to EIA-422 interface converter

(Photo courtesy of B&B Electronics Manufacturing Co.)

3.5. Protocol Analyzers

The tools I have discussed in the previous sections have all been designed to test hardware, such as cables, the power system, and various interfaces. We now turn to tools that can help solve software problems—protocol analyzers.

As you can see in Figure 3-25, there are two types of protocol analyzers for LANs: LAN protocol analyzers and gateway protocol analyzers. LAN protocol analyzers selectively eavesdrop on all LAN transmissions, allowing you to capture, monitor, and digest frames of information. Gateway protocol analyzers scan output from internetworking devices such as bridges, routers, or gateways to assure their proper operation. For a definitive confirmation of the gateway's operation, you can use both the LAN protocol analyzer and the gateway protocol analyzer to capture the information into and out of the device, then compare the results.

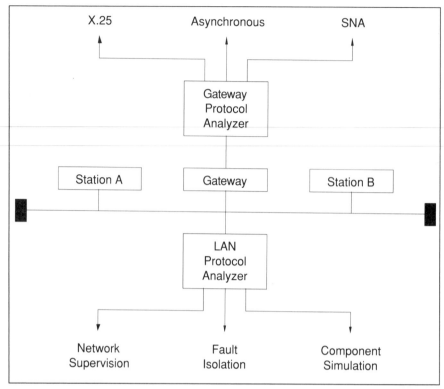

Figure 3-25. Using protocol analyzers on a LAN

Protocol analyzers attach to the LAN just as any other workstation would. They contain a NIC for the particular LAN and attach to the backbone cable. Figure 3-26 shows a representative LAN protocol analyzer, the Distributed Sniffer System from Network General Corp. (Menlo Park, Calif.). Chapters 5, 6, 7, 8, and 9 show examples of frames that have been captured and analyzed with the Sniffer.

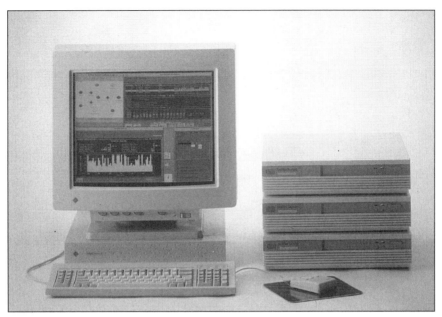

Figure 3-26. The Distributed Sniffer System
(Photo courtesy of Network General Corp.)

Gateway protocol analyzers attach to a digital interface on the output (that is, non-LAN) side of an X.25, 3270, or asynchronous gateway. One example of a gateway analyzer is the Feline ParaScope protocol analyzer from Frederick Engineering, Inc. (Columbia, Md.) shown in Figure 3-27. The Feline ParaScope attaches to a PC via the parallel port and analyzes physical and data-link layer protocols, including X.25, X.75, ISDN, HDLC, SDLC, DDCMP, and BSC.

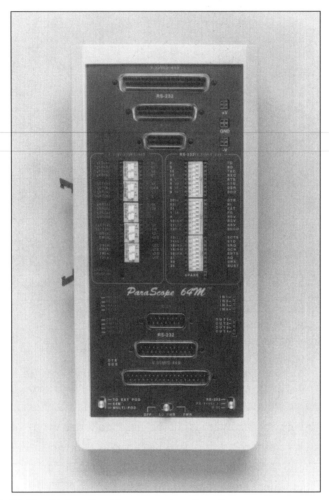

Figure 3-27. The Feline ParaScope protocol analyzer
(Photo courtesy of Frederick Engineering, Inc.)

3.6. Other Useful Tools

Other additions to the network toolkit might include the following:

- *Walkie-talkies*. Easily obtained from Radio Shack stores, walkie-talkies can prove invaluable for tracing cable faults.

- *PC diagnostic software*. Since many network failures are PC-related, programs such as the PC-Technician from Windsor Technologies, Inc. (San Rafael, Calif.) and the System Sleuth from Dariana, Inc. (Cypress, Calif.) can be very useful.
- *Technical database software*. Keeping up to date with all the latest hardware and software options, compatibilities, and potential conflicts can be a real challenge. The Support On Site for Networks from Ziff Communications Co. (New York, N.Y.), is a subscription database containing product data sheets for hundreds of products. It can assist in solving many configuration problems.
- *Network-specific test equipment*. Several devices are available to test specific network interfaces. These include the Fluke 670 LAN-Meter, a token ring network analyzer made by John Fluke Manufacturing Co., Inc. (Everett, Wash.) as shown in Figure 3-28. This device, designed to work with one type of network, can quickly verify operation of a specific hardware component.
- *NIC diagnostic software*. Many NIC manufacturers provide a diagnostic disk with the board. Make sure that you become familiar with the loop-around tests, internal diagnostic tests, and other built-in exercises available on these disks. It is one of the most valuable and timesaving tools.
- *Public domain utilities*. A variety of useful programs are available from public domain and shareware sources for diagnosing data communications problems. Programs included with this handbook are listed in Appendix F.

3.7. Assembling a Toolkit for Your LAN

After seeing this smorgasbord of equipment, you might ask, How can I possibly select the right tools for my network? Here are some guidelines:

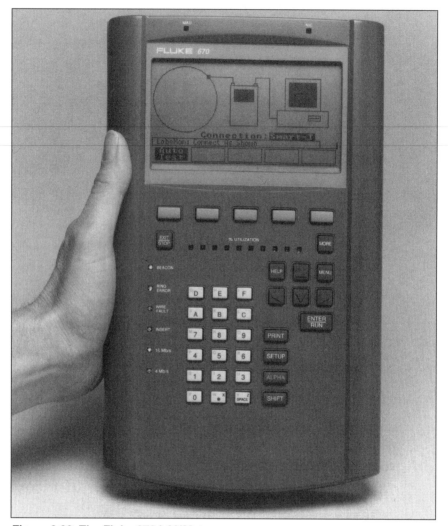

Figure 3-28. The Fluke 670 LANMeter
(Photo courtesy of John Fluke Manufacturing Company, Inc.)

1. Obtain any network-specific tools, such as the NIC diagnostic disk, from the manufacturer. These tools are inexpensive and provide a great deal of diagnostic power.
2. Prepare for cable failures. Surveys indicate that a high percentage of network failures are related to the network wiring. Therefore, have the tools required to test your twisted-pair, coax, or fiber-optic cables.

3. Be able to test the network interfaces. Compile a list of all the various interfaces (EIA-232, EIA-422, Centronics, and so on) on your LAN, and purchase test equipment that can test these points.

4. Consider software analyzers if either multiple LAN protocols or gateways are part of your network. If the network is relatively large (100 or more workstations) or heavily utilized, a LAN protocol analyzer can also assist with network optimization.

5. Make sure that you have an adequate supply of hand tools. A good solution is to purchase a network-specific kit, which contains all the tools that you are likely to use for network installation and troubleshooting. Jensen Tools, Inc. (Phoenix, Ariz.) assembles kits such as the JTK-5 networking toolkit shown in Figure 3-29.

In the next chapter we will begin to see how these tools are used by considering troubleshooting scenarios for cabling systems and LANs.

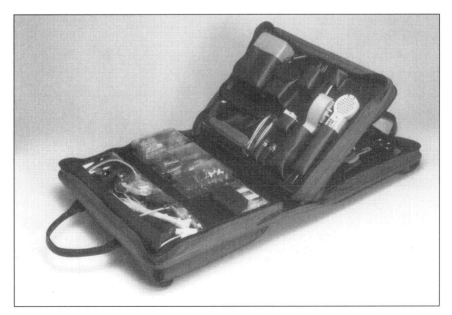

Figure 3-29. The JTK-5 networking toolkit
(Photo courtesy of Jensen Tools, Inc.)

CHAPTER 4

Troubleshooting Cabling Systems

4.1. Transmission Line Fundamentals

The transmission line is the physical medium that carries the electrical signal from a workstation to and from the network server. The transmission line may consist of twisted-pair, coaxial, or fiber-optic cables. Cabling is divided into two general categories: copper-based and fiber-optic media. This chapter begins with copper-based media.

A copper-based (or metallic) transmission line is characterized by four line parameters, known as primary constants. The primary constants determine the characteristics of the transmission line that impact maximum transmission distance, transmission speed, and other physical layer characteristics (see Figure 4-1). These constants, usually expressed on a per distance basis, include DC resistance (R), inductance (L), mutual capacitance (C) and conductance (G). The DC resistance is measured in ohms, the inductance in millihenries, the capacitance in picofarads, and the conductance in micro-ohms.

From the primary constants you can derive the characteristic impedance, Z_0, of the cable:

$$Z_0 = \sqrt{\frac{R + j\omega L}{G + j\omega C}} \quad \text{ohms}$$

Although both resistance and impedance are measured in units of ohms, there's a major difference between them. Resistance measures the opposition to direct current (DC); impedance measures the opposition to alternating current (AC). For copper transmission media, three of the parameters discussed in the previous paragraph are commonly specified: R, C, and Z_0. Chapter 5 of AT&T's *Telecommunications Transmission Engineering* (Reference 4-1) discusses these electrical characteristics.

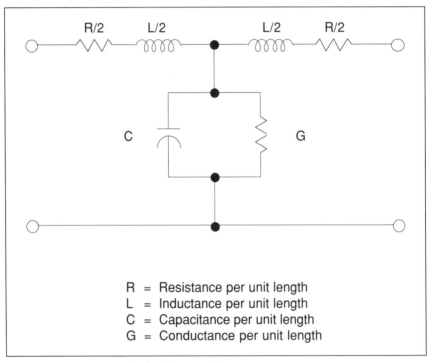

Figure 4-1. The transmission line model

4.1.1. Balanced and unbalanced transmission

Often you'll see the terms balanced and unbalanced used to describe transmission lines. Figure 4-2a shows a balanced line; Figure 4-2b shows an unbalanced line.

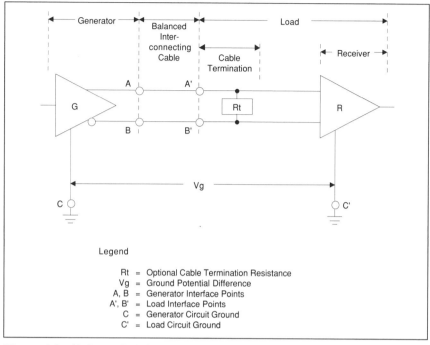

Figure 4-2a. Balanced digital interface circuit

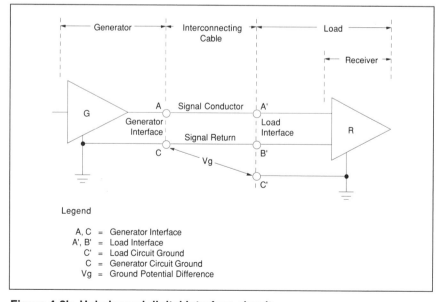

Figure 4-2b. Unbalanced digital interface circuit

In a balanced design (also called differential mode), the currents flowing between the generator and receiver in each of the wires are equal in magnitude but opposite in direction. The voltages in these wires with respect to the ground reference are also equal in magnitude and opposite in polarity. A ground potential difference (shown as Vg in Figure 4-2a) may exist between generator and receiver. Twisted-pair and twinaxial cables are examples of balanced transmission lines.

In an unbalanced design the current flowing from the signal conductor returns via a ground connection that other circuits may share. Both the current and voltage in the signal conductor are measured with respect to this signal return conductor. Coaxial cable is an example of an unbalanced transmission line.

To convert between a balanced and unbalanced transmission line, you use a balun (short for balanced to unbalanced) transformer. To eliminate a length of coaxial cable, you can use a pair of baluns (one on each end of the twisted-pair transmission line) to obtain the necessary conversions from coax to twisted pair and back to coax. Baluns are frequently used with Ethernet and ARCNET networks, since they provide an economical replacement for coaxial cables. However, if you use baluns, make sure that the manufacturer has certified them for your LAN.

4.1.2. Crosstalk

Crosstalk occurs when adjacent cables interfere with each other's signals. A common example is the background conversations you may hear when you're talking on the telephone. Crosstalk results from the inductive (or magnetic field) coupling of one line onto another line. It is most pronounced in cables with bidirectional transmission in the same sheath, such as twisted pair. Figure 4-3, taken from Reference 4-2, depicts crosstalk.

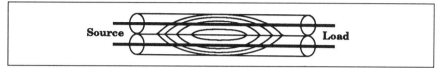

Figure 4-3. Crosstalk
(Courtesy of Trompeter Electronics, Inc.)

Crosstalk is measured in decibels (dB), as follows:

$$dB = 10 \log_{10} \frac{P_{out}}{P_{in}} = 20 \log_{10} \frac{V_{out}}{V_{in}}$$

where P_{out}/P_{in} and V_{out}/V_{in} are the power and voltage measurements, respectively, of the interfered-with and interfering signals. The "log" designates the base 10 logarithm of the power or voltage ratio. For example, a power ratio of 10:1 yields 10 dB, 100:1 yields 20 dB, and so on. When P_{out} is less than P_{in}, a loss results, and this measurement yields a negative value. For example, if the input power was 10 watts and the output power measured 7 watts, the loss would be

$$Loss = 10 \log_{10} \frac{7}{10} = 10 \, (-0.15) = -1.5 \, dB$$

In many cases, a reference power of 1 milliwatt or a reference voltage of 1 millivolt is used as the denominator of the equation:

$$dBm = 10 \log_{10} \frac{Power}{1\ mW} \quad or \quad dBmV = 20 \log_{10} \frac{Voltage}{1\ mV}$$

This yields the values in units of decibel milliwatts (dBm) and decibel millivolts (dBmV), respectively. The interfering (or crosstalk) signal disrupts normal communication from generator to receiver. Thus, it's a good idea to keep the crosstalk signal as low as possible and signal-to-noise ratios as high as possible. The easiest way to do so is to keep the LAN cables as far away as possible from sources of interference, known as noise.

4.1.3. Noise

Noise is any unwanted signal that enters the transmission line from another source and impairs communication signals. Noise is generally classified in two ways: radio frequency interference (RFI) from radio and television transmitters and electromagnetic interference (EMI) from fluorescent lights, arc welders, fan motors, light dimmers, and so on. Figures 4-4a and 4-4b illustrate the effects of RFI and EMI on a transmission line.

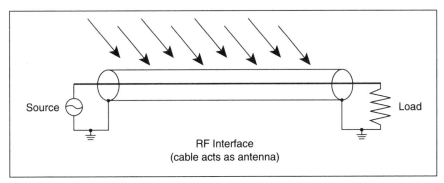

Figure 4-4a. RFI
(Courtesy of Trompeter Electronics, Inc.)

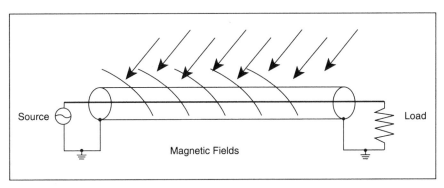

Figure 4-4b. EMI
(Courtesy of Trompeter Electronics, Inc.)

All systems have a built-in threshold of immunity to noise. To measure when noise will begin to disrupt the signal, you calculate a ratio (again given in dB) between the signal and noise powers as follows:

$$dB = 10 \log_{10} \frac{S}{N}$$

where S and N are signal and noise powers measured in watts or milliwatts (see Reference 4-1). This ratio is called the signal to noise ratio.

4.1.4. Effects of crosstalk and noise

In order for the mathematics in the previous sections to be meaningful, you need to relate them to practical LAN applications. The question you need to answer is, How much interference (crosstalk and/or noise) can the LAN cable tolerate before data errors occur? This question becomes even more significant when you're thinking of reusing building wiring already in place.

Because of the intermittent nature of noise, measurements (either as a signal-to-noise ratio or in terms of noise amplitude in millivolts) can be very misleading. Nevertheless, I can make some generalizations.

The ARCNET receiver contains an extremely sensitive filter that passes only the proper frequency (5 MHz) and severely attenuates other frequencies. As a result, ARCNET cabling is extremely tolerant of induced noise, and users have reported that ARCNET cables were able to run next to sources of great EMI, such as arc welders. The IEEE 802.3 and 802.5 standards specify the receiver characteristics, and thus, a minimum receive signal level (measured in millivolts) or crosstalk (measured in millivolts or dB of attenuation). Depending on the particular standard, the maximum noise amplitudes range from 50-300 millivolts. Any interfering signal that exceeds these values could cause data corruption. One tool that can measure these noise amplitudes is the Microtest, Inc. MT350 cable scanner shown in Figure 3-5.

The safest approach, however, is prevention. Keep your LAN cables away from potential noise sources, such as AC power, analog telephones, and so on. By doing so, you'll minimize network maintenance in the long run.

4.2. Standards for LAN Cables

While it may not directly affect network troubleshooting, the type of LAN cable installed can certainly affect the network cost, building code compliance, fire insurance premiums, and so on. In the United States the National Electric Code (NEC), published by the National Fire Protection Association (NFPA), specifies numerous safety regulations concerning the placement of cable in buildings (see Reference 4-3). The NEC covers many types of cable, including twisted-pair, coaxial, and fiber-optic, used for both horizontal and vertical signal distribution. Underwriters Laboratories (UL) has devised tests to certify specific types of cables for plenum, nonplenum, or other uses.

The plenum is the space (usually about two feet) between the false ceiling and the floor above. It is used for circulating warm and cold air throughout the building. Fire codes are quite explicit in stating requirements for any wire placed in the plenum. Plenum cable must pass the UL910 Modified Steiner Tunnel Test. It is certified to be fire resistant and to produce a minimum of smoke. It can be installed in air handling spaces without conduit. Riser (vertical) cables must pass the UL1666 Riser Cable Flame Test and must not carry the fire from one floor to the next. You can install riser cables in vertical runs without conduit. An excellent reference on plenum cable is DuPont Company's (Wilmington, Del.) "How to Specify, Bid and Install Plenum Cable" (Reference 4-4).

4.2.1. National Electric Code (NEC) cable categories

The NEC contains five articles relating to building cables:

- NEC Article 72 covers remote-control signaling and power limited circuits, such as LANS.
- NEC Article 760 covers fire protection signaling systems operating at 600 volts or less, such as smoke detectors.
- NEC Article 770 deals with fiber-optic cables used for data processing.
- NEC Article 800 covers communication cables for telephone, telegraph, burglar alarms, and PBXs.
- NEC Article 820 covers coaxial cables for RF signals, such as those used with CATV or broadband systems.

Of these cable types, Article 725 and Article 800 cables are most frequently used with LANs.

Article 725 cables are divided into two classes: Class 2, rated up to 150 volts, and Class 3, rated up to 300 volts. Each category is further specified for either riser or plenum cable:

- CL2R   Class 2 Riser Cable
- CL2P   Class 2 Plenum Cable
- CL3R   Class 3 Riser Cable
- CL3P   Class 3 Plenum cable
- PLTC   Power Limited Tray Cable

Ethernet transceiver and trunk cables are examples of Article 725 cables.

Article 800 cables were once strictly telephone cable but now include shielded and unshielded twisted pair, as well as coaxial cable. Cable markings are as follows:

- CM   Communications Cable
- CMR   Communications Riser Cable
- CMP   Communications Plenum Cable
- CMX   Communications Cable, Limited Use

Examples of Article 800 cables include the IBM Type 1 (shielded twisted pair), IBM Type 3 (unshielded twisted pair), and telephone cable that you can use with StarLAN and IEEE 10BASE-T networks.

The 1990 NEC introduced a multi-purpose cable type, which includes elements of NEC articles 725, 760, and 800. Cable markings for this cable type include

- MP   Multi-Purpose (General)
- MPP   Multi-Purpose Plenum
- MPR   Multi-Purpose Riser

Building wiring codes may be subject to revisions, updates, and local regulations. Therefore, check the latest standards before planning any network cabling jobs to ensure compliance with any new regulations.

4.2.2. ANSI/EIA wiring standards

As LAN transmission rates have increased, cable manufacturers have tightened their specifications and improved the overall quality of their products. To provide consistency between cable testing and application specifications, the Telecommunications Industry Association (TIA) has developed a series of standards for twisted-pair cabling. These standards are the ANSI/EIA-568 (see Reference 4-5) and related documents EIA/TIA TSB-36 (see Reference 4-6), and EIA/TIA TSB-40 (see Reference 4-7).

The ANSI/EIA-568 defines a telecommunications wiring system— including topological rules, cable types, and connectors—for commercial buildings that products from a variety of manufacturers can implement. Thus, if you've properly planned and installed your cabling infrastructure, you can connect a piece of LAN equipment from any manufacturer to the wiring system, as long as it adheres to these cabling specifications.

The standard allows four types of cables: 100-ohm unshielded twisted pair, 150-ohm shielded twisted pair, 50-ohm coax, and 62.5/125 micron fiber. It defines five categories of cables for unshielded twisted pair:

- Category 1 and 2 are used for voice and low-speed data transmission (not part of ANSI/EIA-568).
- Category 3 is used for voice and data. It specifies transmission characteristics up to 16 MHz. This category is typically used for 4 Mbps token-ring and 10 Mbps IEEE 802.3 10BASE-T applications.
- Category 4 is used for voice and data with transmission characteristics specified up to 20 MHz. This category is intended for 16 Mbps token-ring applications.
- Category 5 is used for voice and data, with transmission characteristics specified up to 100 MHz. This category is intended for 16 Mbps token-ring and 100 Mbps Twisted-pair Distributed Data Interface (TPDDI), or Fiber Distributed Data Interface (FDDI) over unshielded twisted-pair applications.

The ANSI/EIA-568 specifications apply to four-pair, 24 AWG cable having the following color code:

Pair	Color Code
1	Blue/white
2	Orange/white
3	Green/white
4	Brown/white

The specifications also delineate cable characteristics, such as attenuation and crosstalk. For complete details, consult the standards (see References 4-5 through 4-7). A related standard, EIA/TIA-606 (Reference 4-8) considers the documentation requirements for cabling infrastructures. Recent journal articles of interest include Russel Sanders' "Mapping the Wiring Maze" (Reference 4-9); Mark Johnson's "Cable Troubleshooting—Getting Down to the Wire" (Reference 4-10); and Steven Saunders' "Premises Wiring Gets the Standard Treatment" (Reference 4-11).

4.3. Twisted-pair Cable

Twisted-pair cable is the most popular medium for voice and data transmission in the office environment (see Figure 4-5). Twisted pairs get their name because the two wires (or one pair) are twisted longitudinally to minimize crosstalk between the pairs. The tightness of the twisting is referred to as the "pitch" and varies from two to twelve twists per foot. Telephone cables have a lower pitch; special-purpose data cables have a higher pitch.

Data grade or shielded twisted pairs are also used with LANs, principally token-ring networks. The shield reduces interference (see Figure 4-6).

4.3.1. Electrical characteristics

Twisted pairs have four principal electrical characteristics: the gauge of the conductors, which determines the DC resistance in ohms per kilofoot

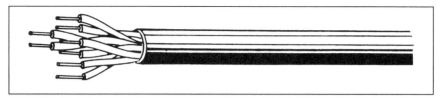

Figure 4-5. Twisted-pair cable
(Courtesy of Mohawk Wire and Cable)

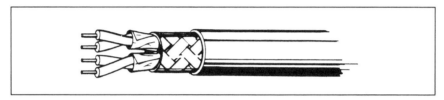

Figure 4-6. Shielded twisted-pair cable
(Courtesy of Mohawk Wire and Cable)

(Kft); the mutual capacitance between the two conductors in picofarads per foot (pF/ft); the characteristic impedance, Z_0, measured in ohms at a given reference frequency, such as 1 MHz; and the attenuation in decibels (dB). Optimum transmission is achieved when the resistance, mutual capacitance, and attenuation of the cable are minimized. The characteristic impedance is determined by the geometry and materials, such as insulation, used in manufacturing the cable and is a constant for a given type of cable.

4.3.2. Twisted-pair color codes

Most twisted-pair cable follows the telephone industry's standard color code, which is based upon a cluster of 25 pairs, known as a binder group. Smaller cables are allowed, and larger cables simply add binder groups inside the sheath, thus yielding 50-pair, 100-pair, 300-pair, or larger cables.

The color code uses five primary and five secondary colors, which yield 25 color combinations when the primary and secondary colors are paired:

Primary Color	Secondary Color
White	Blue
Red	Orange
Black	Green
Yellow	Brown
Violet	Slate

Pair 1 thus consists of a white wire with blue tracer and a blue wire with white tracer. Pair 7 is red/orange, Pair 18 is yellow/green, and so on. These wire pairings must be consistent; that is, two white/blue wires make a pair, one white/blue wire plus one white/green wire do not.

4.3.3. Twisted-pair termination blocks

Most twisted-pair cables are terminated on a modules block that allows easy access to and reconfiguration of the individual pairs. One such termination block is known as the 66-type block, shown in Figure 4-7. The block consists of four columns of 50 pins each, onto which the 50 wires of the 25-pair binder group are placed. Each wire is placed in a pin, then "punched" into place, which strips the insulation. Again looking at Figure 4-7, note that the pins in Columns 1 and 2 are shorted together, as are the pins in Columns 3 and 4. This creates an input and an output side of the block. To connect the two halves, you use bridging (or shorting) clips between Pins 2 and 3 of any particular row.

In addition to the 66-type block, modular blocks, known as the 110-type, and manufacturer-specific blocks are available. Manufacturers of these systems include Mod-Tap, Inc. (Harvard, Mass.) and Krone (Englewood, Colo.).

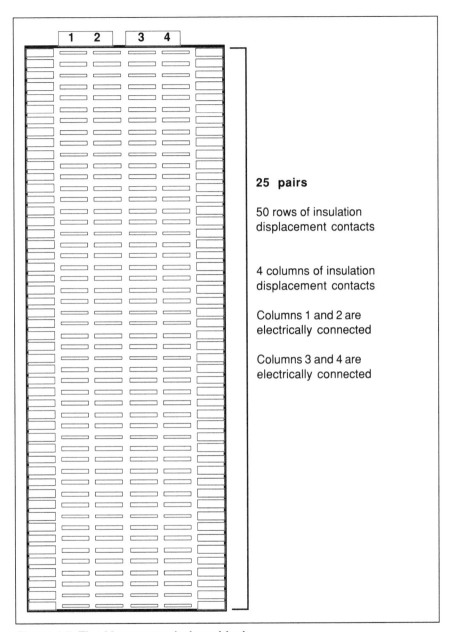

25 pairs

50 rows of insulation displacement contacts

4 columns of insulation displacement contacts

Columns 1 and 2 are electrically connected

Columns 3 and 4 are electrically connected

Figure 4-7. The 66-type punch-down block

4.3.4. Measuring twisted-pair lengths

At some point during the installation, you may need to determine the distance between two points connected via twisted pairs. The easiest way to determine the length of a twisted pair is to measure its DC resistance with a VOM. To do so, connect the VOM leads to one pair, and short the wires at the far end of the same pair together, as shown in Figure 4-8. You can make this measurement either with the cable on the reel, or with the cable already installed. If the cable pair is in place, however, make sure that it does not contain a live circuit. The DC resistance constraints are as follows:

Table 4-1. DC Resistance of twisted-pair cable

Wire Gauge	DC Resistance (Ohms/Km)	DC Resistance (Ohms/Kft)
22	53	16
24	84	26
26	134	41

Record the resistance as measured by the VOM, then divide by the appropriate factor: for example, 26 ohms/Kft for 24 gauge cable. This measurement will be the round-trip distance from your end of the twisted-pair cable to the short and back again. Divide that distance in half for the end-to-end measurement. For example, if a 24-gauge twisted-pair cable showed a resistance reading of approximately 19 ohms when the far end wires were shorted together, that reading would convert to 730 feet of wire. Since this is a round trip distance, the cable actually measures 365 feet.

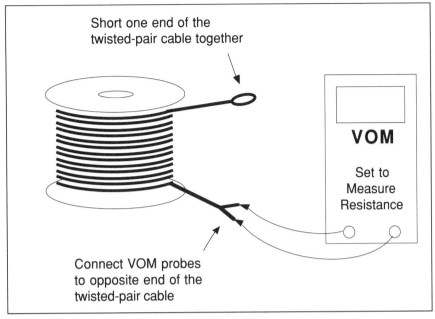

Short one end of the
twisted-pair cable together

VOM

Set to
Measure
Resistance

Connect VOM probes
to opposite end of the
twisted-pair cable

Figure 4-8. Measuring twisted-pair cable lengths

4.3.5. Using modular cords and connectors

Many LANs use modular cords for connections between NICs, transceivers, hubs, and so on. Most networks specify that the cables must have
pin-to-pin continuity; Pins 1, 2, 3, and 4 must be wired to Pins 1, 2, 3, and
4, respectively, on the other end. Some modular cords are not wired straight
through, but instead invert the pins. In other words, Pins 1, 2, 3, and 4 are
wired to Pins 4, 3, 2, and 1, respectively. Make sure that you know the wiring
your modular cord uses. If in doubt, use a VOM or cable continuity tester
to verify. If you assemble your own modular cords, make sure that the modular connector crimp is making a good connection to each wire.

Another challenge associated with the use of modular connectors is determining the correct plug, jack, and wiring configuration for each application. Modular connectors are available in 1, 2, 3, or 4 pair configurations. The wiring connections depend on the intended application and/or the standard specified. Options include the EIA/TIA 568A and 568B, AT&T 258A, Universal Service Order Code (USOC), IEEE 802.3 10BASE-T, IEEE 802.5 (token ring), ANSI X379.5 Twisted-pair-Physical Medium Dependent (TP-PMD), or the DEC Modified Modular Jack (MMJ). Figure 4-9 shows configurations and pinouts for four options. Further details are available in The Siemon Company's (Watertown, Conn.) excellent brochure "The Siemon Guide to Modular Hardware" (see Reference 4-12).

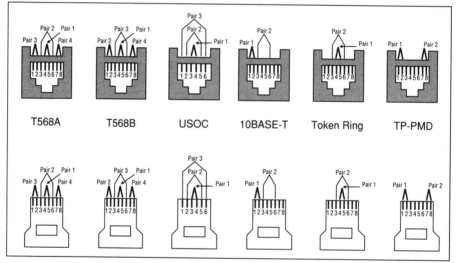

Figure 4-9. Modular Connector configurations and pinouts
(Courtesy of The Siemon Company)

4.4. Coaxial Cable

Coaxial cable gets its name from the center or common axis that the center conductor, shields or braids, and insulating materials share (see Figure 4-10). The shield prevents extraneous signals (noise) from entering the center conductor, and prevents the center conductor from interfering with or suffering from noise from another cable.

Figure 4-10. Coaxial cable
(Courtesy of Mohawk Wire and Cable)

4.4.1. Electrical characteristics

Coaxial cables have five principal electrical characteristics: the DC resistance of the center conductor and shield, measured in ohms per kilofoot; the characteristic impedance, Z_0, at a given frequency such as 1 MHz, measured in ohms; the attenuation, measured in decibels; the capacitance between the center conductor and shield, measured in picofarads per foot; the nominal velocity of propagation (NPV) or speed of transmission relative to the speed of light in a vacuum (C, equal to 300,000 meters/second); and the propagation delay, measured in nanoseconds per foot (ns/ft).

Like twisted pairs, coaxial cables obtain their optimum transmission rates when the attenuation and capacitance are minimized. The characteristic impedance, velocity of propagation, and propagation delay are usually fixed parameters that the system engineers have used to design the transmitter and receiver circuitry. These parameters may also define protocol parameters, such as response timeouts, maximum end-to-end signal propagation delays, and so on.

4.4.2. Coaxial cable used for LANs and data communication

Four types of coaxial are used with LANs:

Table 4-2. Coaxial cables used with LANs

Cable Type	Application	Diameter	Z_0(@ 1 MHz)
Ethernet	IEEE 10BASE5	0.40 inch	50 ohms
RG-58A/U	IEEE 10BASE2	0.18 inch	50 ohms
RG-59/U	CATV, ARCNET	0.25 inch	75 ohms
RG-62/U	ARCNET, IBM Terminals	0.25 inch	93 ohms

Note that RG-58A/U, RG-59/U, and RG-62/U all have diameters of about 1/4 inch. Take care not to mix these up during the installation process.

4.5. Troubleshooting Metallic Cable

Because twisted-pair and coaxial cables share similar types of faults and corresponding solutions, the following discussion of fault isolation will consider both types of cable together.

There are two types of cable problems: faults caused by the connectors, splices, punch-down blocks, terminators, or other mechanical devices; and those caused by the cable itself, such as opens, shorts, crimps, and kinks. Connectors tend to cause more failures than cables. I'll look at two methods for identifying these faults.

4.5.1. Continuity or DC resistance tests

A continuity test measures a DC signal's ability to follow a continuous path or circuit within the cable. Figure 4-8 demonstrated a test to determine the length of a twisted-pair cable. You can use a continuity test to verify the length of a reel of twisted-pair or coaxial cable when you receive it from the vendor. Return any defective spools if you find significant differences between the spool length, which is usually stamped on the reel, and your measured length. Remember that your measurement (when shorting the far ends together) results in a distance calculation of double the actual length.

Cables used with token-ring networks also measure twice the actual distance if you've used a hermaphroditic (genderless) connector at one end. Shorting bars inside the connector connect the Transmit + and Receive +, and Transmit - and Receive - conductors when the connector is separated from its mate. (More about the token-ring wiring in Section 6.3.4)

You can use a VOM to check terminator resistors easily. For terminators in a BNC or N-type connector, measure between the center conductor of the connector and its outer shell. For terminators in modular plugs, measure between the appropriate pins, usually the two pins in the center. Consult your NIC installation manual for the proper terminator wiring. The results you should obtain are as follows:

Table 4-3. Terminator values for LAN cable

Cable Type	Terminator Resistance
Ethernet	50 ohms
RG-58A/U	50 ohms
RG-59/U	75 ohms
RG-62/U	93 ohms
Unshielded twisted pair	100-120 ohms
Shielded twisted pair	150 ohms

Figure 4-11a shows an Ethernet cable with 50-ohm terminators attached, and an access point (either transceiver tap or BNC T connector) identified. If you make a resistance measurement at the access point, you should obtain a value close to 25 ohms. Remember that this is DC ohms (resistance), not AC ohms (impedance). If the DC resistance is much different from 25 ohms (for example, 60 ohms), then one end of the cable is not properly terminated. The reason is evident from the equivalent circuit in Figure 4-11b. When properly installed in parallel, the two terminators will measure approximately 25 ohms.

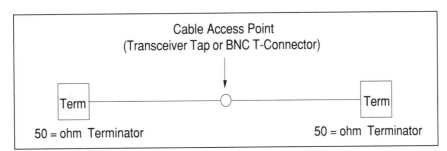

Figure 4-11a. Measuring Ethernet terminators

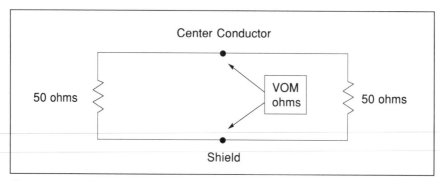

Figure 4-11b. Ethernet cable equivalent circuit

4.5.2. TDR tests

A TDR is a combination pulse generator, voltage sampler, and output amplifier, supplying readings on a display or an oscilloscope. A TDR's operation is similar to radar. It transmits an electrical pulse of known amplitude and duration from one end of the cable. Any changes in the cable's characteristic impedance will cause reflections of the transmitted pulse. If no cable faults exist, and the cable is terminated at the far end, its characteristic impedance (Z_0) will occur.

A variety of cable problems, such as shorts, opens, faulty or improper terminations, kinks, bends, crimps, shorted taps, or impedance mismatches (from mixing different types of coaxial cable) produce a unique signal reflection, known as a TDR fault signature. References 4-13 and 4-14 discuss these technical details in greater depth and illustrate various cable faults that you can diagnose using the Tektronix, Inc., metallic TDRs. Figure 4-12 shows some representative cable faults and associated TDR outputs.

Another TDR, the cable scanner from MicroTest, Inc., which was discussed in Chapter 3, is a microprocessor-based unit that includes several helpful features for cable testing. The cable scanner adds and then measures ambient noise on the cable to help you determine whether crosstalk or noise problems are likely to occur. It also traces the location of existing cable within walls, floors, or ceilings. And finally, it offers various measurements of network activity. See Section 3.1.4 for further details.

When using a TDR to test ARCNET, token-ring, StarLAN, and IEEE 10BASE-T networks, which all use a distributed-star topology, it's best to isolate and deactivate a specific segment. You can, however, use a TDR on a live Ethernet if you use a very short pulse (less than 10 nanosecond duration), and if that pulse is of a negative polarity. Don't use positive pulse TDRs, since they can affect transceiver operation.

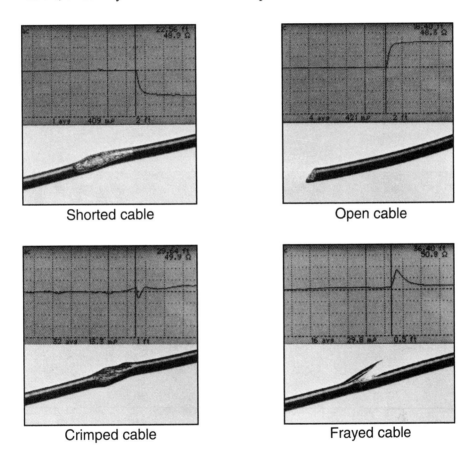

Shorted cable   Open cable

Crimped cable   Frayed cable

Figure 4-12. TDR signatures for various cable faults

(Photo courtesy of Tektronix, Inc.)

4.6. Fiber-optic Cable

The past decade witnessed considerable growth in both LANs and fiber-optic communication. The user has realized many advantages from the marriage of these two technologies. Because optical fibers emit no radiation, they are immune from the typical EMI and RFI that plague many LAN installations. Fiber-optic cables allow ground isolation between buildings, since the material used for the fiber cable, typically silica, is a nonconductor. The small size and light weight of fiber is useful in many installations; for example, you can run far more fiber-optic cables than coax above a false ceiling. And the high bandwidth, hundreds of Mbps, guarantees against the obsolescence of your cable system. Figure 4-13 shows examples of fiber-optic cables. I'll begin by investigating the physical characteristics of fiber-optic transmission.

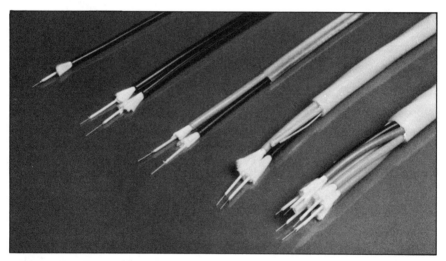

Figure 4-13. Fiber-optic cable
(Photo courtesy of Belden/Cooper Industries, Inc.)

4.6.1. Fiber-optic transmission characteristics

Figure 4-14 illustrates a simple fiber-optic link, which is described in greater detail in Reference 4-15. The input signal in the transmitter drives an optical source, which can be either a laser diode or an LED. The optical source operates in the infrared spectrum, emitting light in one of three wavelength ranges: 800-900 nanometers (nm), 1100-1300 nm, and around 1500 nm. The optical source and cable provide optimum transmission in one of these three ranges.

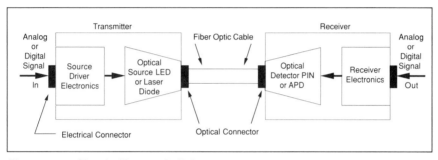

Figure 4-14. Simple fiber-optic link
(Photo courtesy of Belden/Cooper Industries, Inc.)

An optical detector in the receiver, which consists of either a positive-intrinsic-negative (PIN) diode or an avalanche photodiode (APD), captures the light pulses and hands them off to the electronic receiver circuitry. The optical transmission link in between is point-to-point.

This discussion will concentrate on the transmission link. Figure 4-15 illustrates the three types of fiber-optic transmission: single index (monomode); graded index (multimode); and step index (multimode). In single mode (or monomode) applications, light travels along a single path. Monomode cables are used for applications requiring extremely high data rates, such as long-distance telephone transmission. Multimode cables contain many different light rays, and can be step index or graded index. In step index cable, a dramatic change occurs between the core and cladding's index of refraction. In graded index, a more gradual change occurs. The step index cable yields a zigzag light pattern; the graded index bends light more gradually.

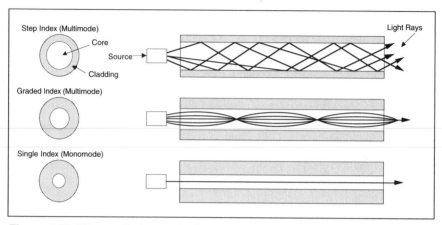

Figure 4-15. Fiber-optic transmission
(Courtesy of Belden/Cooper Industries, Inc.)

Both types of multimode cables experience a phenomenon known as modal dispersion, which means that the received light pulse spreads. When this occurs, the receiver has difficulty distinguishing one pulse from another, which, in turn, limits the effective upper frequency of the cable. The nodal dispersion is measured in nanoseconds per kilometer (ns/km) or alternatively in megahertz-kilometers (MHz-km). The product of the highest frequency (in MHz) and cable distance (in km) yields this model dispersion (or bandwidth) parameter.

The core of a fiber-optic cable is a cylinder that provides a conduit for light; the cladding that surrounds the core reflects the light. The diameter of the cable, measured in microns (micrometers), is usually described as two numbers. For example, a 62.5/125 micron cable has a core diameter of 62.5 microns and a cladding diameter of 125 microns.

The attenuation (or loss) of the optical power is measured in decibels per kilometer (dB/km), in a similar fashion to copper media measurements, where

$$dB = 10 \log_{10} \frac{\text{Power Out}}{\text{Power In}}$$

The typical optical source (power in) is in the milliwatt (mW) range, and a typical power loss would be 30 dB over the length of the transmission link.

The cable and the splices and connectors associated with the link are two sources of optical power loss. Splices have a loss of approximately 0.15-0.5 dB, while connectors have a loss of about 0.5-2.0 dB. Fiber-optic cable used with LANs have a typical loss of around 5 dB/km at 850 nm wavelength. Note that the loss for fiber is specified at a particular wavelength, where the attenuation of copper media is specified at a particular frequency. This attenuation is constant for a particular type of cable.

4.6.2. Fiber-optic cable used with LANs

The five network architectures discussed in this book—ARCNET, token ring, Ethernet, StarLAN, and FDDI—all support fiber-optic cabling. When the transmission system is designed, a total loss budget (in dB) is specified for the optical link between source and detector. In addition, the source wavelength, cable diameter, and cable transmission parameters, such as bandwidth (model dispersion), attenuation, and so on, are given.

Two major standards have emerged for fiber-optic cable, one from AT&T and the other from IBM. The AT&T Premises Distribution System (PDS) specifies 62.5/125 micron cable; the IBM cabling system uses 100/140 micron cable. References 4-16 and 4-17 provide further information.

A variety of fiber-optic connectors are available as well. Figure 4-16, taken from Reference 4-18, shows the most common connectors and their designations.

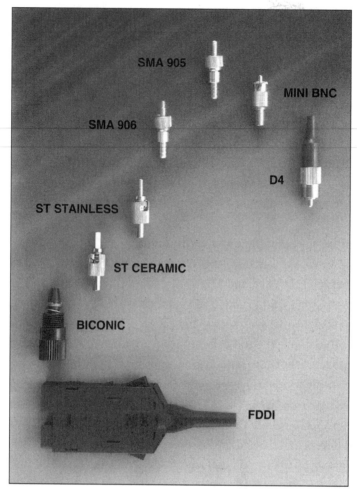

Figure 4-16. Fiber-optic connectors and designations
(Courtesy of Remee Products Corp.)

4.7. Troubleshooting Fiber

As stated in Chapter 3, you can use either an OTDR or an optical source and optical power meter to test fiber transmission links with LANs. Because of the high cost of OTDRs, the second alternative is most commonly used.

To test the fiber-optic transmission link, you first verify the proper operation of the optical power source using a short piece of fiber supplied with the unit. Next, measure the attenuation (loss) of the fiber under consideration. As you can see in Figure 4-17, you attach the optical source to one end of the cable, and the optical power meter to the opposite end. (This is a good time to use walkie-talkies.) Take the optical measurements and compare them with the maximum loss allowed for that type of system. Excessive loss indicates a broken cable, or improperly seated or dirty connectors. All optical systems have specific loss characteristics—refer to the vendor's literature for these details and suggestions for system testing. Optical test equipment vendors, such as Fotec, Inc. (Boston, Mass.) can also offer guidance (see Reference 4-19).

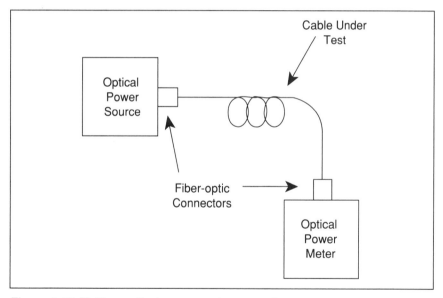

Figure 4-17. Making optical power measurements
(Courtesy of Fotec, Inc.)

4.8. Troubleshooting Summary

To summarize, here's a checklist to assist with troubleshooting cable system failures. Network-specific cabling issues are discussed in Chapters 5, 6, 7, 8, and 9.

1. Know where your cable goes. If you don't know, consult your network documentation (see Chapter 2) or use cable tracing tools (see Chapter 3) and then record the cable location.

2. Define the most likely location of the cable failure, and isolate the problem to one segment of cable. Remember that repeaters also can fail (or blow a fuse), isolating one cable section from another.

3. Look for any recent cable or connector additions or rearrangements, such as a new Ethernet tap that is shorting the backbone cable.

4. Look for obvious disconnections:

   - *ARCNET.* T-connectors, terminators, modular cords, and connectors.
   - *Token ring.* Media filters used with unshielded twisted-pair cable, or hermaphroditic (data) connectors at the MAUs.
   - *Ethernet.* BNC T-connectors, N-connectors, terminators, transceiver, or AUI cables.
   - *StarLAN and IEEE 10BASE-T.* Modular connectors, cross-connect fields and cables attached to termination blocks.
   - *FDDI.* MIC connectors, or cables plugged into an improper port.

5. Consider the less-than-obvious problems, such as open or shorted BNC connectors, miswired modular plugs, or open terminators.

6. Look for cable damage, such as cuts, frays, or breaks in the insulation.

7. When using TDRs, make measurements from both ends of the cable, and be aware of minimum and maximum cable distances that can be tested.

8. For suspected fiber-optic cable failures, use an optical light source to verify fiber continuity. Never look directly into a live fiber, however, since doing so may damage your eyes. Verify that the connectors are not dirty, and clean with isopropyl alcohol and a lint-free swab if necessary.

In this chapter, I have explored one major nemesis of the network manager, the cabling infrastructure. No piece of cable test equipment can make up for a well-planned design and a thoughtful installation. Take a little extra time on the front-end of a LAN installation project, and you'll save countless hours later. Cable vendors are more than eager to assist with the proper section of LAN cabling. References 4-20, 4-21, and 4-22 are three sample vendor publications that can assist with cable design and installation.

In the following five chapters, I will discuss five popular LAN architectures: ARCNET, token ring, coaxial Ethernet, StarLAN, and twisted-pair Ethernet and FDDI. Now the real work begins!

4.9. References

4-1.   AT&T. *Telecommunications Transmission Engineering*, 2d ed., vol. 1, 1977.

4-2.   Trompeter Electronics, Inc. (Westlake Village, Calif.). Catalog T-18A, 1992.

4-3.   National Fire Protection Association (Batterymarch Park, Quincy, Mass.). National Electrical Code—1992.

4-4.   E.I. duPont de Nemours and Company (Wilmington, Del.). "How to Specify, Bid and Install Plenum Cable," 1992.

4-5. Electronic Industries Association. "Commercial Building Telecommunications Wiring Standard." EIA/TIA-568, July 1991.

4-6. Electronic Industries Association. "Additional Cable Specifications for Unshielded Twisted-pair Cables." TSB-36, November 1991.

4-7. Electronic Industries Association. "Additional Transmission Specifications for Unshielded Twisted-Pair Connecting Hardware." TSB-40, August 1992.

4-8. Electronic Industries Association. "Administration Standard for Telecommunication Infrastructure of Commercial Buildings." EIA/TIA-606, 1992.

4-9. Russel Sanders. "Mapping the Wiring Maze." *LAN Technology* (October 15, 1992): 27-36.

4-10. Mark Johnson. "Cable Troubleshooting—Getting Down to the Wire." *MSM* (October 1992): 26-34.

4-11. Steven Saunders. "Premises Wiring Gets the Standard Treatment." *Data Communications* (November 1992): 105-115.

4-12. The Siemon Company (Watertown, Conn.). "The Siemon Guide to Modular Hardware." 1992.

4-13. Tektronix, Inc. "Time Domain Reflectometry Applications for Ethernet." Application Note 22W6360, November 1989.

4-14. Tektronix, Inc. "Time Domain Reflectometry Applications for Token Ring Networks." Application Note 22W6362, November 1989.

4-15. Belden/Cooper Industries, Inc. (Richmond, Ind.). "Guide to Fiber Optics System Design." Belden Fiber-Optic Catalog, 1990.

4-16. AT&T. *Premises Distribution System Fiber Installation Manual*. Document 555-401-102, 1988.

4-17. IBM. *Cabling System Planning and Installation Guide*. Document GA27-3361-7, October 1987.

4-18. Remee Products Corp. (Florida, N.Y.). *Remfo Fiber-Optic Cables*. 1993.

4-19. Fotec, Inc. (Boston, Mass.). "Testing the IBM Fiber-Optic Systems Using a Fotec Test Kit." Fotec Applications Bulletin ABI-868-5K, 1986.

4-20. Berk-Tek (New Holland, Pa.). "The Seven Secrets to Specifying Cable," November 1992.

4-21. Anixter Bros., Inc. (Skokie, Ill.). *Wire and Cable Technical Information Manual*. November 1991.

4-22. Mohawk Wire and Cable Corp. (Leominster, Mass.) *Network Cabling Systems—Computer and LAN Cables*. 1992.

CHAPTER 5

Troubleshooting ARCNET and ARCNETPLUS

Datapoint Corporation (San Antonio, Tex.) developed ARCNET in 1977 as a token-passing bus architecture, transmitting at 2.5 Mbps, a rate equal to the transfer rate of the then-current Datapoint disks (see Reference 5-1). ARCNET remained a proprietary network until 1981 when Standard Microsystems Corporation (SMC, Hauppauge, N.Y.) licensed the technology and began producing two integrated circuits: the COM9026, a LAN controller that implements the ARCNET protocol (see Reference 5-2); and the COM9032, a LAN transceiver that generates the clock signals. SMC subsequently integrated these two devices into the COM90C66 (see References 5-3 through 5-5). NCR Microelectronics (Fort Collins, Colo.) also manufactures CMOS versions of the LAN controller and transceivers, such as the 90C26, 90C32, and 90C98A (see Reference 5-6). In addition to the controller and transceiver, each ARCNET NIC contains the following components: a driver for coaxial, twisted-pair, or fiber-optic cable, a RAM buffer to store both incoming and outgoing frames, and miscellaneous logic to control the bus interface.

SMC introduced the first ARCNET NIC for the IBM PC in 1983. SMC, along with manufacturers such as Datapoint, Contemporary Control Systems, Thomas-Conrad, LANMaster, Quam, Pure Data, and Earth Computer, supplies ARCNET cards for a variety of computer buses. These buses include the PC, AT, Microchannel, and industrial bus structures, such as Intel Corporation's Multibus and the IEEE STD bus.

ARCNET also boasts an organization of users and vendors, called the ARCNET Trade Association (ATA) (708-255-3003), which sponsors conferences and architecture improvements. The ATA was instrumental in persuading ANSI to formalize the ARCNET standard as ANSI/ATA 878.1 (Reference 5-7). This standard officially recognizes the ARCNET architecture, and provides a benchmark for interoperability between different vendors' products.

ARCNETPLUS, which Datapoint announced in February 1992, is the most recent enhancement. ARCNETPLUS operates at 20 Mbps and can coexist with the earlier version. ARCNETPLUS provides an eight-fold increase in the data transmission rate, and much longer transmission frame sizes. These improvements provide an economical upgrade path for existing ARCNET networks. ARCNETPLUS is implemented in a two-chip set, the DPT1474 ARCNETPLUS Protocol Controller (APC) and the DPT 1457 Line Interface Coupler (LIC). References 5-8 and 5-9 discuss both of these devices in detail. Section 5.9.6. discusses the operation and protocols for ARCNETPLUS in detail.

5.1. ARCNET Topology

ARCNET offers the most flexible architecture of all the major topologies. It can use a star or bus topology, or a combination that you could call a distributed star with branches. In addition, you can use and interconnect all three media choices: coax (RG-62/U), a single twisted-pair (100 ohm impedance, 2 twists/foot, 22, 24, and 26 gauge solid, or 24 and 26 gauge stranded), and duplex fiber-optic cable (50, 62.5, 100, or 200 micron core). Thus you could easily design a network with coax in the computer room, twisted pair throughout the office, and fiber-optics outside to the guard station. You use media converters (called optical or twisted-pair links from SMC) to connect dissimilar media types. The only major constraint on the transmission medium is that the signal propagation delay between any two workstations cannot exceed 31 microseconds. In addition, the attenuation characteristics of the different cable types affect the number of workstations you can attach in a bus topology. The maximum signal attenuation between workstation and active hub, or between two workstations connected via a passive hub, must not exceed 11 dB (see Reference 5-10).

The simplest topology is a star with a passive hub, and RG-62/U coax extending to three workstations (see Figure 5-1). Maximum workstation-to-hub distance is 100 feet. Notice that you must connect the unused port to a termination resistor (93 ohms in this case) to provide an impedance match. See Section 5-3 for more on this requirement.

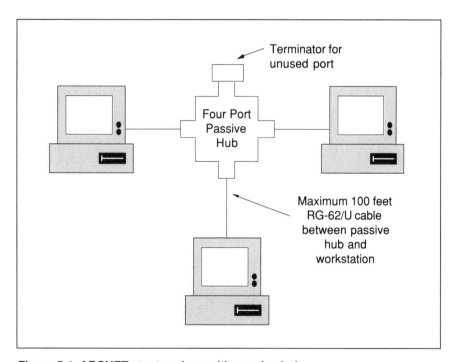

Figure 5-1. ARCNET star topology with passive hub

A star topology with an active hub is another alternative (see Figure 5-2). The active hub repeats the signal, allowing you to extend the hub-to-workstation distance to 2,000 feet. Active hub ports are self-terminating, so they do not require termination resistors.

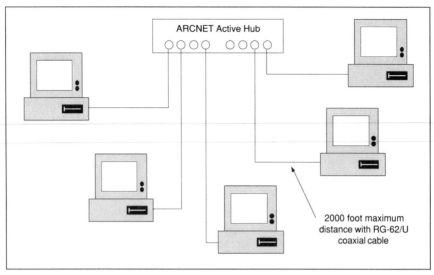

Figure 5-2. ARCNET star topology with active hub

Figures 5-3a and 5-3b show a third option, a bus topology. You can use RG-62/U coax or unshielded twisted-pair cable. Note that the number of workstations changes with the type of cable you select: Coax can support as many as eight workstations; twisted pair as many as ten.

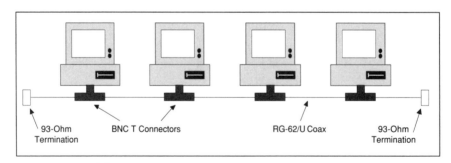

Figure 5-3a. ARCNET coaxial bus topology

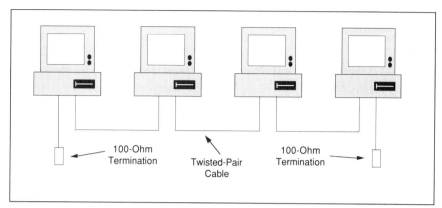

Figure 5-3b. ARCNET twisted-pair bus topology

A distributed star ARCNET topology can combine coaxial, twisted-pair, and fiber-optic media with bus and star connections (see Figure 5-4).

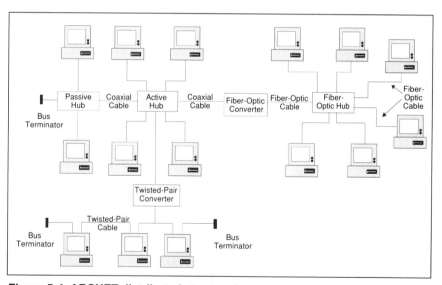

Figure 5-4. ARCNET distributed star topology

5.2. ARCNET Cabling

Because of its flexible topology, you can use a variety of transmission media with ARCNET. Table 5-1 lists the cables acceptable for ARCNET use (see Reference 5-11). Note that any one segment can have a maximum of 11 dB of signal attenuation; hence the 2,000-foot limit from active hub to workstation when using RG-62/U coax (5.5 dB/Kft * 2 Kft = 11 dB total attenuation). Other manufacturers of ARCNET products may have different recommendations or offer other options, such as fiber optics.

Table 5-1. Recommended ARCNET cabling

Cable Type	Nominal Impedance	Attenuation per 1,000 ft @ 5 MHz	Propagation Velocity	FCC RFI Compliance
RG-62 Belden #86262	93 ohms	5.5 dB	85%	OK
RG-59/U Belden #89108	75 ohms	7.0 dB	84%	OK
RG-11U Belden #89292	75 ohms	5.5 dB	80%	OK
IBM Type 1 Belden #89688	150 ohms	7.0 dB	78%	OK with IBM balun
IBM Type 3 Telephone Twisted Pair; Belden #1155A	100 ohms	17.9 dB	66%	Requires filter/ balun

(Source: Datapoint Corporation)

114

5.3. ARCNET Hardware Components

A typical ARCNET network consists of a NIC in each workstation, active and/or passive hubs, repeaters or media converters, and the appropriate cables.

5.3.1. ARCNET NICs

Figure 5-5 shows a sample ARCNET NIC, the PC600FS from Standard Microsystems Corporation. Key components include the eight-position DIP switch for setting the node address; another bank of DIP switches for setting the base I/O port address and memory buffer address; the ARCNET LAN Controller IC, COM9026; the LAN Transceiver IC, COM9032; jumpers for setting the IRQ line; the interface's connector to the cable; and a socket for an autoboot PROM for diskless PCs.

Figure 5-5. A sample ARCNET NIC
(Photo courtesy of Standard Microsystems Corp.)

You use a standard modular connector (RJ-11, RJ-14, or RJ-45) for twisted-pair cable installations. For each connector size (4-pin, 6-pin, or 8-pin, respectively) you use the two center pins for the two signal leads. For example, Figure 5-6 shows the twisted-pair interface that the Standard Microsystems' PC270E NIC uses for twisted-pair cable. Note that the wire connections are sensitive to polarity. The wires connecting Pins 3 and 4 must go straight through; for example, Pin 3 must connect to Pin 3, and Pin 4 must

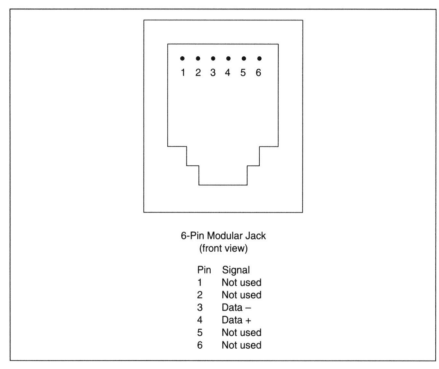

6-Pin Modular Jack
(front view)

Pin	Signal
1	Not used
2	Not used
3	Data −
4	Data +
5	Not used
6	Not used

Figure 5-6. Pin assignments for the ARCNET unshielded twisted-pair cable interface

connect to Pin 4. You need a minimum of six feet of cable between two PC270s. Terminators for use with twisted-pair NICs consist of a 100-ohm resistor connected between the center two pins (3 and 4 in this case) of the 6-pin modular connector.

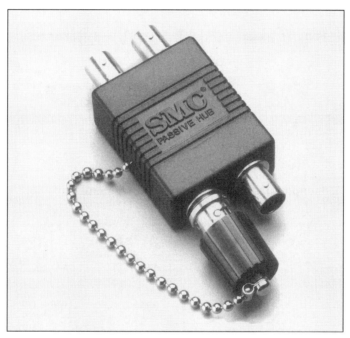

Figure 5-7. SMC passive hub
(Photo courtesy of Standard Microsystems Corp.)

5.3.2. ARCNET passive hubs

Figure 5-7 shows a four-port passive hub module from SMC, and Figure 5-8 shows the internal wiring. The passive hub is simply a resistive network divider designed to match the source impedance (93 ohms for coaxial cable) and the load impedance. For example, assume that you wish to calculate the impedance for Port D in Figure 5-8.

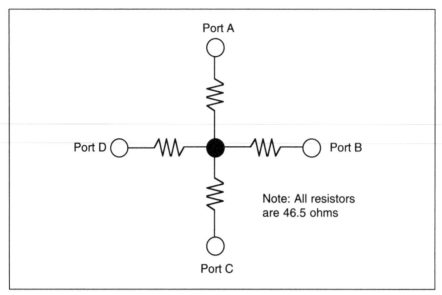

Figure 5-8. Four-port passive hub wiring (coax version)

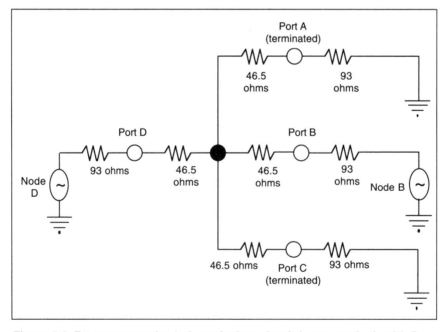

Figure 5-9. Four-port passive hub equivalent circuit (coax version), with B and D as active ports, and A and C as terminated ports

Further assume that Ports A and C are terminated, and Port B has another workstation attached, as shown in Figure 5-9. If the passive hub resistors have a value of 46.5 ohms, and each port has a 93-ohm impedance, the combination of ports A, B, and C yields an effective load on Port D of 93 ohms, thus achieving the impedance match. The following equation shows the result:

$$Z_{in} = 46.5 + \cfrac{1}{\cfrac{1}{139.5} + \cfrac{1}{139.5} + \cfrac{1}{139.5}} = 93 \text{ ohms}$$

See Reference 5-11, Section 8, for further details on these calculations.

Manufacturers, such as Datapoint and SMC, use 33-ohm and 36-ohm resistors in their passive-hub networks. The Datapoint design uses 33-ohm resistors. If you make three (or four) connections to the passive hub, you needn't terminate the unused port. Check the documentation for your network hardware for details.

5.3.3. ARCNET active hubs

Active hubs are bit level repeaters that regenerate the signal. Most active hubs have 8- or 16-port capacities. Figure 5-10 shows one example, the Mod Hub 16 from Contemporary Control Systems, Inc. (Downer's Grove, Ill.). The Mod Hub 16 supports combinations of coaxial, twisted-pair, and fiber-optic cable. Some products distinguish themselves by offering built-in diagnostics, usually in the form of LED indicators. At the very least, the hub should indicate activity on each port and whether or not a network reconfiguration is underway. Section 5.6 discusses reconfiguration further.

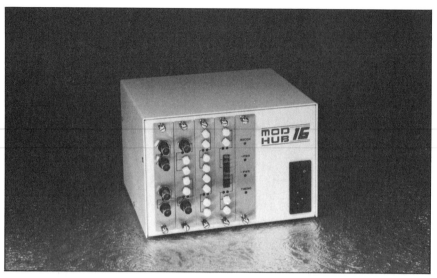

Figure 5-10. ARCNET modular active hub
(Photo courtesy of Contemporary Control Systems, Inc.)

5.4. ARCNETPLUS Hardware Compatibility

When developing ARCNETPLUS, Datapoint made sure that the new product would be backward compatible with the old one. As a result, an ARCNETPLUS node operating at 20 Mbps can communicate with an ARC-NET node operating at 2.5 Mbps.

Datapoint achieved this compatibility in two ways. First, ARCNET-PLUS derives its electrical signal characteristics from the ARCNET signal, although it adds amplitude and phase modulation. Thus an ARCNETPLUS node's transmitter can revert to the simpler ARCNET signaling scheme. Reference 5-8 describes the electrical signaling characteristics in detail.

Second, ARCNETPLUS supports the ARCNET frame formats. The enhanced version, however, adds capabilities. For example, ARCNETPLUS data frames can contain up to 4,224 octets of data, a significant improvement over ARCNET's limit of 508 octets per frame. (Section 5.9 considers both of these frame formats.)

Because of the signaling differences between ARCNETPLUS and ARC-NET, you should exercise some caution when combining the two topologies into one network (see Figure 5-11). Because ARCNETPLUS is designed to communicate with either ARCNETPLUS or ARCNET nodes, you can use an ARCNETPLUS hub to connect both ARCNETPLUS and ARCNET hubs (Hub 2 in Figure 5-11). You can also extend one ARCNETPLUS hub by connecting to another ARCNETPLUS hub (Hub 3 in Figure 5-11). The converse is not true; ARCNET hubs may only connect to ARCNET nodes (Hub 1 in Figure 5-11).

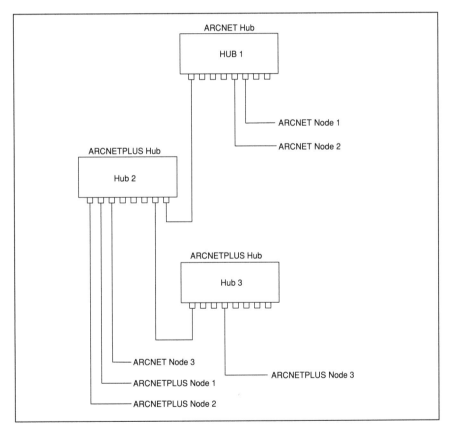

Figure 5-11. Combination of ARCNET and ARCNETPLUS
(Courtesy of Datapoint Corp.)

An internal table within the ARCNETPLUS Protocol Controller (APC) chip records all active nodes on the network. The record notes whether the remote node is an ARCNET or ARCNETPLUS device and adjusts the signaling scheme and transmission rate accordingly. This internal table is populated during the system reconfiguration process, which is discussed in Section 5.6.

5.5. ARCNET and ARCNETPLUS Addressing

The heart of ARCNET and ARCNETPLUS is a token-passing bus architecture that passes the permission to transmit (token) in a logical ring but is physically connected as a bus (or star). As such, each workstation's opportunity (or turn) to transmit is independent of its physical location in the network.

For the logical ring to operate, each NIC must have a unique address between 1 and 255; address 0 is reserved for broadcast messages. You use an 8-position DIP switch to make these assignments. Each workstation must know its own address (Source ID, or SID) and the address of the next workstation (Next ID, or NID) in the logical ring progression.

One of the easiest ways to disable an ARCNET network is to duplicate a node address. If duplication occurs because of human error in setting the address DIP switches, the reconfiguration process will fail, terminating network communication. ARCNETPLUS includes a duplicate ID detection algorithm that requires a new node to listen to a complete circulation of the token before joining the network. Should the node detect a duplicate ID, it will abort the login process and deliver a message to the higher-layer software regarding the problem. This process is not foolproof, however. An ARCNET node with SID = 222 (but without the built-in duplicate ID detection algorithm) could still join the network after an ARCNETPLUS node with SID = 222, and disrupt operation.

Figures 5-12a and 5-12b show a sample ARCNET LAN with four nodes, addressed 4, 32, 65, and 203. Figure 5-12a shows the physical topology, Figure 5-12b the logical topology. Each NIC passes the token to its NID node; the highest-addressed node then wraps around to the lowest-addressed node, completing the logical ring progression.

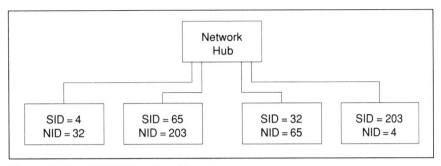

Figure 5-12a. ARCNET node addressing

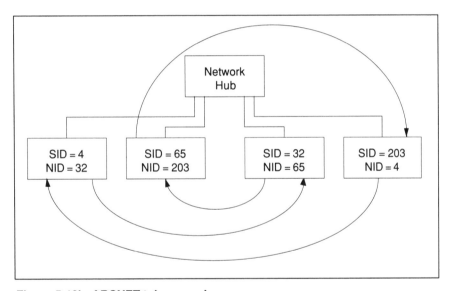

Figure 5-12b. ARCNET token passing

5.6. ARCNET and ARCNETPLUS Network Reconfiguration

Any time a node wishes to enter or exit the ring, the logical ring must be modified. The process, called system reconfiguration or recon, proceeds as follows: Any node that turns on, or has not received an Invitation to Transmit frame for 840 milliseconds, makes a system reconfiguration transmission: 8 marks + 1 space repeated 765 times. This transmission is longer than any other transmission. It disrupts normal token passing, causing all stations to set their Next ID (NID) register to their own (or Source) ID (SID) so that NID (SID). In addition, it initializes a timer as follows:

Timeout = 146 * (255-SID) microseconds

The highest node address times out first and issues the first Invitation to Transmit frame, or token. If it does not hear a response within 74 microseconds, the first node assumes that the NID address does not exist, increments the NID, and tries again. Any response will cause the node to save the current value of NID in its buffer and pass the token to the NID station. That station then searches for its upstream neighbor in the logical ring.

In the network in Figures 5-12a and 5-12b with node addresses 4, 32, 65, and 203, node 203 would issue the first token to node 204. Since node 204 does not exist, node 203 would increment NID to 205, 206,...255 then to 1, 2,...4 until node 4 seizes control of the process and begins the search for its nearest neighbor. The process continues until node 4 finds node 32, node 32 finds node 65, and node 65 finds node 203. Node 203 already knows about node 4, thus completing the logical ring.

If a node is removed from the network, a similar (but less disruptive) search takes place. Again referring to Figures 5-12a and 5-12b, if node 32 was turned off, node 4 would continue to increment its NID register until it passed control of the network to node 65. No other changes in the logical ring are required.

System reconfiguration time depends on the total number of nodes and the cable's propagation delay, and ranges from 24 to 61 milliseconds. As a result, a normal network reconfiguration is nearly transparent to users, and any deviation from the prescribed reconfiguration protocols disrupts the network.

For ARCNETPLUS networks, the reconfiguration algorithm within the controller chip limits the number of transmittable recon bursts to one in five seconds. This algorithm allows the network to remain in operation, but prevents the failed node from disrupting network communication. Network software (such as Novell's NetWare version 3.11 server monitor program) can detect these periodic recon bursts, allowing for easy identification.

5.7. Typical ARCNET and ARCNETPLUS Hardware Failures

One of the most common causes for passive hub hardware failure is the omission of a termination resistor at an unused passive hub port, or at the end of a bus topology cable. Such an omission affects the impedance balance and causes signal reflections.

To test the terminator, use a VOM and measure the DC resistance between the two contacts of the internal resistor. For a BNC terminator, you measure between the center pin and the outside shell and look for a value close to 93 ohms; for a modular (RJ-11) terminator, measure between the two center pins (2 and 3, 3 and 4, or 4 and 5, as appropriate) and look for a value close to 100 ohms. The correct impedance is 93 ohms for coax buses, and 100 ohms for twisted-pair buses and twisted-pair repeaters. Active hubs for coax cable are self-terminating.

You can avoid many problems with ARCNET simply by obeying the configuration rules. For example, remember limitations, such as a maximum of 10 NICs per twisted-pair segment or a minimum twisted-pair bus length of 400 feet.

The other major cause of hardware failure is a dysfunctional (or nonfunctional) NIC or active hub. These problems are relatively easy to diagnose because most manufacturers include a diagnostic LED on the NIC or active hub. Unfortunately, there are no standards for these LED indicators, so you'll have to consult the manual for your network hardware for proper interpretation. Many active hubs also provide another LED to indicate that a network reconfiguration is in progress.

5.8. Isolating the Failing Component

ARCNET's and ARCNETPLUS's modular architecture makes it easy to isolate network failures. Since most NICs and active hubs include diagnostic LEDs, the first step is to check the LED at each port for any indication of problems.

For example, in Figure 5-13 assume that the active hub LED indicates that a network reconfiguration is in progress. The reconfiguration (sometimes labeled Recon) LED normally lights for a few seconds, even though the actual network reconfiguration completes in less than 61 milliseconds.

Although a Recon LED indicates that a reconfiguration has occurred, it does not indicate its source. Most likely, a NIC's defective receiver is causing the problem. The next challenge is to find the failure.

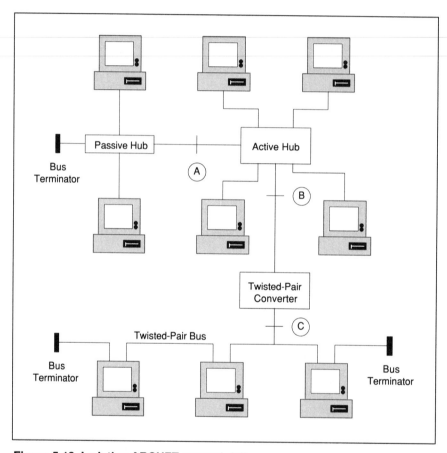

Figure 5-13. Isolating ARCNET network failures

To isolate the problem, first segment the network. In Figure 5-13 you would disconnect the cable between the active hub and passive hub (point A), and see if the problem clears. If it does, the problem lies in a component within the disconnected section. Reconnect the cable between the passive and active hubs at point A, and start disconnecting workstations from the

126

passive hub ports one at a time. Remember to terminate the unused port when the cable is disconnected. If the network recovers (Recon goes out), you've found the problem; if not, continue the process.

Now return to the first scenario, and assume that segmenting at point A did not clear the problem. Disconnect at point B (the input of the twisted-pair converter), and check the network. If the problem clears, reconnect at point B, and disconnect at point C, which is the output of the twisted-pair converter. Remember to terminate any unused port on the converter. If the problem clears, reconnect at point C and methodically segment the twisted-pair bus, terminating each open endpoint, until you've isolated the faulty NIC or cable section. If a cable section appears to be the problem, test it as discussed in Chapter 4. If you suspect a NIC, replace it with a known good spare, being careful to check all option settings, and making sure to avoid duplicating another NIC node address.

5.9. ARCNET and ARCNETPLUS Software Considerations

One strength of the ARCNET and ARCNETPLUS networks is their simple hardware configurations. ARCNET software, specifically Datapoint's ARCNET protocols, is similarly easy to configure.

5.9.1. ARCNET frame formats

The ARCNET protocol implemented on the COM9026, COM 90C66, or other controller chips is a character-oriented protocol having five types of frames, as shown in Figure 5-14. All ARCNET frames begin with a starting delimiter of six ones. Each character within the frame, called an Information Symbol Unit (ISU), consists of an 11-bit sequence: one + one + zero + 8-bit character. As a result, the network throughput is actually 1.8 Mbps (8/11 * 2.5 Mbps). The five frame formats are defined as follows:

1. *Invitation to Transmit (ITT)* passes the token from one node to another. It is identified by the ITT character (04H, where H represents hexadecimal notation).

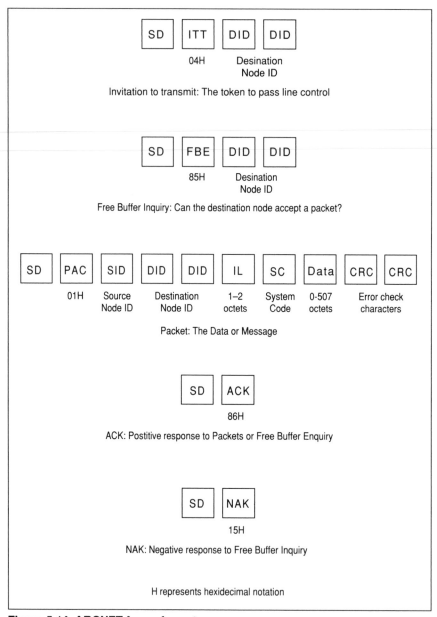

Figure 5-14. ARCNET frame formats

2. *Free Buffer Enquiry (FBE)* asks an intended destination node whether it can accept a data packet from the node currently holding the token. It is identified by the FBE character (85H).

3. *Data Packet (PAC)* transports the data itself and can contain up to 508 octets (delineated in the Information Length, the IL field). It is transmitted from the token holder to the intended destination. (The frame type indicator indicates the contents of the frame and the PAC character (01H) indicates the packet.) The IL field is a Continuation Pointer (CP) that locates the packet in the memory buffer. Packets of length 0-253 use a one octet IL; packets from 257-508 octets use a 2-octet IL. Note that packet lengths of 254-256 are not allowed. For packets of 253 octets or less, CP = 256 - length; for packets greater than 256 octets, the first octet CP = 0, and the second octet CP = 512 - length. The first octet of data is a System Code (SC), which is a unique protocol identifier administered by the ATA.

4. *Acknowledgment (ACK)* indicates correct receipt of a packet or an affirmative response to an FBE frame. It is identified by the ACK character (86H).

5. *Negative Acknowledgment (NAK)* is a negative response to a FBE frame. It is identified by the NAK character (ISH).

5.9.2. ARCNET protocol operation

When a node receives a token, it can either play (by initiating the transmit sequence) or pass (by sending the Invitation to Transmit to another node). If the node wishes to transmit, the source issues an FBE to the intended destination to confirm its ability to accept a message. Either an ACK or a NAK is returned. If the FBE receives an ACK, it transmits a packet. When the destination node receives the packet, it uses the CRC to verify the accuracy of the data. If the data passes the CRC, it sends an ACK. If the data fails the CRC, the destination node is silent, which signals to the transmitting node that the transmission failed, and that the node should retransmit the next time it obtains the token. See References 5-5 and 5-12 for additional details.

5.9.3. Network response times

Because ARCNET is a deterministic network where aberrations such as collisions never occur, you can easily calculate overall response times. Figure 5-14 illustrates the five types of ARCNET transmissions. Each begins with a starting delimiter (six ones) and a transmission of 11 bits per character. Each bit requires 400 nanoseconds (1/2,500,000), or a total of 4.4 microseconds (11 x 400 nanoseconds) to send each character. Response times are as follows for the five frame types shown in Figure 5-14:

Invitation to Transmit (ITT)

Starting Delimiter:	6 bits	= 2.4 microseconds
ITT, DID, DID	3 * 11 = 33 bits	= 13.2 microseconds

Total 15.6 microseconds

Free Buffer Enquiry (FBE)

Starting Delimiter:	6 bits	= 2.4 microseconds
FBE, DID, DID	3 * 11 = 33 bits	= 13.2 microseconds

Total 15.6 microseconds

Data Packets (PAC)

Starting Delimiter:	6 bits	= 2.4 microseconds
PAC,SID,DID,DID,IL	5 * 11 = 55 bits	= 22.0 microseconds
SC	1 * 11 = bits	= 4.4 microseconds
n characters	n * 11 = 11n bits	= 4.4n microseconds
CRC, CRC	2 * 11 = 22 bits	= 8.8 microseconds

Total 37.6 microseconds
+
4.4n microseconds

IL is one octet in this example (0-252 octets of data)

For PACs with n = 256 - 507 octets of data, IL = 2 octets, and the resulting response time is: 42.0 microseconds = 4.4 x n microseconds.

Acknowledgment (ACK)

Starting Delimiters:	6 bits	= 2.4 microseconds
ACK	1 * 11 = 11 bits	= 4.4 microseconds

Total 6.8 microseconds

Negative acknowledgment (NAK)

Starting Delimiters:	6 bits	= 2.4 microseconds
NAK	1 * 11 = 11 bits	= 4.4 microseconds

Total 6.8 microseconds

In addition to the transmission times associated with the individual frames, the protocol includes several other delays or timers (see Reference 5-7). To assure compatibility, ARCNETPLUS uses the same timers. The timers are as follows:

- *Timer, Lost Token (TLT)* = 840 milliseconds. TLT initiates network reconfiguration when a token is not received.
- *Timer, Identifier Precedence (TIP)* = 146 microseconds (default). TIP determines when a given node will begin the token circulation after a TAC has expired.
- *Timer, Activity Timeout (TAC)* = 82.4 microseconds. TAC is the maximum time the network is allowed to be idle; once the TAC expires, the reconfiguration sequence begins.
- *Timer Response Timeout (TRP)* = 74.6 microseconds. TRP is the maximum time allowed for a response to a transmission, equal to Tpm + Tta + Tpm (twice the message propagation time plus the turnaround time).

- *Timer, Recovery Time (TRC)* = 3.4 microseconds. TRC is measured between a response timeout and the subsequent pass of the token.
- *Timer, Line Turnaround (TTA)* = 12.6 microseconds. The TTA is measured from the end of a received transmission to the start of the response.
- *Timer, Medium Quiescent (TMQ)* = 4.0 microseconds. TMQ determines whether a transmission is occurring on the medium.
- *Timer, Receiver Blanking (TRB)* = 5.6 microseconds. TRB is the time after the end of the transmission from a node that the receiver is blanked (and the data ignored to allow the transmission line to stabilize) before it can receive valid network activity.
- *Timer, Broadcast Delay (TBR)* = 15.6 microseconds. TBR begins when a node has completed broadcast of a message and ends at the start of the next token pass. Note that no FBE is sent before the broadcast message, and no ACK generated after; TBR is thus fixed at 15.6 microseconds.
- *Media Propagation Delay (Tprop)* = 0-31 microseconds. Tprop is measured from the time one node transmits a signal until another node receives it. This time is a measure of the propagation delay of the cable and hubs, and must not exceed 31 microseconds.

Two examples of ARCNET response time calculations are the Token Pass and a Token Pass plus Messages. For additional examples, see Reference 5-10 and Reference 5-12.

Token Pass. The originating node passes the token to the next station (NID) in the logical ring:

ITT	15.6 microseconds
TTA + Tprop	12.6 + Tprop microseconds
	Total 28.2 + Tprop microseconds

Given the worst case, Tprop at 31 microseconds, maximum Token Pass time would be 59.2 microseconds.

Token Pass plus Messages. A workstation initiates a packet transmission to another workstation:

ITT	15.6	microseconds
TTA + Tprop	12.6 + Tprop	microseconds
FBE	15.6	microseconds
TTA + Tprop	12.6 + Tprop	microseconds
ACK	6.8	microseconds
TTA + Tprop	12.6 + Tprop	microseconds
PAC	33.2 + 4.4n	microseconds
TTA + Tprop	12.6 + Tprop	microseconds
ACK	6.8	microseconds
TTA + Tprop	12.6 + Tprop	microseconds

Total   141.0 + 4.4n + 5 Tprop microseconds

Again, assuming the maximum case: n = 508 characters and 31 microseconds for Tprop, the Token Pass and Message would occur in 2531.2 microseconds.

5.9.4. Memory buffers

The longest data packet (508 octets for ARCNET) requires an external RAM buffer of at least 2K. This buffer must be located somewhere in the PC's address space, usually in segment D, address D0000 Hex. Make sure that this buffer does not interfere with the address space for any PC boards installed in your system. If you suspect a conflict, remove all add-on cards in the PC, and add them back one at a time, starting with the ARCNET card.

5.9.5. Software options

ARCNET boards are sensitive to I/O-related options, such as IRQ lines, DMA channels, and I/O Base Addresses of the PC. These options must also be consistent with the network operating system or higher-layer software (for example, NetWare, NetBIOS, and so on). Refer to a NIC installation manual (such as Reference 5-13) or the manufacturer if any questions arise.

5.9.6. ARCNETPLUS frame formats

The ARCNETPLUS protocol, implemented in the Datapoint DPT1474 chip, includes all of the ARCNET frames described in Section 5.9.1, plus enhancements that improve data transmission speed and throughput. The signaling differences between the two versions (discussed in Section 5-4) have changed some of the fundamental information transfer elements. Consider the Starting Delimiter fields (elements unique to ARCNETPLUS begin with the letter X):

ARCNET Starting Delimiter (SD) = 111111

ARCNETPLUS Starting Delimiter (XSD) = S [F] S [7]

In the first case (SD) the transmitted signal is six binary ones. The second case (XSD) introduces a silence interval (S) and two amplitude and phase modulated symbols with 4-bit hexadecimal values: [F] = 1111 and [7] = 0111.

Network analysts do not see this difference because their protocol analyzer performs the necessary decoding. Systems programmers, however, should be aware of these differences, since the transmission times of similar ARCNET and ARCNETPLUS elements differ. In the preceding example, the SD takes 2.4 microseconds; the XSA takes 0.8 microseconds.

Another change in ARCNETPLUS is an Information Symbol Unit (ISU) of 8 bits (not 11 as in ARCNET), denoted as XISU. An additional symbol, the Calibration Symbol Unit (CSU) is inserted in the data stream at periodic intervals to synchronize the receiver clock. References 5-8 and 5-9 provide the details.

The ARCNETPLUS enhancements include seven additional frames: XITT, XTOK, XENQ, XRSP, XPAC, ADM, and XADM. These frames provide the following functions (see Figure 5-15).

1. *The Extended ITT (XITT)*. XITT passes the token from an ARC-NETPLUS node to an ARCNET node or a node whose capabilities (ARCNET or ARCNETPLUS) are known. Three control fields define the ARCNETPLUS format flag, protocol version, and maximum packet size (either 508 or 4,224 octets).

2. *ARCNETPLUS Token (XTOK)*. XTOK passes the token from one ARCNETPLUS node to another. The STAT symbols contain the compatibility table, indicating the node's status, type, protocol version, and maximum packet size.

3. *ARCNETPLUS Enquiry (XENQ)*. XENQ initiates control functions, such as a Free Buffer Enquiry.

4. *ARCNETPLUS Response (XRSP)*. XRSP responds to a XENQ or XPAC.

5. *ARCNETPLUS Data Packet (XPAC)*. XPAC transfers information from one ARCNETPLUS node to another. The Length field indicates the amount of data transmitted, which may be 1 to 4,224 octets. The rest of the frame consists of data and error check characters.

6. *Administrative Packet (ADM)*. ADM transfers 0-506 octets of administrative information from one node to another using ARCNET signaling.

7. *ARCNETPLUS Administrative Packet (XADM)*. XADM transfers up to 4,224 octets of supervisory or control information from one node to another and does not interfere with the normal data transfer mechanism.

Note that for the XPAC and XADM frames, the Data, CSU, and FCS fields are integrated for enhanced error control.

Control	ITT	DID	DID

Flag Format, Protocol   04H   Destination Node ID
Version and Packet Size

Extended ITT (XITT): The token to pass line control from an ARCNETPLUS node to a standard node, or a node whose capabilities are not known

XSD	1	XDID	XDID	STAT	STAT

   1H   Destination Node ID   Compatibility Table
        (12 bits each)   (4 bits each)

ARCNETPLUS Token (XTOK): The token to pass line control from an ARCNETPLUS node to another ARCNETPLUS node

XSD	9	XDID	XDID	CTL	LEN	LEN

   9H   Destination Node ID   Control   Packet Length
       (12 bits each)   Function   (12 bits each)

ARCNETPLUS Enquiry (XENQ): Used to initate control functions

XSD	D	STAT	STAT	FCS Interval	FCS Interval

   DH   Response Status   Interval of the Frame Check Sequence
       (12 bits each)   (1 octet each)

ARCNETPLUS Response (XRSP): Used to respond to an XENQ or XPAC

XSD	F	XSID	XDID	Length	Reserved	FCS Interval

   FH   Source   Destination   Datafield   (1 octet)   Interval of the Frame
      Node ID   Node ID   Length   Check Sequence
      (12 bits)   (12 bits)   (2 octets)

CSU	FCS	Data	CSU	FCS

Calibration   Error Check   0–4,224   Calibration   Error Check
Symbol Unit   Characters   octets   Symbol Unit   Characters
(12 bits)   (2 octets)   (12 bits)   (2 octets)

ARCNETPLUS Data Packet (XPAC): Used to transfer information from one ARCNET node to another

SD	ADM	XSID	XSID	Length	SC	Data	FCS

   94H   Source   Destination   Length of Datafield   System   0–506   Error Check
       Node ID   Node ID   Code   octets   Characters

Administrative Packet (ADM): Used to transfer administrativel information from one node to another using standard ARCNET signaling

XSD	B	XSID	XDID	Length	SC	Data	CSU	FCS

   BH   Source   Destination   Length of Datafield   System   0–4,224   Calibration   Error Check
      Node ID   Node ID   Code   octets   Symbol Unit   Characters
                                          (12 bits)   (2 octets)

ARCNETPLUS Administrative Packet (XADM): Used to transfer supervisory or control information from one node to another without interferering with the normal data transfer mechanism

* for the XPAC and XADM frames, the DATA, CSU and FCS are intergrated for enhanced error control
H represents hexidecimal notation

Figure 5-15. ARCNETPLUS frame formats
(Source: Datapoint Corporation)

136

5.10. Protocol Analysis with NetWare

According to many market surveys, Novell's NetWare is the most popular LAN operating system. One reason for its popularity is the number of hardware and software platforms that it supports, including Macintosh, DECnet, and OS/2. Figure 5-16, which compares NetWare and the ISO/OSI reference model, further details this broad protocol support. Another reason for NetWare's wide acceptance is that NetWare drivers are available for more than 100 different NICs. See References 5-14 and 5-15 for further details.

OSI MODEL	Media Interface	Workstation Driver	IPX/SPX Transport	OS/2 Workstation	NetBIOS Workstation	Workstation/Server Communications	Streams Environment	Remote Execution	OSI MODEL
Application						NetWare Core Protocol (NCP)			Application
Presentation									Presentation
Session				OS/2 Requester	NetBIOS Emulator			NetWare Remote Procedure Calls (RPC)	Session
Transport			Sequenced Packet Exchange (SPX)				Transport Layer Interface (TLI)		Transport
Network			Internetwork Packet Exchange (IPX)				Streams		Network
Data Link		Link Support Layer (LSL) / ODI LAN Driver							Data Link
Physical	Network Interface Card								Physical

Figure 5-16. Comparing the NetWare Protocol Suite to the OSI Model

(Courtesy Novell, Inc.)

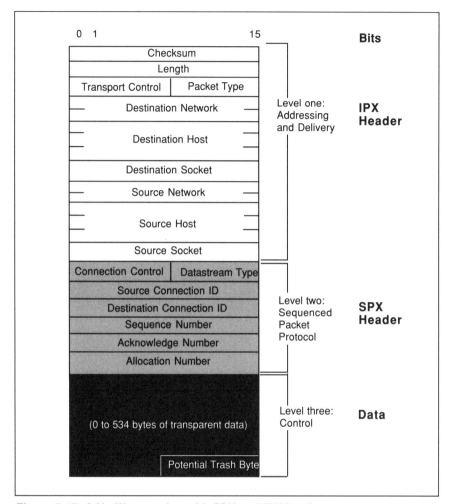

Figure 5-17. A NetWare packet with SPX and IPX headers

The NetWare communication protocols is the Internetwork Packet Exchange/Sequenced Packet Exchange (IPX/SPX) transport protocols detailed in Figure 5-17. IPX provides connectionless communication service. The IPX header, an implementation of the Xerox Networking Systems (XNS) Internet Datagram Protocol (IDP), consists of fifteen 16-bit words or 30 octets. The Network, Host, and Socket fields identify the specific network on the Internet (32 bits), the host's node address (48 bits), and the application process queue (16 bits), respectively.

SPX provides for connection-oriented data transfer. The 12-octet SPX header, an implementation of Xerox's Sequenced Packet Protocol (SPP), is built on top of IPX. Immediately following the IPX and SPX headers are up to 534 octets of transparent data.

For workstation-to-server communication, the Network Core Protocol (NCP) is used with IPX transport, as shown in Figure 5-18. The data field of the ARCNET frame encapsulates the NCP packet and IPX header. Note the ARCNET fragmentation header. The ARCNET data field can contain up to 508 octets. A NetWare packet (IPX header, NCP header, and data) that exceeds this length must be divided into multiple frames for transmission over an ARCNET network. The Fragmentation header controls this, providing information that allows the entire NCP message to be reassembled at the receiver (see Reference 5-16).

When viewing the contents of a frame using a protocol analyzer such as the Network General Corp. Sniffer Network Analyzer, you should be aware that these tools are selective in the portion of the frame that they capture. For example, the Sniffer captures only the address and data fields of the ARCNET frame (see Figure 5-19). This limitation optimizes higher-layer protocol processing.

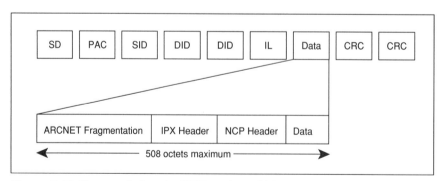

Figure 5-18. Encapsulating the NCP packet within an ARCNET frame

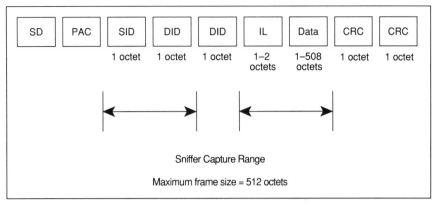

Figure 5-19. Capture range of the Network General Sniffer protocol analyzer for ARCNET networks

Traces 1 and 2 are examples of NCP packets transmitted over an ARCNET network and captured by the Network General Sniffer protocol analyzer. The first frame (Trace 5-1) is an NCP Get Station Number Request. The second frame (Trace 5-2) is a Get Station Number Reply. The notations along the left-hand side of the trace indicate the protocol layer being decoded. DLC indicates Data Link Control (ARCNET), NOV indicates the Novell ARCNET fragmentation header, XNS indicates the Xerox Network Systems header (IPX), and NCP indicates the NetWare Core Protocol is in use.

```
Sniffer Network Analyzer data 23-December-92 at 11:54:17, NW.arc,
Pg 1

DLC: ----- DLC Header -----
DLC:
DLC: Frame 11 arrived at 13:39:34.3424; frame size is 45 (002D hex) bytes.
DLC: Destination: Station 44, NetWare-XT
DLC: Source     : Station 20, IBM PC
DLC: ARCNET system code = FA
DLC:
NOV: ----- Novell ARCNET fragmentation header -----
NOV:
NOV: Unfragmented frame
NOV: Sequence number = 8
NOV:
XNS: ----- XNS Header -----
XNS:
XNS: Checksum = FFFF
XNS: Length = 37
XNS: Transport = 0
XNS: Packet type = 17 (Novell Netware)
XNS:
XNS: Dest   network = 00001111, host = 10005A0033BF, socket = 1105
XNS: Source network = 00002222, host = 000000000020, socket = 16385
XNS:
XNS: ----- Novell Advanced NetWare -----
XNS:
XNS: Request type = 2222 (Request)
XNS: Seq no=5    Connection no=1    Task no=1
XNS:
NCP: ----- Get Station Number Request -----
NCP:
NCP: Request code = 19
NCP:
NCP: [Normal end of Netware "Get Station Number Request" packet.]
NCP:
```

Trace 5-1. Novell NetWare Get Station Number Request packet transmitted over ARCNET and captured by the Network General Sniffer protocol analyzer

```
Sniffer Network Analyzer data 23-December-92 at 11:54:17, NW.arc,
Pg 1


DLC:  ----- DLC Header -----
DLC:
DLC:  Frame 12 arrived at 13:39:34.3457; frame size is 49 (0031 hex) bytes.
DLC:  Destination: Station 20, IBM PC
DLC:  Source     : Station 44, NetWare-XT
DLC:  ARCNET system code = FA
DLC:
NOV:  ----- Novell ARCNET fragmentation header -----
NOV:
NOV:  Unfragmented frame
NOV:  Sequence number = 28633
NOV:
XNS:  ----- XNS Header -----
XNS:
XNS:  Checksum = FFFF
XNS:  Length = 41
XNS:  Transport = 0
XNS:  Packet type = 17 (Novell Netware)
XNS:
XNS:  Dest   network = 00002222, host = 000000000020, socket = 16385
XNS:  Source network = 00001111, host = 10005A0033BF, socket = 1105
XNS:
XNS:  ----- Novell Advanced NetWare -----
XNS:
XNS:  Request type = 3333 (Reply)
XNS:  Seq no=5   Connection no=1   Task no=0
XNS:
NCP:  ----- Get Station Number Reply -----
NCP:
NCP:  Request code = 19 (reply to frame 11)
NCP:
NCP:  Completion code = 00 (OK)
NCP:  Connection status flags = 00 (OK)
NCP:  ASCII Station Number = 01
NCP:  Station number = 1
NCP:
NCP:  [Normal end of Netware "Get Station Number Reply" packet.]
NCP:
```

Trace 5-2. Novell NetWare Get Station Number Reply packet transmitted over ARCNET and captured by the Network General Sniffer protocol analyzer

Several elements of these trace files illustrate the uniqueness of the ARC-NET protocols. You can see that both frames fit within the ARCNET data field (less than or equal to 508 octets) since the frame is not fragmented. Reviewing Figure 5-17, the IPX (XNS) header delineates the network, host, and socket addresses, with socket 1105 indicating the NCP process. The NCP header includes fields for a request type, sequence number, connection number, task number, and function (request) code. These parameters communicate connection-related information between workstation and server. Novell has defined hundreds of NCP packet types, which illustrates the rigor built into NetWare. Reference 5-17 provides further information on ARC-NET protocol analysis.

5.11. ARCNET and ARCNETPLUS Troubleshooting Summary

In summary, here's a quick checklist to assist in troubleshooting your ARCNET network:

1. Check for duplicate node addresses. Make sure that the DIP switches are making positive contact, and that they are actuated as far as possible (either in/out or up/down).
2. Check for unterminated passive hubs, T-connectors, cable ends, or unused jacks on twisted-pair hubs or NICS.
3. Verify correct IRQ and DMA channel options, plus I/O base address, and memory (on-board RAM) buffer locations.
4. Observe the status of the diagnostic LEDs on the NIC or active hub, and verify correct network operation.
5. Check the network topology for any recent violations, such as number of PCs per segment, length of the segment, and so on.
6. Verify power connections to any active hubs; also check for any blown fuses or incorrect power (120/240 VAC) settings.
7. If the entire network has failed, start at the server and disconnect segments until proper operation is restored. Then begin adding back disconnected sections until you can isolate the failing element.

This chapter has explored ARCNET and its successor technology, ARC-NETPLUS. While ARCNET does not receive the press exposure of token-ring or FDDI networks, it's nonetheless a popular architecture. A recent survey estimated an installed base of 4 million ARCNET nodes worldwide (Reference 5-18). ARCNET's main advantages lie in its user friendliness; it's easy to install, maintain, and troubleshoot. The next chapter will look at another token-passing architecture, the token ring.

5.12 References

5-1.   Some of the material in this chapter first appeared in "Troubleshooting ARCNET," by Mark A. Miller. *LAN Technology Magazine*, (May 1989.): 44-49.

5-2.   Standard Microsystems Corp. *COM9026 Local Area Network Controller Circuit Description*, 1984.

5-3.   Standard Microsystems Corp. *COM9032 Local Area Network Transceiver Circuit Description*, 1984.

5-4.   Standard Microsystems Corp. "Using the COM9026 and COM9032," Technical Note TN5-2, 1985.

5-5.   Standard Microsystems Corp. COM90C66 Local Area Network Controller/Transceiver with AT Interface and On-Chip RAM Data Sheet, 1991.

5-6.   NCR Corp. *Microelectronic Products Short Form Catalog*, 1992.

5-7. ARCNET Trade Association. *Local Area Network: Token Bus (2.5 Mbps).* ANSI/ATA 878.1, 1992.

5-8. Datapoint Corp. *ARCNETPLUS Design Specification.* Document 51385, September 1992.

5-9. Datapoint Corp. *ARCNETPLUS Programmer's Reference Guide.* Document 51384, September 1992.

5-10. Datapoint Corp. *ARCNET Designer's Handbook,* 2d ed. Document 61610, 1988.

5-11. Datapoint Corp. *ARCNET Cabling Guide,* 2d ed. Document 51087, 1988.

5-12. Contemporary Control Systems. *ARCNET Factory LAN Primer,* 1987.

5-13. *Configuration Guide for ARCNET.* PC600/650 Network Controller Boards, Publication 900.095, September 1991.

5-14. Novell, Inc. *NetWare System Calls for DOS.* Document 101-000571-001, 1989.

5-15. Stephen Bearnson. "Communication Basics and Open Data-Link Interface Technology." *Netware Application Notes* (November 1992): 51-82.

5-16. Novell, Inc. "ARCNET Packet Header Definition Standard." Document 100-000721-001, November 1990.

5-17. Network General Corp. *ARCNET Network Portable Protocol Analyzer Operation and Reference Manual*, 1986-1988.

5-18. Bonny Hinners. "Pulling the Plug." *LAN Magazine* (January 1993): 99-120.

CHAPTER 6

Troubleshooting the Token Ring

In 1982 IBM and Texas Instruments announced an agreement to develop a chipset to support the token ring. That agreement culminated in the TMS380 five-chip set in 1985. When the token-ring standard advanced from 4- to 16-Mbps transmission speed, TI enhanced the chipset, announcing the TMS380C16 in 1988. IBM has also developed a single chip, known as the Token Ring Protocol Interface Controller (TROPIC) that National Semi-conductor Corporation now markets. A number of LAN manufacturers—including Apple Computer, Cabletron Systems, IBM, Proteon, Racal-Datacom, 3Com, Standard Microsystems and others (see Reference 6-1) also manufacture products that adhere to the IEEE 802.5 standard.

This chapter looks at how the token-ring architecture works, how specific details of the IEEE 802.5 standard fit into the ISO/OSI model, and how to troubleshoot a token-ring network.

6.1. Token-Ring Architecture

Although its name implies that it's a ring, the token ring is actually a physical star and an electrical ring. Figure 6-1 shows a sample network with two Multistation Access Units (abbreviated MSAU so as not to confuse it with the Medium Attachment Unit used with 802.3 networks) and various workstations. You can add media repeaters (for copper or fiber) between two MSAUs to increase the transmission distance. Each node acts as a bit repeater; it receives the serial bit stream from its Nearest Active Upstream Neighbor (NAUN), processes it when necessary, then sends the bit stream on to the next node. Each workstation requires only a few bit times of delay for these functions. The serial transmission follows a complete ring or loop (hence the name token ring); in other words, the sending station eventually gets the information it transmitted back after it has completed one trip around the ring.

The token is the bit sequence that circulates among the nodes, polls each workstation to determine whether it needs access to the network, and grants permission to transmit. For this reason, token-ring networks are often described as distributed polling environments. A node on a token-ring network can transmit a message from its output buffer only when it possesses a token; otherwise, it is in bit repeat (receive and process) mode.

The star-wired ring architecture has two troubleshooting advantages over other topologies: (1) The wiring center (MSAU in this case) allows ready access to both ends (workstation and wire center) of the cable for testing. (2) You can easily bypass a faulty node or wire center by rearranging jumpers on the patch panel, or by using your network management software to eliminate the failing section automatically.

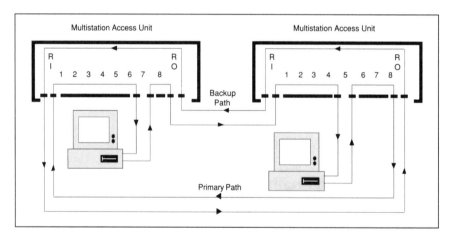

Figure 6-1. Token-ring architecture

6.2. The Token-Ring Standard

Because it adheres to the IEEE 802.5 standard (see Reference 6-2), the token-ring network offers some features that help with troubleshooting. For example, the MSAU provides some physical layer fault tolerance; and the architecture provides some built-in fault tolerance.

6.2.1. The token-ring physical layer

The 802.5 physical layer has the following characteristics:

- *Symbol Encoding*. The 802.5 physical layer uses Differential Manchester encoding with no DC component. This encoding scheme permits inductive or capacitive coupling between the cable and the network interface. The Differential Manchester signal is encoded always to have a transition in the middle of the bit cell (see Figure 6-2). To represent a binary zero, a change of state occurs at the beginning of the bit cell. To represent a binary one, the change of state occurs in the middle of the bit cell. Violations to the Differential Manchester code provide special framing characters. The timing will be important in the discussion of the active and standby monitors.

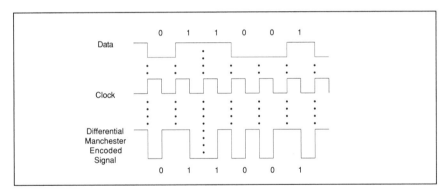

Figure 6-2. The Differential Manchester encoded signal

- *Signal Rate*. 4 or 16 Mbps.
- *Cable*. Balanced shielded twisted pairs, 150 +/- 15 ohms impedance, or unshielded twisted pairs, 100 +/- 15 ohms impedance (typically 24 to 22 AWG cable).
- *Connector*. Use a four-conductor, hermaphroditic (genderless) connector (shown in Figure 6-3a) for shielded cable. The connector is wired as follows:

Signal Lead	Pin Designation
Receive +	Red (R)
Receive -	Green (G)
Transmit +	Orange (O)
Transmit -	Black (B)

Shorting bars connect pins R and O and pins G and B. This feature is important to remember when testing for defective cables.

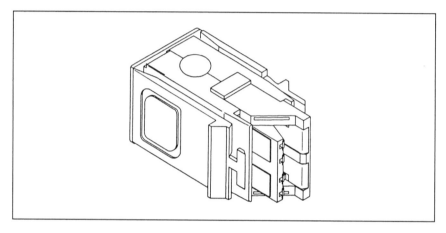

Figure 6-3a. A hermaphroditic connector

- *For unshielded twisted-pair (UTP) cable*, you typically use an eight-pin modular connector. Of the eight pins, one pair is used for the transmit (Tx) circuit, and a second pair for the receive (Rx) circuit (see Figure 6-3b). Reference 6-3 details the use of UTP with token-ring networks.
- *Latency Buffer*. In order for the token (a 24-bit sequence) to circulate properly when all stations are repeating, the ring must have at least a 24-bit time propagation delay. This delay guarantees that the token will not return to the sending station before it is completely transmitted. Since most rings are not physically long enough

← 6-Pin Jack →						← 8-Pin Jack →							
Terminal No.	1	2	3	4	5	6	1	2	3	4	5	6	7	8
Designator	U	Tx	Rx	Rx	Tx	U	U	U	Tx	Rx	Rx	Tx	U	U

Station Signal Assignment	6-Pin Jack (Pin No.)	8-Pin Jack (Pin No.)	Data Connector Code	TCU Pin Function
Tx	2	3	B	Rx
Rx	3	4	R	Tx
Rx	4	5	G	Tx
Tx	5	6	O	Rx

U: Unassigned, not used by token ring
Tx: Transmit
Rx: Receive
TCU: Trunk Coupling Unit

Figure 6-3b. The token-ring medium interface connection
(Courtesy of IEEF)

(at 4 Mbps, the cable would have to be about 4,500 feet long to hold the entire token), the Active Monitor station inserts a minimum of 24-bit times of delay.

- *Phantom Power.* The NIC uses the four-wire transmit/receive circuit to supply DC current to a relay in the MSAU. When the station is not plugged in or is turned off, the relay bypasses its MSAU port, maintaining the continuity of the ring. When the station is plugged in and turned on, the relay changes state, enabling the NIC to transmit and receive. For unpowered MSAUs, you should use an initialization tool to set the correct state of the electronic relay when you first install the MSAU. Powered MSAUs initialize the relays when the MSAU is powered up.

6.2.2. The token-ring MAC layer

The 802.5 MAC layer controls access to the transmission medium or cable and performs the following functions:

- *Frame Formats.* The 802.5 standard defines three transmission frames: the token, a 24-bit sequence authorizing network access; the MAC frames used for network management and the LLC frames for data transmission; and the abort sequence, used when a frame transmission terminates prematurely. Section 6.5 discusses the use of these frames.
- *Error Control.* This function generates the 32-bit Frame Check Sequence (FCS).
- *Ring Maintenance.* Ring maintenance functions include active and standby monitor functions, error isolation, recovery, and ring management. The functions of the ring monitors, which are especially interesting, are discussed in Section 6.2.4.

6.2.3. The LLC layer

The LLC layer defines the virtual data paths between communicating end points that work with the physical data paths defined in the MAC and physical layers. Multiple links to multiple logical entities (called Service Access Points or SAPs) are possible. For example, one NIC, with a unique 48-bit address (defined at the MAC layer) can provide a communication path to several higher-layer protocols, such as NetBIOS or SNA protocols. To review from Chapter 1, there are three different types of LLC services:

- *Type 1—Unacknowledged Connectionless.* LLC frames are sent and received with no delivery acknowledgment.
- *Type 2—Connection-Oriented.* Frames are transmitted sequentially with acknowledgments.
- *Type 3—Acknowledged Connectionless.* Datagram service with transmission acknowledgments but no virtual circuit connection.

As we saw in Chapter 1, a Class 1 LAN station supports Type 1 LLC services, while a Class II LAN station supports either Type 1 or Type 2. Texas Instruments' TMS380 chipset and National Semiconductor's TROPIC chip support Class II service.

6.2.4. The token-ring monitors

The Active Monitor is the active node with the highest address; it wins active monitor status via a claim token process that takes place between all active nodes. The Active Monitor performs the following functions: It provides the master clock for the network from which all other workstations receive their timing; it monitors the network, looking for a frame or token every 10 milliseconds; it removes any continuously circulating priority tokens or frames (with a priority greater than zero); it inserts a latency buffer (24 bits long when operating at 4 Mbps, 32 bits long at 16 Mbps) to guarantee a ring length and ensure token circulation; and it periodically notifies the other nodes of its existence by sending the Active Monitor Present MAC frame, which is one of 25 MAC frame types.

All other nodes become Standby Monitors that determine whether the Active Monitor is functioning properly.

Ring error isolation, recovery, and management involve a number of MAC-defined frames that are "built-in" to the token-ring chipsets. Section 6.8 details these services.

6.3. Token-Ring Hardware Components

Token-ring networks use more sophisticated hardware components than other networks because token-ring chipsets offer built-in network management functions. Therefore, I will briefly discuss the chipset before exploring other hardware components.

6.3.1 Token-ring network controller chips

Texas Instruments' TMS380 chipset implements the IEEE 802.5 standard for token-ring LANs. Two versions of the chipset exist. The first generation, TMS380, is a five-chip set that operates at 4 Mbps and consists of:

- *TMS38051* Ring interface transceiver
- *TMS38052* Ring interface controller
- *TMS38010* Communication protocol processor
- *TMS38021* Protocol handler for 802.5 functions
- *TMS38030* DMA controller between the NIC and host system bus

155

The TMS380C16 second-generation token-ring COMMprocessor, which operates at 16 Mbps, incorporates the functions of the TMS38010, TMS38021, and TMS38030 into a single 132-pin device using 1-micron complementary metal-oxide semiconductor (CMOS) technology. The device also combines the TMS38051 and TMS38052 ring interface transceiver and controller chips into the TMS38053 ring interface. The ring interface processes the signal from the transmission media, then sends a data stream to the COMMprocessor. Second-generation devices have dramatically reduced the size of the NIC to less than 10 square inches. Among the companies currently using the TMS380 chipset in products are Andrew Corp., Crosscomm Corp., Cisco Systems, Inc., Olicom, Proteon, Inc., Racore Computer Products, and Vitalink Communications Corp. The TMS380 User's Guide (Reference 6-4) provides further information on the design and use of the T.I. chipset.

Although IBM and Texas Instruments jointly developed the first generation TMS380 chipset, the companies went their separate ways for subsequent generations of token-ring controllers. IBM developed and manufactures the TROPIC, a single-chip solution. In February of 1992, IBM announced that National Semiconductor Corporation would market and support the TROPIC as the DP8025 (see Reference 6-5).

As a single chip solution, the TROPIC includes a high level of integration. This chip integration means fewer components on the token-ring NIC itself. The NIC consists of the TROPIC chip, transmit and receive buffers, Programmable Read-Only Memory (PROMs) containing MAC/LLC and addressing functions, an interface to the host system, and an interface to the cable.

In addition to IBM, a number of hardware manufacturers are using the TROPIC chip in their products, thus assuring compatibility and interoperability with IBM products. Currently, these vendors include Alta Research, Asante Technologies Corp., Compex Inc., Eagle, Madge Networks Inc., Microdyne and Thomas-Conrad Corp., and 3Com Corp.

6.3.2. Token-ring NICs

Figure 6-4 shows an example of a token-ring NIC, the p1392 ProNet 4/16 AT NIC from Proteon, Inc. (Westborough, Mass.). Note that the NIC offers both shielded twisted-pair (DB-9) and unshielded twisted-pair (RJ-45) connectors. You can see the TMS380C16 chip in the upper left-hand corner of the board.

Figure 6-4. The p1392 ProNet 4/16 AT NIC
(Photo courtesy of Proteon, Inc.)

6.3.3. Token-ring Multistation Access Units (MSAUs)

The MSAU is the token ring's wiring hub. Figure 6-5 shows a sample MSAU, the Proteon Series 70 Intelligent Hub. On the front panel, you can see eight ports for workstations and Ring In (RI) and Ring Out (RO) connectors for connecting to other MSAUs. One of the Proteon product's strengths is its support for various transmission media. Products in the Series 70 family can support STP and UTP at the node ports, and STP, UTP, or fiber-optic connections at the RI/RO ports.

Figure 6-5. The Proteon Series 70 Intelligent Hub
(Photo courtesy of Proteon, Inc.)

Another important feature of the Proteon products is their integration into the TokenView Plus and OneView network management systems, which use the troubleshooting capabilities incorporated into the 802.5 standard. The Proteon Intelligent Hubs also include relays in the RI and RO ports to facilitate remote fault isolation. Other vendors' products use the hermaphroditic connectors (with the internal shorting bars) for RI and RO instead. Recall from Figure 6-1 that you should connect the first RI to the last RO to provide a backup wiring path for MSAUs on the same wiring rack.

Figure 6-6 shows the MSAU's internal wiring. Note that attached, activated workstations have opened the relay connections at the ports; the relay contacts are closed for disconnected or inactive ports to maintain the electrical continuity of the ring. As the station inserts into the ring, you can hear an audible "click" when the relay operates. It's a good idea to listen for this sound at the MSAU enclosure to verify proper port operation.

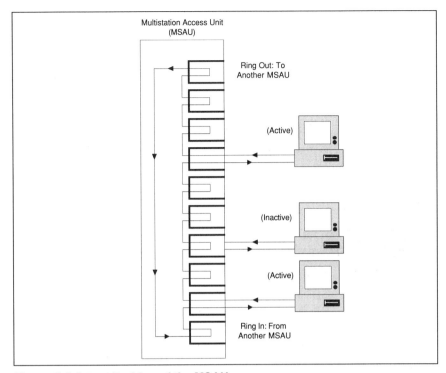

Figure 6-6. Internal wiring of the MSAU

6.3.4. Token-ring cabling systems

Section 6.2.1 noted that the 802.5 standard specifies shielded twisted pairs with a characteristic impedance of 150 ± 15 ohms, or unshielded twisted pairs with a characteristic impedance of 100 ± 15 ohms. IBM defines the cable types for its token-ring network by number, as follows:

- *Type 1*. Two shielded, solid wire, twisted pairs, 22 AWG. Available for plenum or nonplenum interior use and underground or aerial exterior use. Use of Type 1 permits transmission at 16 Mbps, and a maximum of 260 stations on the network.
- *Type 2*. Two shielded, solid wire, twisted pairs, 22 AWG, plus four twisted pairs of solid 26 AWG wires added between the shield and the insulating cable sheath. Type 2 also supports 16 Mbps transmission.

- *Type 3*. Unshielded, telephone-grade (22 or 24 AWG) twisted pairs, typically found inside a building. Requires a media filter at (or within) the NIC, and limits the transmission rate to 4 Mbps, and the number of workstations to 72.
- *Type 5*. 100/140 micron fiber-optic cable, used to connect distant MSAUs with fiber-optic repeaters.
- *Type 6*. Patch cables consisting of data-grade, stranded, shielded twisted pairs, 26 AWG. The distance limits are 66 percent of Type 1.
- *Type 8*. Undercarpet cable, data-grade twisted-pair cable, 26 AWG. The distance limits are 50 percent that of Type 1.
- *Type 9*. Shielded twisted pair, 26 AWG approved for plenum installations. The distance limits are 66 percent that of Type 1.

Many vendors, including Anixter Brothers, Belden, and Mohawk, also supply various components and assemblies for the IBM cabling systems. References 6-6 and 6-7 provide further details on the cable types and specifications.

6.3.5. Token-ring repeaters

Both copper and fiber-optic repeaters are available to connect MSAUs in distant wiring closets. Specific details on distance limitations and other characteristics are beyond the scope of this book; see References 6-7 and 6-8 for further information.

6.4. Token-Ring Hardware Troubleshooting

Any time a ring is malfunctioning, you should first look for problems resulting from human error, such as unplugged cables, improper transmission speed settings (4 versus 16 Mbps), and so on. Because of the myriad of patch cord connections typically found on a token-ring network, be sure to have copies of the network documentation on hand. IBM, for example, offers a problem determination guide that walks you though the analysis of very complex problems (see References 6-7 and 6-8). After that, it's relatively straightforward to isolate the defective portion of the ring (called the failure domain), remove (or patch around) the failing section, repair the defective component, and restore the ring to full operation.

6.4.1. Identifying failure domains

The IEEE 802.5 standard defines the term *failure domain* as the station reporting a failure, its Nearest Active Upstream Neighbor (NAUN), and the cable (and possibly repeaters) in between.

This means that a downstream station discovers failures in an upstream node or cable. When it recognizes a failure, the downstream station initiates the Beacon process. The Beacon process first transmits a MAC frame called a Beacon frame to notify the other network stations of the failure. A protocol analyzer or the diagnostic disk that accompanies most token-ring cards can decode the Beacon frame, which includes the NAUN station address and Beaconing station address. Once you define these two end points, you know that the hardware failure must be somewhere in between. The Beacon process also performs an autoreconfiguration, in which the nodes within the failure domain automatically perform cable and node diagnostics. Thus, in many cases, failure recovery is automatic.

When the network has just one wiring closet, you can isolate the failure to an individual MSAU and bypass the failed MSAU by rearranging jumper cables. When there are multiple wiring closets, first isolate the problem to a single closet, then identify the failed MSAU. Further troubleshooting involves testing (or replacing) both NICs, MSAUs, or repeaters, and thoroughly testing the cable system in between. As part of your cable plant testing, be sure to check any noise filters used with unshielded twisted-pair cable. Reference 6-9 further details these analysis processes.

6.4.2. Token-ring cable system testing

Since many token-ring failures involve cable and wiring difficulties, several companies have developed tools to specifically test token-ring cabling. One such tool is the RingOut cable tester from Bytex Corp. (Southborough, Mass.) shown in Figure 6-7. The RingOut includes both DB-9 and RJ-45 connectors, and offers a number of token-ring-specific tests. These tests can verify the cable, the MSAU port relay, and proper ring operation as well as locate a Beaconing node on an inoperable ring.

Figure 6-7. The RingOut cable tester
(Photo courtesy of Bytex Corp.)

Figure 6-8 shows the nine-pin (DB-9) hermaphroditic connector that the NIC uses to connect to the MSAU port. You can do a quick test of the shorting bars within the hermaphroditic connector by using a VOM to measure the resistance between pins 1 and 9, and pins 5 and 6 on the DB-9 connector at the other end of the pigtail cable (see Figure 6-9). If the shorting bars are operating properly, both of these measurements will be very close to a short (0 ohms) since transmit + should be shorted to receive +, and transmit - should be shorted to receive -.

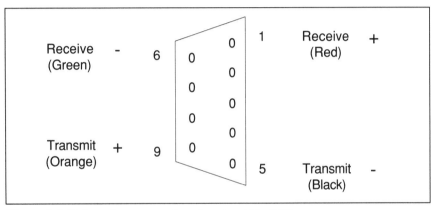

Figure 6-8. Token-ring connector pinouts at the NIC

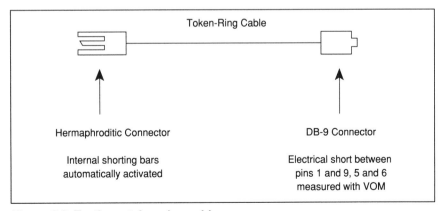

Figure 6-9. Testing a token-ring cable

6.5. Token-Ring Frames

The token ring employs three frame formats: the token, the frame, and the abort sequence, shown in Figures 6-10a, b, and c, respectively. In addition, two classes of frames (types of data) are possible: LLC Frames transmit user data, and MAC frames manage the ring.

Starting Delimiter	Access Control	Ending Delimiter	
1	1	1	octets
VV0VV000	PPPTMRRR	VV1VV1IE	

V = Differential
    Manchester
    Violations
0 = Binary ZERO

P = Priority Mode
T = Token Bit
M = Monitor Count
R = Priority
    Reservation

V = Differential
    Manchester
    Violations
1 = Binary ONE
I = Intermediate
E = Error Detect

Figure 6-10a. Token-ring token format

6.5.1. The token format

The token circulates the ring, controlling access to the network. As you can see in Figure 6-10a, the token's 24 bits are divided into three octets: the starting delimiter, which contains violations to the Differential Manchester Code and binary zeros; the access control field; and the ending delimiter.

The access control field grants network access. It begins with three Priority (P) bits that set the priority of the token. Each workstation is assigned a priority (see the Change Parameters MAC frame) for their transmissions: 000 is the lowest; 111 is the highest. The Token (T) bit delineates either a Token (T=0) or a Frame (T=1). The Monitor (M) bit prevents high priority tokens or any frames from continuously circulating the ring. It is set to M=0 by the transmitting station, and M=1 by the active monitor. If the monitor sees an incoming priority token or frame with M=1, it assumes that the transmitting station did not remove the token or frame after one round trip, removes it, purges the ring, and issues a new token. The workstation can use Priority Reservation (R) bits to reserve the next token as a transmission passes by. For a workstation to transmit, its priority must be greater than or equal to the priority of the token.

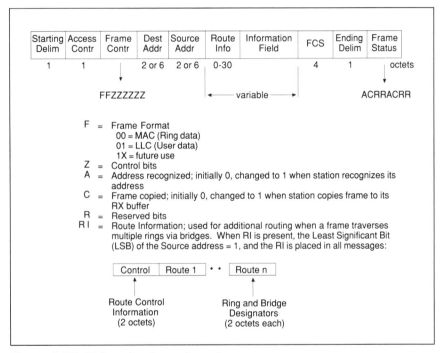

Figure 6-10b. Token-ring frame format

The ending delimiter signals the end of the transmission to the receiver. The ending delimiter also includes Differential Manchester Code violations and binary ones; an Intermediate frame (I) bit, which indicates that a frame is part of a multiframe transmission; and an Error detect (E) bit that is set when a frame contains a Frame Check Sequence (FCS) error, a nonintegral number of bytes, or a Differential Manchester Code violation between starting and ending delimiters.

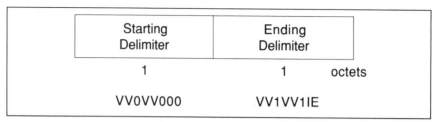

Starting Delimiter	Ending Delimiter	
1	1	octets
VV0VV000	VV1VV1IE	

Figure 6-10c. Token-ring abort sequence

6.5.2. The frame formats

As you can see in Figure 6-10b, the first two octets of the frame, the Starting Delimiter and Access Control fields, come from the token format described previously. The two types of frames, MAC and LLC, are identified by the first two bits of the third octet, or frame control field:

00ZZZZZZ	= MAC frame
01ZZZZZZ	= LLC frame
1XZZZZZZ	= Reserved for future use
Z	= Represents control bits

Next the Destination and Source Address fields can be 2 or 6 octets long, although the longer addresses are commonly used. The Address field format is the same as that used for the IEEE 802.3 networks, and is described in Figure 7-11b. The Routing Information field is optional, and is used for multiring networks, as described in Reference 6-10. The information field is variable in length, although length is generally limited by the manufacturer and the transmission rate (4 Mbps or 16 Mbps). Within the Information field is an LLC or MAC Protocol Data Unit (PDU).

The Frame Check Sequence (FCS) field is a 32-bit CRC. The ending delimiter field is also from the token format. Last, the Frame Status field provides feedback to the transmitter about the condition of the frame. The receiving station sets the Address Recognized (A) bits equal to one to indicate that the intended receiver recognized its address. The receiving station sets the Frame Copied (C) bits equal to one to indicate that it copied the frame into its buffer. Both the A and C bits are repeated for redundancy. By reading the A and C bits, the transmitter can verify proper reception of a frame.

6.5.2.1. The LLC frame format. Figure 6-11 shows the LLC frame. Imbedded within the information field of the 802.5 frame are: The LLC Protocol Data Unit (PDU), which contains the Destination and Source Service Access Point Addresses (DSAP and SSAP); a Control field that defines three types of PDUs and finally another Information field. The Control field may designate an Information (I), Supervisory (S), or Unnumbered (U) transfer of data. The Information field within the LLC PDU contains user data from the higher layers of the ISO/OSI model; that is, 3 through 7. Reference 6-11 explains these items in detail.

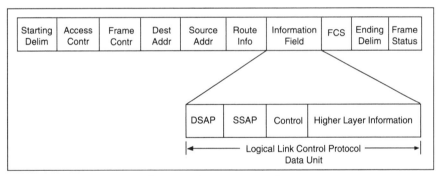

Figure 6-11. The 802.2 LLC PDU within an 802.5 frame

6.5.2.2. The MAC frame format. Figure 6-12 illustrates the MAC frame. The Information field within the MAC PDU consists of a Length field, indicating the PDU's length in octets; a Class field, indicating the source and destination class (for example, Ring Station, Network Manager, Ring Parameter Server, Ring Error Monitor, and so on); Commands for the intended receiver to perform; and Parameters, called subvectors, that elaborate on the commands. Section 6.9 provides more details on these functions.

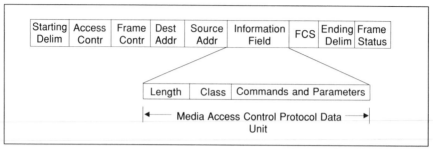

Figure 6-12. The MAC PDU within an 802.5 frame

6.5.3. The abort sequence format

Certain error conditions, such as hard errors internal to the workstation, cause the transmission of the abort sequence shown in Figure 6-10c. Note that the starting delimiter and ending delimiter fields are the same as in the token frame, discussed in Section 6.5.1.

6.6. Token-Ring Management

Each token-ring NIC, regardless of manufacturer, includes the network management functions provided by the 802.5 standard. These functions include monitoring soft and hard errors; maintaining configuration details, such as the NAUN; and controlling various parameters, such as the token priority, ring number, and so on. The network management "agent" located in each NIC provides these functions and communicates with the network management "product" located somewhere on the network. The product could be a dedicated program, such as Proteon's TokenVIEW Plus software, IBM's LAN Network Manager (see Reference 6-12), or integrated into an intelligent wiring hub, such as Cabletron Systems' MultiMedia Access Center (MMAC). Figure 6-13 illustrates the relationship between the agent on the NIC or Ring Station (RS), and the product (attached somewhere on the network).

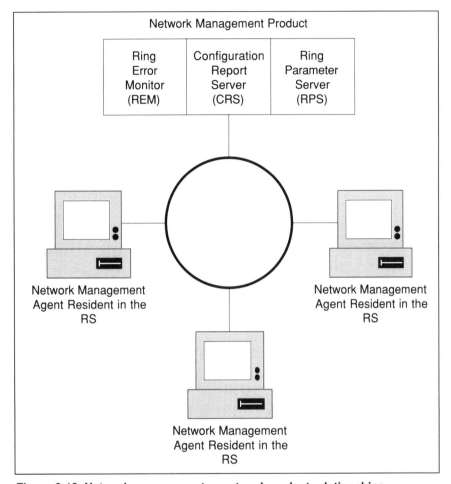

Figure 6-13. Network management agent and product relationships

The product implements four functions:

1. *The Active and Standby Monitors* supervise the network operation.

2. *The Ring Error Monitor (REM)* is responsible for collecting error reports from the NICs and Active and Standby Monitors.

3. *The Configuration Report Server (CRS)* keeps track of the current network configuration and controls individual NIC para-

169

meters, such as access priority, or signals a particular station to remove itself from the ring.

4. *The Ring Parameter Server (RPS)* assigns operational parameters to the station at the time of insertion onto the ring.

Since the product may exist anywhere on the ring, the agent communicates with the product through a series of 25 MAC frames transmitted to one of several functional (or well-known) addresses, shown here as 12 hexadecimal characters (or 6 octets):

C00000000001: Active Monitor
C00000000002: Ring Parameter Server
C00000000008: Ring Error Monitor
C00000000010: Configuration Report Server

When the agent wants (or is asked) to communicate with the product, it builds a MAC frame, as shown in Figure 6-12, and transmits it to the appropriate functional address above. The host system (for example, a workstation on the network) is oblivious to these transmissions since they're used for network management, not for transmitting user data. Should a fault, such as a noisy section of cable, occur on the network, the human network administrator can use the software network management product for diagnostic assistance. Protocol analysis tools can also capture, record, and decode various MAC frames to help you isolate faults and optimize the network. Since the active monitor, ring parameter server, ring error monitor, and configuration report server have unique addresses, you can capture any information sent to one of these entities for further analysis, as discussed in Section 6.10.

6.7. Token-Ring Processes

To understand the various MAC frames, it helps to review the processes that occur between workstations on a token-ring network. These processes include ring insertion, claim token, ring purge, neighbor notification, beacon, transmit forward, hardware error, and soft error counting. For more information, see Section 2.4.4 of Reference 6-4.

6.7.1. Ring insertion

When any host system wishes to attach to the ring, it issues an open command to the network to initiate the ring insertion process. The process has five phases:

Phase 0. The Lobe Media check verifies the cable by looping the station transmit signal to the station receiver at the wiring concentrator. It then issues the Lobe Media Test MAC frame.

Phase 1. Physical insertion. The NIC applies phantom drive DC current to the transmit pair to activate the relay at the wire concentrator port, thus activating the relay at the MSAU port. The NIC is now physically connected to the network.

Phase 2. Address verification. The station verifies that its address is unique within the ring. It uses the Duplicate Address Test MAC frame.

Phase 3. Neighbor notification. The station learns its upstream neighbor's address and sends its own address to the nearest downstream neighbor.

Phase 4. Request initialization. The workstation sends the Request Initialization MAC frame to the RPS, which responds with an Initialize Ring Station MAC frame containing that station's parameters, such as the local ring number. If no RPS is present, the station will insert onto the ring with its default parameters.

When Phase 4 is completed, the station is physically and logically attached to the network.

6.7.2. Claim token

One of the active RS's must be designated as the active monitor (AM); all others are standby monitors. When an RS detects the absence of the AM, it originates the claim token (also called monitor contention) process by transmitting a Claim Token MAC frame. The active RS with the highest address wins the process and becomes the new active monitor.

6.7.3. Ring purge

There are two cases in which the AM uses the ring purge process: to put the ring in a token-passing mode after it wins the monitor contention process, or when it detects a token error condition. The AM initiates the Ring Purge MAC frame, and all downstream stations repeat it. When the Ring Purge frame returns to the AM without errors, the AM transmits a new token, thus initiating token passing.

6.7.4. Neighbor notification

This process allows each RS to obtain the 6 octet (or 12 hex character) address of its upstream neighbor, and also provides the CRS with an ordered list of all active stations.

6.7.5. Beacon

The Beacon process alerts downstream stations to a hard error, causing network failure. Examples of such a failure would include a broken or shorted cable, or a defective NIC. The Beacon MAC frame also informs the downstream stations about the nature of the failure. If a station's downstream neighbor sends the Beacon frame (that is, points to a fault at the upstream station or the cable in between), the upstream neighbor automatically tests itself and may remove itself from the ring.

6.7.6. Transmit forward

Transmit forward transmits (or relays) information around the ring to test the communication path between stations.

6.7.7. Hardware error

Hardware error detects a wire fault (absence or improper DC phantom drive from the NIC); frequency error (a frequency difference between the incoming signal and the station's crystal oscillator); or loss of signal (either insufficient signal level or major phase difference).

6.7.8. Soft error counting

Soft error counting is a log of network errors that degrade performance but don't cause network failure, such as corrupted tokens. The higher-layer protocols use the log to initiate a recovery process, and the CRS uses it to isolate potential problem areas.

6.8.   Token-Ring MAC Frames

The MAC frames, which provide communication for the token-ring processes described above, can be divided into four categories: medium control; station initialization; error monitoring; and network management. Recall that the MAC frames are transmitted from the network management agent (on the NIC or RS) to one of several functional addresses: AM, RPS, REM, or the CRS. Delving into these frames with, say, a protocol analyzer will provide further insight into the network's internal operation. The 25 MAC frame formats are shown in Sections 6.8.1 through 6.8.4. For further information on the MAC frames, see Section 2.4.4 of Reference 6-4.

6.8.1 Medium control frames

Medium control frames are concerned with the reliable operation of the network. They include

- *Beacon (RS to all RS)*. Beacon frames are transmitted when an RS detects a hard failure, such as a wire fault, signal loss, or streaming station.
- *Claim Token (RS to all RS)*. Any station that detects the absence of the AM transmits the claim token to start the claim token

process; claim token frames are also transmitted during the contention process that determines the new AM.

- *Ring Purge (AM to all RS)*. The AM uses ring purge frames to recover from a temporary error condition, release a new token, and reinitialize the token passing process; or to conclude the claim token process.
- *Active Monitor Present (AM to all RS)*. The AM transmits the Active Monitor Present frame every 7 seconds or at the end of the Ring Purge process to indicate that it is present.
- *Standby Monitor Present (RS to all RS or AM)*. This frame is transmitted in response to an Active Monitor Present or another Standby Monitor Present frame during the neighbor notification process.

6.8.2 Station initialization frames

Station initialization frames are used when a station wishes to join the ring. They include

- *Lobe Media Test (RS to itself)* is used during the initial phase of the ring insertion process to test the transmission media from the station to the wire center and back.
- *Duplicate Address Test (RS to all RS's)* verifies the uniqueness of a station's address.
- *Request Initialization (RS to RPS)* asks the RPS for operational parameters (local ring number, physical drop number, and error report timer value) during the ring initialization process.
- *Initialize Ring Station (RPS to RS)* transmits the parameters from the RPS to the station.

6.8.3 Error monitoring frames

Error monitoring frames indicate soft errors. They include

- *Report Error (RS to REM)* counts the soft errors that higher-layer protocols may be able to recover from.

174

- *Report Monitor Error (RS to REM)* informs the REM of a problem in the claim token process, or a problem with the AM.
- *Report Neighbor Notification Incomplete (RS to REM)* indicates that the station has not received a transmission from its upstream neighbor during the neighbor notification process.

6.8.4 Network management frames

Network management frames control the network configuration and station parameters:

- *Report New Monitor (AM to CRS)*. The winning station transmits this frame at the end of the claim token process.
- *Report SUA Change (RS to CRS)*. This frame reports a change in the station's stored upstream address as a result of information gathered during the neighbor notification process.
- *Remove Ring Station (CRS to RS)*. The Configuration Report Server sends this frame to force a station to withdraw from the ring.
- *Change Parameters (CRS to RS)*. These parameters allow the Configuration Report Server to change the local ring number, physical drop number, soft error report timer value, function class, and access priority number; they may also be used during the station initialization process.

The Configuration Report Server uses the following frames to gather information about a particular station:

- *Request Station Address (CRS to RS)*
- *Report Station Address (RS to CRS)*
- *Request Station State (CRS to RS)*
- *Report Station State (RS to CRS)*
- *Request Station Attachment (CRS to RS)*
- *Report Station Attachment (RS to CRS)*
- *Transmit Forward (CRS to RS)* tests the path between various stations by retransmitting a given message.

175

- *Report Transmit Forward (RS to CRS)* is a confirmation from the station to the CRS that a frame has been forwarded in the transmit forward process.
- *Response (RS to CRS or RPS)* acknowledges a response to a Change Parameters (from CRS) or an Initialize Ring Station (from RPS) frame.

6.9. Token-Ring Software Considerations

Many software failures require you to use a protocol analyzer to decode at OSI layers 3-7; these are discussed in Section 6.10. You should be aware of several software-configurable parameters that may cause difficulties.

6.9.1. NIC address

The token-ring frame format specifies a 2 or 6 octet (16 or 48 bit) address for source and destination nodes. These addresses can be universally administered (and burned into a ROM chip on the NIC) or locally administered (set in RAM on the NIC). While it is always safest to use the ROM address (in theory, these are never duplicated), you may on occasion require the locally administered address. For example, the network administrator may wish to correlate the physical workstation location with a locally administered address (LAA). If this is done, the LAA will begin with a hexadecimal 4; that is, 400000000001H could represent workstation, port, or location number 1.

If you use LAAs, be sure not to select a duplicate address. Some vendors recommend using a specific prefix for LAAs; for example, Proteon suggests 4000C9XXXXXXH, where the network administrator assigns the Xs. IBM recommends that the LAA fall within the range of 400000000000 to 40007FFFFFFFH. Consult vendor-specific references, such as IBM's (see Reference 6-8), or Proteon's (see Reference 6-13) for further information.

6.9.2. Memory considerations

The TROPIC token-ring chipset shares its memory with the workstation's address space; NICs based upon the TMS380 chipset use DMA. Therefore, when you use TROPIC-based NICs, be careful to select the RAM address to avoid conflict with other system boards. As with other workstation add-in cards, check for conflicts with the interrupt level, I/O base address, and so on.

6.9.3. NIC priority

The token format includes two fields (the network priority and priority reservation) that comprise eight priorities (000 = lowest and 111 = highest) for tokens. These fields allow a high priority transmission to grab the next token, regardless of its physical position in the ring. In most cases, all nodes will have the same priority, such as a default of 000; however, in fine-tuning the network, you may need to set a host or bridge at a higher priority. If a particular node experiences response time delays when the network is heavily used, make sure the software driver hasn't incorrectly set that NIC's priority lower than the other nodes on the network.

6.9.4. Routing information

The routing information field is inserted in the frame anytime the source-to-destination route includes one or more bridges. You obtain the parameters that identify the bridge-ring paths via special frames that discover routes. Should a particular workstation have trouble accessing another node via a bridge, double-check the routing information (review Reference 6-10).

6.10.   Protocol Analysis with NetBIOS Frames

IBM and Sytek, Inc. developed NetBIOS as a programming interface to IBM's PC Network LAN. In its initial release, NetBIOS came on the IBM PC Network board itself; in subsequent releases of the token-ring network, workstations emulate NetBIOS. Many other vendors also offer NetBIOS emulators (see References 6-14 and 6-15, Chapter 5).

Table 6-1. NetBIOS frames available with the IBM Token Ring Network

Command Name	Code	Function
ADD_GROUP_NAME_QUERY	'00'H	Check for duplicate group name on network
ADD_NAME_QUERY	'01'H	Check for duplicate name on network
ADD_NAME_RESPONSE	'0D'H	Negative response: add name is duplicate
NAME_IN_CONFLICT	'02'H	Duplicate names detected
NAME_QUERY	'0A'H	Request to locate a name on the network
NAME_RECOGNIZED	'0E'H	Name recognized: NAME_QUERY response
SESSION_ALIVE	'1F'H	Verify session is still active
SESSION_CONFIRM	'17'H	SESSION_INITIALIZE acknowledgment
SESSION_END	'18'H	Session termination
SESSION_INITIALIZE	'19'H	A session has been set up
DATA_ACK	'14'H	DATA_ONLY_LAST acknowledgment
DATA_FIRST_MIDDLE	'15'H	Session data message-first or middle frame
DATAGRAM	'08H'	Application-generated datagram
DATAGRAM_BROADCAST	'09'H	Application-generated broadcast datagram
DATA_ONLY_LAST	'16'H	Session data message—only or last frame
NO_RECEIVE	'1A'H	No receive command to hold received data
RECEIVE_CONTINUE	X'1C'	Indicated receive outstanding
RECEIVE_OUTSTANDING	'1B'H	Retransmit last data—receive command up
STATUS_QUERY	'03'H	Request remote node status
STATUS_RESPONSE	'0F'H	Remote node status information
TERMINATE_TRACE	'07'H	Terminate traces at remote nodes
TERMINATE_TRACE	'13'H	Terminate traces at local and remote nodes

Many applications are NetBIOS compatible, which means that they use the NetBIOS functions for network communication. In terms of the ISO/OSI model, NetBIOS is a session-layer interface that establishes and terminates the communication session between two users on the network, or between a user and the network server. NetBIOS does not rigorously address functions at the transport and network layers, specifically end-to-end reliability and internetworking. For these functions, other protocols, such as TCP/IP, are used in addition to NetBIOS. References 6-16 and 6-17 discuss using NetBIOS with TCP/IP; Chapter 8 discusses TCP/IP.

When using NetBIOS, the host machine builds a Network Control Block and transmits the appropriate NetBIOS frame. Table 6-1, from Reference 6-15, lists the NetBIOS frames available with the IBM Token Ring network; see Chapter 3 in that reference for further details.

Figure 6-14, also from Reference 6-15, shows how a NetBIOS frame is encapsulated within the token-ring information field. Note the NetBIOS command field (CMD)—the 1 octet code specifying the NetBIOS frame in use.

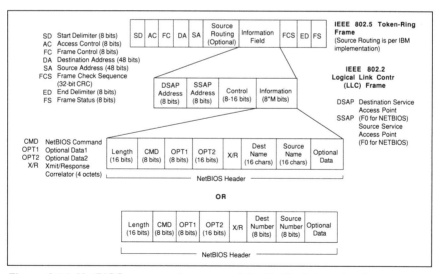

Figure 6-14. NetBIOS commands encapsulated in the token-ring frame

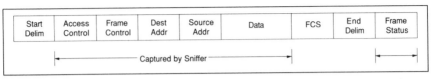

Figure 6-15. Capture range for the Network General Sniffer protocol analyzer for token-ring networks

Figure 6-15 shows the capture range of the Network General Sniffer protocol analyzer. Traces 6-1 and 6-2 show NetBIOS frames used with a token-ring network and captured with the Sniffer. The summary trace (Trace 6-1) shows the processes required to establish a NetBIOS session between two token-ring nodes, then transmit data over the connection. In frame 65, workstation Proteon 1 transmits a NetBIOS Name Query (code 0AH in Table 6-1), looking for the name "Boomer." Note that the destination address is C00000000080H, which is a functional address assigned for NetBIOS service. Workstation Proteon 6 recognizes that name in frame 66. (Some breaks in the frame numbers appear because I have filtered the trace to remove frames irrelevant to this discussion.) In frame 71A (code 19H in Table 6-1), the session is initialized and confirmed (frame 73). Data transfer begins in frame 75.

The detail trace of the captured data provides further insight into the NetBIOS frames (see Trace 6-2). The notations along the left-hand side of the figure indicate the protocol layer being decoded. DLC indicates Data Link Control (in this case, token-ring), RI indicates Routing Information, LLC indicates Logical Link Control, and NETB indicates NetBIOS. (Reference 6-18 discusses the operation of the Sniffer protocol analyzer in greater detail.)

In frame 65, the RI field indicates a single-route broadcast, with all-routes broadcast return. This would be consistent with a name query, since the sending station (Proteon 1) does not know where on the network the desired receiver (Boomer) will be found. Note also that the LLC layer uses the value F0H for both the DSAP and SSAP addresses. The NetBIOS Name Query Packet uses the first header structure shown in Figure 6-14, specifying the destination and source names, rather than destination and source numbers.

Trace 6-1. Summary of NetBIOS frames transmitted over a token-ring network and captured by the Network General Sniffer protocol analyzer

Sniffer Network Analyzer data 16-May-91 at 17:36:50, NETB.TRC, Pg.1

SUMMARY	Delta T	Destination	Source	Summary
65	2.835	C00000000080	Prteon 1	NETB Find name Boomer
66	0.004	Prteon 1	Prteon 5	NETB Name Boomer recognized
71	0.011	Prteon 5	Prteon 1	NETB D=23 S=01 Session initialize
73	0.004	Prteon 1	Prteon	5NETB D=01 S=23 Session confirm
75	0.003	Prteon 5	Prteon	1NETB D=23 S=01 Data 128 bytes
79	0.332	Prteon 1	Prteon	5NETB D=01 S=23 Send more now
81	0.003	Prteon 5	Prteon	1NETB D=23 S=01 Data 128 bytes

Trace 6-2. Details of NetBIOS frames transmitted over a token-ring network and captured by the Network General Sniffer protocol analyzer

Sniffer Network Analyzer data 16-May-91 at 17:36:50, NETB.TRC, Pg.1

```
- - - - - - - - - - -- - - - - Frame 65 - - - - - - - - - - - - - -


    DLC:  —- DLC Header —-
    DLC:
    DLC:  Frame 65 arrived at  17:37:50.079; frame size is
            63 (003F hex) bytes.
    DLC:  AC: Frame priority 0,  Reservation priority 0,
            Monitor count 1
    DLC:  FC: LLC frame,  PCF attention code: None
    DLC:  FS: Addr recognized indicators: 11, Frame copied
            indicators: 11
    DLC:  Destination = Functional address C00000000080
    DLC:  Source     = Station Prteon  1
```

```
DLC:
RI :  —- Routing Indicators —-
RI :
RI :  Routing control = C2
RI :        110. .... = Single-route broadcast,
             all-routes broadcast return
RI :        ...0 0010 = RI length is 2
RI :  Routing control = 70
RI :        0... .... = Forward direction
RI :        .111 .... = Largest frame is unspecified maximum
              value
RI :        .... 0000 = Reserved
RI :
LLC:  —- LLC Header —-
LLC:
LLC:  DSAP = F0, SSAP = F0, Command, Unnumbered frame: UI
LLC:
NETB: —- NETBIOS Name Query —-
NETB:
NETB: Header length = 44, Data length = 0
NETB: Delimiter = EFFF (NETBIOS)
NETB: Command = 0A
NETB: Local session number = 1
NETB: Caller's name type = 00 (Unique name)
NETB: Receiver's name = Boomer
NETB: Sender's name = <Brutus>
NETB:


- - - - - - - - - - - - - - Frame 66 - - - - - - - - - - - - -


DLC:  —- DLC Header —-
DLC:
DLC:  Frame 66 arrived at  17:37:50.083; frame size is
           61 (003D hex) bytes.
DLC:  AC: Frame priority 0,  Reservation priority 0,
           Monitor count 1
DLC:  FC: LLC frame,  PCF attention code: None
DLC:  FS: Addr recognized indicators: 11, Frame copied
           indicators: 11
```

```
DLC:  Destination = Station Prteon  1
DLC:  Source      = Station Prteon  5
DLC:
LLC:  —- LLC Header —-
LLC:
LLC:  DSAP = F0, SSAP = F0, Command, Unnumbered frame: UI
LLC:
NETB: —- NETBIOS Name Recognized —-
NETB:
NETB: Header length = 44, Data length = 0
NETB: Delimiter = EFFF (NETBIOS)
NETB: Command = 0E
NETB: Local session number = 35
NETB: Caller's name type = 00 (Unique name)
NETB: Transmit correlator = 0005
NETB: Response correlator = 03D7
NETB: Receiver's name = <Brutus>
NETB: Sender's name = Boomer
NETB:


- - - - - - - - - - - - - Frame 71 - - - - - - - - - - - - - -


DLC:  —- DLC Header —-
DLC:
DLC:  Frame 71 arrived at  17:37:50.095; frame size is
         32 (0020 hex) bytes.
DLC:  AC: Frame priority 0,  Reservation priority 0,
         Monitor count 1
DLC:  FC: LLC frame,  PCF attention code: None
DLC:  FS: Addr recognized indicators: 00, Frame copied
         indicators: 00
DLC:  Destination = Station Prteon  5
DLC:  Source      = Station Prteon  1
DLC:
LLC:  —- LLC Header —-
LLC:
LLC:  DSAP = F0, SSAP = F0, Command, I frame, N(R) = 0, N(S) = 0
LLC:
NETB: —- NETBIOS Session Initialize —-
```

```
NETB:
NETB: Header length = 14, Data length = 0
NETB: Delimiter = EFFF (NETBIOS)
NETB: Command = 19
NETB: Flags = 8F
NETB: 1... .... = NO.ACK ability
NETB: .... 111. = Largest frame value = 7
NETB: .... ...1 = Version 2.0 or higher
NETB: Max data receive size = 2000
NETB: Transmit correlator = 03D7
NETB: Response correlator = 0006
NETB: Remote session number = 35
NETB: Local session number = 1
NETB:


- - - - - - - - - - - - - Frame 73 - - - - - - - - - - - - - - -


DLC:  —- DLC Header —-
DLC:
DLC:  Frame 73 arrived at  17:37:50.100; frame size is
          32 (0020 hex) bytes.
DLC:  AC: Frame priority 0,  Reservation priority 4,
          Monitor count 1
DLC:  FC: LLC frame,  PCF attention code: None
DLC:  FS: Addr recognized indicators: 11, Frame copied
          indicators: 11
DLC:  Destination = Station Prteon  1
DLC:  Source      = Station Prteon  5
DLC:
LLC:  —- LLC Header —-
LLC:
LLC:  DSAP = F0, SSAP = F0, Command, I frame, N(R) = 1, N(S) = 0
LLC:
NETB: —- NETBIOS Session Confirm —-
NETB:
NETB: Header length = 14, Data length = 0
NETB: Delimiter = EFFF (NETBIOS)
NETB: Command = 17
NETB: Flags = 00
```

```
NETB: 0... .... = NO.ACK ability
NETB: .... ...0 = Pre version 2.0
NETB: Max data receive size = 936
NETB: Transmit correlator = 0006
NETB: Session correlator = 0000
NETB: Remote session number = 1
NETB: Local session number = 35
NETB:
```

- - - - - - - - - - - - - - - Frame 75 - - - - - - - - - - - - - - -

```
DLC: —- DLC Header —-
DLC:
DLC: Frame 75 arrived at  17:37:50.104; frame size is
         160 (00A0 hex) bytes.
DLC: AC: Frame priority 0,  Reservation priority 0,
         Monitor count 1
DLC: FC: LLC frame,  PCF attention code: None
DLC: FS: Addr recognized indicators: 00, Frame copied
         indicators: 00
DLC: Destination = Station Prteon  5
DLC: Source      = Station Prteon  1
DLC:
LLC: —- LLC Header —-
LLC:
LLC: DSAP = F0, SSAP = F0, Command, I frame, N(R) = 1, N(S) = 1
LLC:
NETB: —- NETBIOS Data Only Last —-
NETB:
NETB: Header length = 14, Data length = 128
NETB: Delimiter = EFFF (NETBIOS)
NETB: Command = 16
NETB: Flags = X1
NETB: .... 0... = No Acknowledge_Included
NETB: .... .0.. = No Ack_with_data_allowed
NETB: .... ..0. = No NO.ACK indicator
NETB: Re-synch indicator = 0
NETB: Response correlator = 0007
NETB: Remote session number = 35
```

```
NETB: Local session number = 1
NETB:
NETB: [128 byte(s) of data]


- - - - - - - - - -- - -- - - Frame 79 - - -- - - - - - - - - -- - - -


DLC:  —- DLC Header —-
DLC:
DLC:  Frame 79 arrived at  17:37:50.456; frame size is
            32 (0020 hex) bytes.
DLC:  AC: Frame priority 0,  Reservation priority 4,
            Monitor count 1
DLC:  FC: LLC frame,  PCF attention code: None
DLC:  FS: Addr recognized indicators: 11, Frame copied
            indicators: 11
DLC:  Destination = Station Prteon  1
DLC:  Source      = Station Prteon  5
DLC:
LLC:  —- LLC Header —-
LLC:
LLC:  DSAP = F0, SSAP = F0, Command, I frame, N(R) = 2, N(S) = 1
LLC:
NETB: —- NETBIOS Receive Outstanding —-
NETB:
NETB: Header length = 14, Data length = 0
NETB: Delimiter = EFFF (NETBIOS)
NETB: Command = 1B
NETB: Data bytes accepted = 0
NETB: Remote session number = 1
NETB: Local session number = 35
NETB:
```

- - - - - - - - - - - - Frame 81 - - - - - - - - - - - -

DLC: —- DLC Header —-
DLC:
DLC: Frame 81 arrived at 17:37:50.460; frame size is
         160 (00A0 hex) bytes.
DLC: AC: Frame priority 0, Reservation priority 0,
         Monitor count 1
DLC: FC: LLC frame, PCF attention code: None
DLC: FS: Addr recognized indicators: 00, Frame copied
         indicators: 00
DLC: Destination = Station Prteon 5
DLC: Source   = Station Prteon 1
DLC:
LLC: —- LLC Header —-
LLC:
LLC: DSAP = F0, SSAP = F0, Command, I frame, N(R) = 2, N(S) = 2
LLC:
NETB: —- NETBIOS Data Only Last —-
NETB:
NETB: Header length = 14, Data length = 128
NETB: Delimiter = EFFF (NETBIOS)
NETB: Command = 16
NETB: Flags = X1
NETB: .... 0... = No Acknowledge_Included
NETB: .... .0.. = No Ack_with_data_allowed
NETB: .... ..0. = No NO.ACK indicator
NETB: Re-synch indicator = 1
NETB: Response correlator = 0007
NETB: Remote session number = 35
NETB: Local session number = 1
NETB:
NETB: [128 byte(s) of data]

6.11 Token-Ring Troubleshooting Summary

To summarize, here's a checklist to assist with diagnosing token-ring network failures:

1. Perform the NIC board diagnostics, if a diagnostic disk is available.

2. Check IRQ, DMA Shared Memory, and I/O Base Address for conflicts with other boards. If in doubt, remove all boards but the NIC, and reinsert one at a time. Visually inspect the NIC for any jumpers that may have fallen off, or any loose DIP switches.

3. Verify that the transmission rate for the NIC is properly set for 4 or 16 Mbps.

4. Verify status of power (and fuse) to the MSAUs if they require commercial (110/220 VAC) power. Look for a break in any daisy-chained MSAU power connections.

5. Certain manufacturers' MSAUs include an LED at each port to indicate an in-ring condition of the workstation, plus a switch to force that node off the ring.

6. If using unpowered MSAUs, unplug all cable connections to the MSAU, reset each port with the initialization tool, and reinsert the cable connectors.

7. If the NIC and cable have been tested and pass, but the failure still exists, move the NIC to another port on the MSAU and retest.

8. Listen for the audible "click" that verifies relay operation from the MSAU port when a station inserts into the ring.

9. Replace any type 3 (twisted-pair) media filters if a cable problem proves elusive.

10. For a quick check of the wiring on the NIC to MSAU cable, and to verify that the shorting bars of the hermaphroditic connector are working, check for a short between pins 1 and 9, and 5 and 6 on the DB-9 connector end of the cable.

11. Check for duplicate node addresses with the NIC diagnostic disk, network management software, or protocol analyzer if you've used LAA.

12. Check the DB-9 token-ring connector to make sure that a video monitor isn't connected to this port. (Don't laugh—this is a common error!)

This chapter has discussed the fastest growing LAN architecture, the token ring. Support from major corporations such as IBM, Apple Computer, Proteon, and others has certainly contributed to the token ring's popularity. If you need more information, you can find many sources in the trade literature. The next two chapters explore the popular predecessor to the token ring, Ethernet.

6.12 References

6-1. Some of the material in this chapter first appeared in "Troubleshooting the Token Ring," by Mark A. Miller, *LAN Technology Magazine*, (June 1989): 48-53 and "Token-Ring Management with the TMS380 Chipset," by Mark A. Miller, *LAN Technology Magazine*, (July 1989): 48-53.

6-2. Institute of Electrical and Electronics Engineers. *Token-Ring Access Method and Physical Layer Specifications*, IEEE Std 802.5, 1989.

6-3. Institute of Electrical and Electronics Engineers. *IEEE Recommended Practice for Use of Unshielded Twisted-Pair Cable (UTP) for Token-Ring Data Transmission at 4 Mbps*. IEEE Std 802.5b, 1991.

6-4. Texas Instruments. *TMS380 Second Generation Token Ring User's Guide*. Document SPWU005, 1990.

6-5. National Semiconductor Corp. *Token-Ring Protocol Interface Controller (TROPIC)*. DP8025 Data Sheet and Specifications, 1992.

6-6. Chris Schulman. "Complex Token-Ring Cabling Built on a Simple Foundation." *LAN Times* (November 19, 1990): 48-53.

6-7. IBM. *Cabling System Planning & Installation Guide*. Document GA27-3361, 1986.

6-8. IBM. *Token-Ring Network Introduction & Planning Guide*. Document GA27-3677, 1986.

6-9. IBM. *Token Ring Network Problem Determination Guide*. Document FX27-3710-02, 1992.

6-10. Institute of Electrical and Electronics Engineers. *Media Access Control (MAC) Bridges*. IEEE 802.1D, 1993.

6-11. Institute of Electrical and Electronics Engineers. *Logical Link Control*. IEEE Standard 802.2, 1989.

6-12. IBM. *LAN Network Manager V1.0, IBM 8230 Controlled Access Unit and LAN Management Utilities/2*. Document GG24-3754, August 1991.

6-13. Proteon. *ProNET 4/16 Network Interface Cards User Guide*. Document 42-040295-00, November 1992.

6-14. J. Scott Haugdahl. *Inside the Token Ring*, 3d ed. Architecture Technology Corporation (Minneapolis), 1990.

6-15. J. Scott Haugdahl. *Inside NetBIOS*, 3d ed. Architecture Technology Corp. (Minneapolis), 1990.

6-16. Network Information Center. *RFC-1002: Protocol Standard for a NetBIOS Service on a TCP/UDP Transport—Detailed Specifications, DDN*. March 1987.

6-17. Network Information Center. *RFC-1001: Protocol Standard for a Net-BIOS Service on a TCP/UDP Transport—Concepts and Methods, DDN*. March 1987.

6-18. Network General Corp. *Sniffer Network Analyzer Operations Manual*. Document 20028-001, May 1990.

CHAPTER 7

Troubleshooting Coaxial Ethernet

Developed by DEC, Intel, and Xerox (known collectively as DIX) in 1973, Ethernet was the first LAN to achieve widespread acceptance (see Reference 7-1). The first version, known as Experimental Ethernet, operated at 3 Mbps. It was later upgraded to Ethernet version 1 and finally to the Ethernet version 2 used today, which transmits at 10 Mbps (see Reference 7-2). In the early 1980s DIX turned over the Ethernet standard to the IEEE as a model for today's IEEE 802.3 standard. The IEEE made improvements in the DIX version and published IEEE 802.3 in 1983. As a result, Ethernet and the IEEE 802.3 networks are similar but not identical and are often confused.

The IEEE 802.3 networks include StarLAN (IEEE 802.3 1BASE5), twisted-pair Ethernet (10BASE-T), thin-coaxial Ethernet (10BASE2), thick-coaxial Ethernet (10BASE5), and broadband Ethernet (10BROAD36), which is rarely used (see References 7-3 and 7-4). Recall from Chapter 1 that the names of these networks in 802.3 terminology (for example, 10BASE5) specify the transmission rate in Mbps (10 Mbps), baseband or broadband signaling (BASE), and the maximum length of a segment in hundreds of meters (500 m).

All versions of Ethernet are similar in that they share the same Carrier Sense, Multiple Access with Collision Detection (CSMA/CD) bus architecture. However, because the transmission media significantly impacts the troubleshooting approach, this chapter focuses on the coaxial versions of Ethernet—the original DIX Ethernet, 10BASE2, and 10BASE5. It also notes the differences between the DIX Ethernet standard and the IEEE 802.3 standards. Chapter 8 discusses StarLAN and twisted-pair Ethernet (10BASE-T) networks.

7.1. Ethernet Topology

The Ethernet standard specifies a branching, nonrooted, topology generally described as a bus. It allows you to run cable for a maximum distance of 2.5 kilometers, offers a data rate of 10 Mbps over baseband cable, and allows a maximum of 1,024 workstations. Like all baseband LANs, transmission is half-duplex, allowing only one workstation to transmit at a time.

7.1.1. The CSMA/CD protocol

The CSMA/CD protocol governs access to the media or cable. With the CSMA/CD protocol, each workstation listens for the presence of another station's transmitted signal before transmitting. If the network is active, the station defers. If the network appears inactive, the station transmits but continues to "listen" during transmission for the presence of other signals. If it hears another station during transmission, a collision results.

Because of the analog process required to sense the presence of any other transmitting (and thus colliding) signal, timing parameters for the network are set for the worst-case scenario. Thus workstations at opposite ends of the bus cable have enough time to hear each other's signal in order to defer transmission.

7.2. The CSMA/CD physical layer

As mentioned previously, the coaxial CSMA/CD networks—Ethernet, 802.3 10BASE5 (see Figure 7-1), and 802.3 10BASE2 (see Figure 7-2)—are different in several ways. One difference has to do with naming conventions. The Ethernet standard calls the attachment between the NIC and the coaxial cable a transceiver; 10BASE5 and 10BASE2 refer to it as the Medium Attachment Unit (MAU), although for 10BASE2 the MAU may be built into the NIC. Ethernet calls the cable between the transceiver and

NIC the transceiver cable; 10BASE5 refers to it as the Attachment Unit Interface (AUI) cable. Since 10BASE2 NICs usually attach directly to the backbone cable, no AUI cable is required.

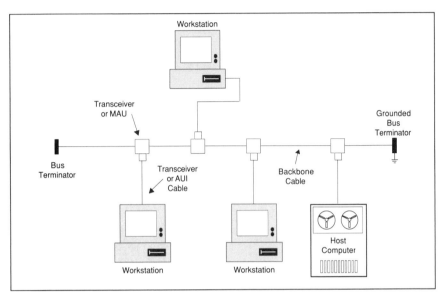

Figure 7-1. Thick Ethernet and IEEE 802.3 10BASE5 topology

Sections 7.2.1 and 7.2.2 discuss the physical layer characteristics of Ethernet, 10BASE5, and 10BASE2. You'll notice that these physical characteristics differ considerably. Thus when selecting products for your LAN, make sure they adhere to the version of the standard you're using.

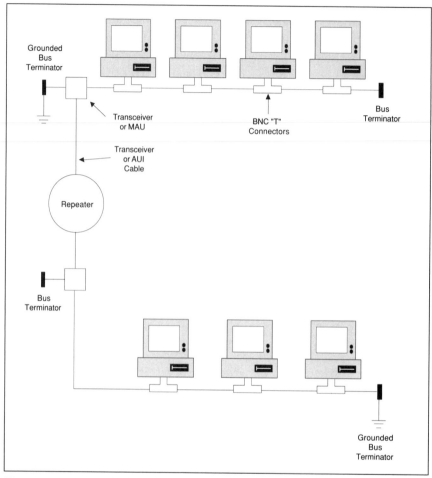

Figure 7-2. Thin Ethernet and 802.3 10BASE2 topology

One word of caution: Some NICs, such as those from Standard Microsystems Corp., offer an option that extends the allowable transmission distance. This enhancement does not adhere to either the Ethernet or the 802.3 standard. Therefore, you can only use these NICs with specified cables and other LAN devices. Consult the NIC documentation for more information.

7.2.1. The Ethernet physical layer

The physical limits of the Ethernet physical layer are summarized below (see Reference 7-2, Section 7, for more information):

- The maximum length of the coaxial cable segment is 500 meters, where the cable has a propagation velocity of 0.77c (c is the speed of light in a vacuum, 300,000 meters per second).
- The cable must be terminated in its characteristic impedance, 50 ± 2 ohms, and grounded only at only one point.
- A maximum of two repeaters can be along a path between two workstations.
- A maximum of 50 meters can be between a transceiver attached to the coaxial cable segment and its associated workstation.
- Each segment can have a maximum of 100 transceivers.

7.2.2. The 802.3 physical layer

The 802.3 specification for CSMA/CD networks defines two types of baseband networks: 10BASE5 (10 Mbps transmission, 500-meter maximum segment length) and 10BASE2 (10 Mbps transmission, 185-meter segment length). These are described as ANSI/IEEE 802.3-1988 and IEEE 802.3a-1990 standards, respectively (see References 7-3 and 7-4). Both use the Manchester encoding scheme shown in Figure 7-3 for transmitting data signals. The physical characteristics are slightly different from the Ethernet specification.

Before looking at the 802.3 physical layer characteristics, you need the following background: A coax segment uses MAUs to connect to the workstations. Link segments (sometimes called interrepeater links, or IRLs) are point-to-point connections between repeaters and have no user or host MAUs attached. Repeaters connect either coax segments or link segments and may attach at any MAU location on a coax segment, but only at the ends of a link segment. Repeater connections count toward the total number of MAU connections allowed on a coax segment.

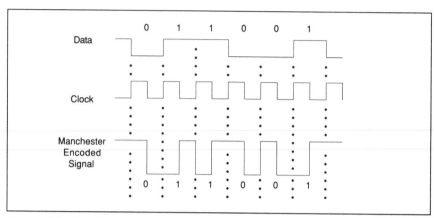

Figure 7-3. Manchester encoded signal

7.2.2.1. 802.3 10BASE5. The physical limits of the 802.3 10BASE5 physical channel are summarized as follows:

- The maximum coaxial segment length is 500 meters, with a minimum velocity of propagation of 0.77c.
- A maximum of five segments (with four repeaters) can be along a path between any two workstations; three may be coax segments having a maximum delay of 2,165 nanoseconds, and two may be link segments having a maximum delay of 2,570 nanoseconds. Note that propagation delay, not distance, determines the maximum length of a link segment, although many manufacturers use 500 meters (for coax) as the maximum network span, commonly quoted as 2,500 meters (5 segments x 500 meters per segment).
- When no link segments are used, three coax segments may exist on a path.
- 10BASE5 typically uses double-shielded, 0.4-inch-diameter coaxial cable.
- Cable is terminated at each end with 50 ± 2 ohms; it is grounded at only one point within the segment.
- You can have a total of 100 MAUs on a cable segment.
- MAUs are placed on the cable at increments of 2.5 meters over the entire length of the cable.

7.2.2.2. 802.3 10BASE2. The physical limits of the 802.3 10BASE2 physical layer are summarized as follows:

- The maximum coaxial segment length is 185 meters, with a minimum velocity of propagation of 0.65c.
- RG-58A/U coax, 0.2 inch in diameter with a stranded center conductor, is typically used.
- A maximum of five segments (with four repeaters) can occur between two workstations: three tapped coax segments and two link segments—the same as 10BASE5.
- Cables are terminated at each end in 50 ± 2 ohms, and grounded at only one point within the segment.
- Cables connect with BNC T adapters.
- You can have a maximum of 30 workstations or nodes per cable segment.
- MAUs must be placed at least 0.6 meter apart.

See Table 7-1 for a comparison between the three standards.

Table 7-1. Ethernet and IEEE 802 parameters

Parameter	Ethernet Version 2.0	IEEE 802.3 10BASE5	IEEE 802.3 10BASE2
Cable Impedance	50 ohms	50 ohms	50 ohms
Maximum Coax Segment Length	500m (1640 ft.)	500m (1640 ft.)	185m (600 ft.)
Maximum Number of Coax Segments Without Link Segments (IRLs)	3	3	3
Maximum Number of Segments Including 2 Link Segments	3	5	5
Maximum Network Span (not including drop cables)	1500m (4920 ft.)	2500m (8200 ft.)	925m (3000 ft.)
Maximum Number of MAUs Per Segment	100	100	30
Minimum Distance Between Nodes	2.5m (8 ft.)	2.5m (8 ft.)	0.6m (1.5 ft.)

Table 7-1. *Continued*

Parameter	Ethernet Version 2.0	IEEE 802.3 10BASE5	IEEE 802.3 10BASE2
Transceiver	external	external	internal or external
Connector Type	N	N	BNC
Maximum Transceiver to Node Distance	50m (164 ft.)	50m (164 ft.)	50m (164 ft.) if external transceiver is used

7.3. Ethernet Hardware Components

Ethernet and 802.3 hardware consists of the NIC, repeaters, and transceivers. Let's look at each component individually.

7.3.1. Ethernet NICs

Ethernet hardware has seen amazing size and cost reductions in the last few years. Figure 7-4 shows three generations of 3Com Corp. NICs: the Etherlink I, II, and III. Notice the reductions in the number of components from the Etherlink I NIC (top) to the Etherlink III NIC (bottom).

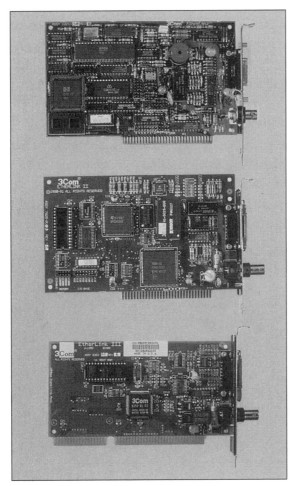

Figure 7-4. Etherlink I, II, and III NICs
(Photo courtesy of 3Com Corp.)

These reductions are possible because of advances in parallel processing technology implemented in custom Application-Specific Integrated Circuit (ASIC) components. (In Figure 7-4 the ASIC is the device with the 3Com logo in the center of the Etherlink III NIC.) Note that each Etherlink NIC provides two connectors: the BNC for thin coax and the DB-15 AUI connector for thick coax networks. The Etherlink III board includes an auto-configuration option that senses whether a cable is connected to the AUI port. If it is not, the NIC automatically activates the BNC port. Other boards include manual jumpers to allow you to specify the appropriate cable type. When you install a new or replacement Ethernet board, double-check the setting of the jumper before closing the workstation case.

7.3.2. Ethernet Repeaters

A repeater regenerates the electrical or optical signal in order to extend the maximum transmission distance. As such, it operates strictly at the physical layer. Figure 7-5a shows an Ethernet/802.3 Intelligent Repeater Module (IRM-2) from Cabletron Systems. Cabletron's MultiMedia Access Center (MMAC) houses the IRM-2, as shown in Figure 7-5b.

Figure 7-5a. Cabletron's 803.3-compliant Intelligent Repeater Module (IRM-2)
(Photo courtesy of Cabletron Systems)

Figure 7-5b. Cabletron's MultiMedia Access Center intelligent wiring hub
(Photo courtesy of Cabletron Systems)

The front panel of the IRM-2 card offers a number of connections. At the top, diagnostic LEDs communicate the status of both the repeater and the network. These indicators can be very useful in troubleshooting the network, since they can describe errors, power, reception, transmission, collisions, port tests, and fiber-optic link status. By becoming familiar with the normal states of these LEDs, you'll know when an abnormal condition arises. Other connectors on the front panel can attach an RS-232 console, AUI connector, or the fiber-optic interrepeater link (FOIRL).

7.3.3. Ethernet Transceivers

The transceiver provides the physical connection between the cable and any attached device. Figure 7-6 shows a Cabletron Systems transceiver and its attachment around a coaxial cable. In Figure 7-7, DB-15 connectors terminate a transceiver cable that extends from the transceiver to the Ethernet or 802.3 NIC.

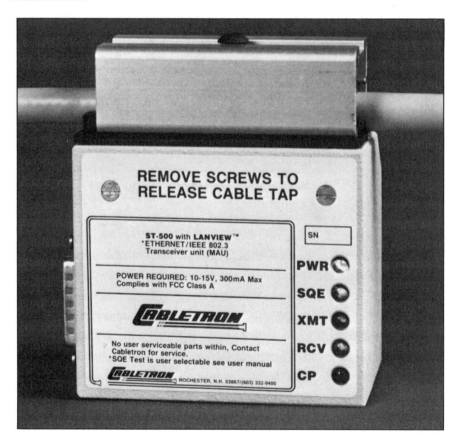

Figure 7-6. Thick Ethernet transceiver
(Photo courtesy of Cabletron Systems)

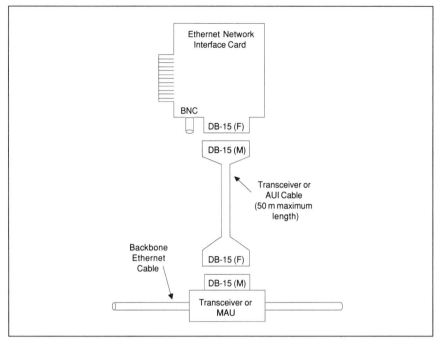

Figure 7-7. Thick Ethernet transceiver attachment

The transceiver uses four pairs of wire: Transmit (called Data Out in 802.3) from NIC to transceiver; Receive (called Data In in 802.3) from transceiver to NIC; Collision Presence (called Control In in 802.3), which indicates a transmission collision with another node; and Power (called Voltage in 802.3), which provides power from the NIC to the transceiver.

Figure 7-8 gives pinouts for the transceiver. Note the differences between Ethernet version 2.0 and IEEE 802.3. It is very important to wire the cable connecting the transceiver to the NIC for either the Ethernet version 2.0 or the IEEE 802.3 configuration. The wrong version may not work because of differences in ground (shield) leads.

Pin No.	Ethernet V2.0	IEEE 802.3
1	Shield	Control in Shield
2	Collision Presence +	Control in A
3	Transmit +	Data Out A
4	Reserved	Data in Shield
5	Receive	Data in A
6	Power Return	Voltage Common
7	Reserved	Control Out A
8	Reserved	Control Out Shield
9	Collision Presence —	Control in B
10	Transmit —	Data Out B
11	Reserved	Data Out Shield
12	Receive —	Data in B
13	Power	Voltage
14	Reserved	Voltage Shield
15	Reserved	Control Out B
Connector Shell	____	Protective Ground

Figure 7-8. Transceiver pinouts for Ethernet version 2.0 and IEEE 802.3

Ethernet version 2.0 transceivers generate a self-test signal, known as the Collision Presence Test and sometimes referred to as the heartbeat. This signal confirms that the collision detect circuitry in the transceiver is working (see Reference 7-2, Section 7.4.7). IEEE 802.3 transceivers generate a signal similar to the Collision Presence Test, known as the Signal Quality Error (SQE) Test (see Reference 7-3, Section 7.2.2.2.4). Transceivers that connect to 802.3 repeaters cannot use the SQE Test signal (see Reference 7-4, Section 9.1).

Many transceiver manufacturers, such as Cabletron and Racal-Datacom, have designed transceivers that can provide the Collision Presence or SQE Test signal when connecting to Ethernet version 2.0 NICs, and turn it off when connecting to 802.3 repeaters. Make sure that this option is set correctly. Reference 7-7 provides information on this issue, plus useful comparisons between the Ethernet and 802.3 standards.

7.4. Ethernet Hardware Troubleshooting

Hardware faults for Ethernet LANs generally fall into three categories: cable failures, transceiver failures, and NIC failures. To find these failures, you need to isolate their location. Examples include a network failure, in which the entire network is nonfunctional; a segment failure, in which only a portion of the network is at fault; or a workstation failure, in which a single node cannot communicate with other nodes.

7.4.1. Ethernet cable failures

Since Ethernet is a bus topology, any damage to the bus will crash the network. To find bus failures, you can perform continuity (DC resistance) or time domain reflectometry (TDR) tests, as discussed in Chapter 4. Of these tests, the TDR tests are considered more reliable.

For a continuity test, go to one end of the cable, disconnect the terminator, and use a VOM to measure the DC resistance between the cable's center conductor and shield. A properly terminated cable can measure about 50 ohms. If the cable is shorted, expect 0 to 10 ohms, and if the cable is open (or the terminator at the far end is missing), you'll get a measurement significantly more than 50 ohms. If you suspect a problem with the terminator, measure the DC resistance between its center conductor and outside shield—it should be close to 50 ohms. If not, replace the terminator.

7.4.2. Testing Ethernet cable segments

For a more accurate measurement of Ethernet cabling, use a TDR. A TDR operates by sending a pulse of known amplitude and duration (and associated rise and fall times) from one end of the cable. When the pulse hits an open or a short, it reflects back to the TDR. An open connection reflects the same polarity; a short reflects the opposite polarity. Since the polarity and time delay (between initial pulse transmission and reflected pulse reception) is known, you can calculate the distance to any open or short using the cable's velocity of propagation. Most cable opens and shorts occur at connector junctions or transceiver connections, or wherever a mechanical device has entered the transmission path. See Chapter 4 for more details on TDR usage.

In addition to shorts and opens, a TDR detects the location of impedance mismatches along the cable. Resulting signal reflections can be caused by cable crimps, kinks, sharp bends, or an improper cable termination. Thus it's a good idea to use a TDR to verify the proper installation of newly installed cable prior to bringing up the network.

7.4.3. Cable connections

Coaxial barrel connectors join thick Ethernet segments; BNC T connectors join thin segments. Should the cable test open, look for disconnected portions of the bus. Typically this problem occurs when someone tries to remove a workstation and detaches the wrong end of the T, thereby opening the bus. An open cable will bring down the network by unterminating two ends.

Many vendors recommend that all cable segments come from the same spool to ensure manufacturing consistency. In addition, Reference 7-3, Section 8.6.2.1, recommends using connectorized lengths that are odd multiples of a half wavelength in the cable at a transmitted frequency of 5 MHz; that is, lengths of 23.4 meters, 70.2 meters, and 117 meters (± 0.5 meters) for all thick coax sections. Add sections as necessary to achieve the 500-meter maximum segment length.

7.4.4. Transceiver failures

For most thin Ethernet networks (10BASE2), the transceiver is built into the NIC, and you must replace the NIC to correct a transceiver failure. For thick Ethernet (10BASE5) networks, the mechanical connection between the transceiver attachment and the cable can cause problems, or the transceiver can fail internally. If an entire cable shows a short, a recently added transceiver may have shorted the cable's center conductor to the outer shield. Use a TDR to determine the location of the short, and if you find a transceiver at that location, replace it.

If only one workstation cannot communicate with the network, the transceiver may be open. A TDR would not indicate the problem because the open appears as a nonexistent node on the network. Some transceivers include LEDs that indicate network and node activities, confirm proper power feed from the NIC, and so on. Inspect these LEDs as part of your diagnostics. When in doubt replace the transceiver with a known good spare.

Transceivers can occasionally fail without causing a cable short or open connection. For a quick test remove the NIC (thus powering down the transceiver) and see whether the network recovers. If the problem persists, remember that the transceiver could still be shorting the cable, and the only cure is to remove it.

7.4.5. NIC failures

A faulty NIC is the easiest failure to correct because you can easily swap in a replacement, assuming you have a spare on hand. Most NICs come with diagnostic disks that allow internal diagnostics without removing the interface board from the PC. One common difficulty, however, occurs because most Ethernet or 802.3 NICs have two connectors: a DB-15 for connecting to the transceiver and thick cable, and a BNC for connecting to thin cable. To select the correct cable connection, you must set a jumper on the NIC. If the jumper is set incorrectly, the NIC cannot communicate with the network. Double-check this option before closing the cover on the PC. See References 7-5 and 7-6 for more information.

7.4.6. Jabbering nodes

Ethernets occasionally suffer from a jabbering node, when garbage data with no known origin appears on the network. When this occurs you need to segment the network to isolate the fault. Suppose you're testing the thick Ethernet network shown in Figure 7-9, and that the network is jammed with garbage data. You must disconnect the repeater at point A to see whether the problem clears. If it does, the jabbering node occurs after the repeater connection. Now suppose you suspect the segment past the repeater. Reconnect the repeater at point A, and then disconnect the individual sections that comprise that segment one at a time, making sure to terminate each new endpoint. Once you've isolated the problem to an individual section of cable, reconnect the section, and isolate the problem down to a particular node by powering down each node on the section individually. When the network recovers you've identified the jabbering node. Further testing can determine whether the fault lies in the transceiver, transceiver cable, or NIC.

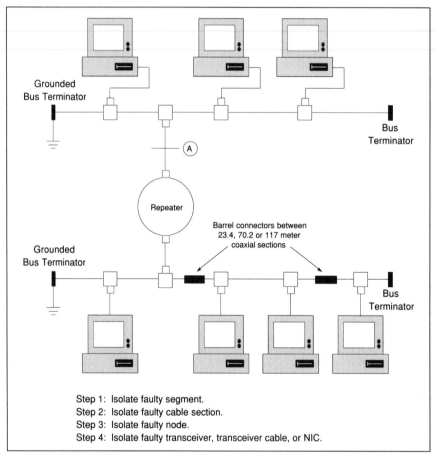

Grounded
Bus Terminator

Bus
Terminator

Repeater

Barrel connectors between
23.4, 70.2 or 117 meter
coaxial sections

Grounded
Bus Terminator

Bus
Terminator

Step 1: Isolate faulty segment.
Step 2: Isolate faulty cable section.
Step 3: Isolate faulty node.
Step 4: Isolate faulty transceiver, transceiver cable, or NIC.

Figure 7-9. Isolating jabbering nodes

7.5. Ethernet Software Considerations

In addition to the differences in hardware, Ethernet and 802.3 differ in their data-link layer frame structure. Figures 7-10a and 7-10b show the Ethernet frame; Figures 7-11a and 7-11b show the 802.3 frame.

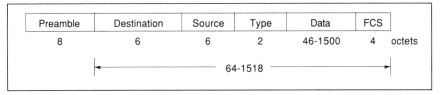

Figure 7-10a. The Ethernet data-link layer frame

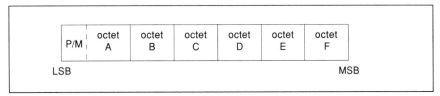

Figure 7-10b. The Ethernet address fields

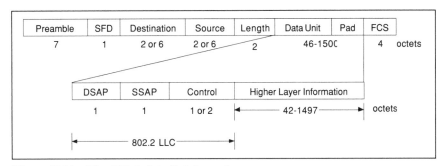

Figure 7-11a. The 802.3 data-link layer frame

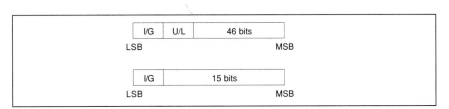

Figure 7-11b. The 802.3 address fields

7.5.1. The Ethernet frame

The Ethernet frame begins with a preamble (eight octets) that provides synchronization. The preamble uses an alternating 1010... pattern that ends in 10101011. The destination address is a six-octet field that defines either a physical address or a multicast address, determined by the least significant bit of the first byte of that field. A physical address (usually burned into a ROM chip) sets LSB=0 and is unique across all Ethernet networks. A multicast address can broadcast to a group or to all stations and has LSB=1. For a broadcast address the destination field is set to all ones—that is, FFFFFFFFFFFFH (where H represents hexadecimal notation). The physical addresses are subdivided further: the IEEE assigns the first three octets (A, B, and C in Figure 7-10b), and the manufacturer assigns the last three (D, E, and F). (In the earlier days of Ethernet development, Xerox Corp. assigned the first three octets of the address.) If the NIC becomes defective, and if you need a consistent node address (such as a well-known address for a gateway), you can remove the ROM chip containing the original address from the old board and insert it onto the new board; or you can set the address in a register using the diagnostic disk. However, be careful when you bypass the safeguards built into the existing address administration system. The source address is specified next and refers to the address of the station originating the frame.

The type field, sometimes referred to as the Ethertype, is a two-octet field that specifies the higher-layer protocol used in the data field. Xerox Corp. administers this field. Some familiar Ethertypes include 0800H (for the IP of TCP/IP), 0600H (XNS), and 6003H (DECnet).

The data field is the only variable length field and can range from 46 octets to 1,500 octets. The contents of this field are completely arbitrary, as specified by the higher-layer protocol used within the frame.

The last field is a Frame Check Sequence, which is a 32-bit CRC based on the contents of the address, type, and data field.

The allowable frame length, not including the preamble, ranges from 64 to 1,518 octets. Frames outside that range are considered invalid. Short frames (sometimes called fragments or runts) generally arise from collisions. Long frames (sometimes called jabbers) usually indicate a defective transmitter at one of the NICs.

7.5.2. The 802.3 frame

Note the differences between the Ethernet and 802.3 frames in Figures 7-10 and 7-11. The 802.3 frame begins with a preamble (seven octets), which is an alternating pattern 1010..., this time ending in 1010. The Start Frame Delimiter (SFD) is next, defined as 10101011. Note that when you combine the 802.3 preamble and SFD fields, a pattern identical to the Ethernet preamble results.

Next is the destination address field (shown in Figure 7-11b), which can be either two or six octets in length, although six octets is the most common. The Individual/Group (I/G) field corresponds to Ethernet's physical/multicast designation; the Universal/Local (U/L) field indicates whether the IEEE administers the address universally or the network administrator administers it locally.

The source address, which comes next, must match the destination address field in length (either two octets for destination and two for source or six for destination and six for source, but not two and six). The length field is two octets long and indicates the number of LLC octets in the data field. A minimum of 46 octets of data is required; when the LLC data is less than 46, the pad field is used. The maximum length of the data and pad fields combined is 1,500 octets. Finally, the Frame Check Sequence (FCS), based on a 32-bit CRC, is computed according to the contents of the destination address, source address, length, data, and pad fields. Reference 7-3, Section 3.2, provides additional details on the frame format.

7.5.3. Data-link layer analysis

One difference between the Ethernet and 802.3 data-link layer frames occurs in the Ethernet Ethertype and 802.3 length fields. For Ethernet the Ethertype defines the higher-layer protocol used within the data field. Within the 802.3 field the length (or number of octets) of the data fields occupies the same position. For 802.3 the 802.2 LLC PDU and its destination service access point (DSAP) and source service access point (SSAP) fields designate the higher-layer protocol type.

In general, older DEC Ethernet backbones used the Ethernet frame format, and newer ones use either Ethernet or 802.3 frames. Most NIC vendors support 802.3. From the point of view of a data-link layer frame, however, both formats' bit streams are the same length. Because of the differences in the Ethernet and 802.3 frame formats, any NIC that wants to communicate with an Ethernet host must transmit the appropriate Ethertype, whereas NICs communicating with 802.3 hosts transmit the length of the data field in the same position. An Ethernet host that expected an Ethertype and received a length field would be confused. To solve this problem, Novell provides a parameter for its LAN driver that allows the network administrator to configure the NIC to either the Ethernet or IEEE 802.3 frame format specifications. If internode communication on an Ethernet or IEEE 802.3 network fails, check this software driver for proper configuration.

7.6. Protocol Analysis with DECnet

Ethernet networks frequently use the DECnet protocol suite because of the historical ties to Digital Equipment Corp. Figure 7-12 illustrates how the DECnet Phase IV Protocol Suite aligns with the ISO/OSI model; see References 7-8 and 7-9 for further details.

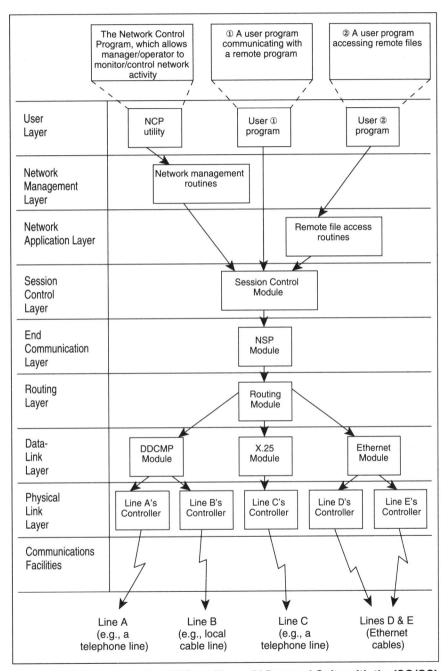

Figure 7-12. Comparing the DECnet Phase IV Protocol Suite with the ISO/OSI model

DECnet Phase I was introduced in 1976. In September of 1987, it was enhanced through the announcement of DECnet Phase V; the current version, introduced in 1991, is DEC's Advantage Networks. The announcement of DEC's Advantage Networks was particularly significant because with it DEC stated its commitment to fully complying with the ISO/OSI model. The individual layers of the DECnet protocol suite are defined as follows:

- *Physical layer.* DECnet recognizes standards from EIA, CCITT, and ISO, such as EIA-232-E, V.24, X.21, and ISO 8802-3.
- *Data-link layer.* DECnet Phase V supports DDCMP (the Digital Data Communications Message Protocol from DEC), HDLC (High-Level Data Link Control from ISO), and IEEE 802 (ISO 8802-3) Ethernet for DECnet Phase IV compatibility.
- *Network layer.* The ISO 8473 (Internetwork Protocol) supports Phase V, and the DECnet Routing Protocol (DRP) supports Phase IV.
- *Transport layer.* ISO 8073 (Transport Protocol Classes 0, 2, and 4) support Phase V, and the Network Services Protocol (NSP), originally defined in Phase I, maintains compatibility with Phase IV.

The Phase V higher layers (session, presentation, and application) maintain compatibility with Phase IV protocols and support the standard OSI protocols defined for those layers. The most common Phase IV protocols include

- Session Control Protocol (SCP)
- Data Access Protocol (DAP), for remote file access
- Network Information and Control Exchange Protocol (NICE), for network management
- Maintenance Operation Protocol (MOP)
- Command Terminal Protocol (CTERM), a virtual terminal protocol used in conjunction with the session layer Foundation Services Protocol (FOUND)
- Server Message Block (SMB)

References 7-8 and 7-9 provide further details on DECnet Phase IV and V, respectively.

Before looking at an example of DECnet Phase IV packets, examine how the Ethernet frame encapsulates the various levels of protocols, as shown in Figure 7-13. The data field contains the higher-layer protocol information, which is further divided by the layer of protocol in use. For example, the DECnet Routing Protocol (DRP) and Network Services Protocol (NSP) might precede some Data Access Protocol (DAP) information. Many other combinations are possible, as you can see in the DECnet Phase IV Protocol Suite in Figure 7-12. The Sniffer Analyzer captures the entire Ethernet frame, less the preamble and Frame Check Sequence (shown in Figure 7-14 and discussed in Reference 7-10).

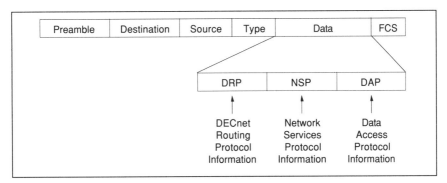

Figure 7-13. DECnet protocols within an Ethernet frame

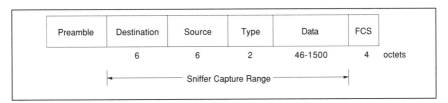

Figure 7-14. Capture range of the Network General Sniffer protocol analyzer for Ethernet networks

Let's look at and example of some routine data being transferred from workstation DECnet 000E14 to workstation DECnet 000214 (see Trace 7-1). Frames 1 and 2 contain DECnet NSP data packets, which are identified by logical link destination and source addresses (20A4 and 3D02, respectively). Also identifying that data is a data segment number, DSEG=1156, and the length, in octets, of that segment (LEN=558). Frame 3 acknowledges the data segment transmitted in Frame 1. Subsequent frames contain data transmitted from DECnet 000E14 to DECnet 000214, and the acknowledgment packets that flow in the opposite direction.

The details of the first three packets show the subfields contained in the DLC, DRP, and NSP layers (see Frames 1, 2, and 4 in Trace 7-2). With the first layer of protocol decoded, the Data-Link Control (DLC) layer identifies an Ethernet, not IEEE 802.3, frame. (For confirmation, compare the frame formats of Figures 7-10a and 7-11a.) The DRP header routes the packet from its source to its destination within the DECnet internetwork. The NSP header precedes the data, identifying the beginning (Frame 1) or the end of data (Frame 2), the logical link destination and source addresses, and the data segment number. Both Frames 1 and 2 contain 558 octets of higher-layer DECnet data (network user information, in this case), which did not require a higher-layer DECnet protocol header. Frame 4 contains an acknowledgment for data segment 1156, which was transmitted in Frame 1. Subsequent frames continue the process of data transmission and acknowledgments.

Trace 7-1. Summary of DECnet data transfer and acknowledgment packets

Sniffer Network Analyzer data 20-Jun-91 at 08:07:04, file TRIG. ENC Pg 1

```
     SUMMARY   Delta T      Destination   Source        Summary

 M    1                  DECnet000214 DECnet000E14  NSP DATA Begin
                                                    D=20A4 S=3D02
                                                    DSEG=1156 LEN=558
      2    0.0054    DECnet000214 DECnet000E14  NSP DATA Middle
                                                    D=20A4 S=3D02
                                                    DSEG=1157 LEN=558
```

```
4    0.0022   DECnet000E14 DECnet000214   NSP ACK  Data
                                            D=3D02 S=20A4
                                            DACK=1156
5    0.0015   DECnet000214 DECnet000E14   NSP DATA Middle
                                            D=20A4 S=3D02
                                            DSEG=1158 LEN=558
6    0.0036   DECnet000214 DECnet000E14   NSP DATA End
                                            D=20A4 S=3D02
                                            DSEG=1159 LEN=384
7    0.0014   DECnet000E14 DECnet000214   NSP ACK  Data
                                            D=3D02 S=20A4
                                            DACK=1157
8    0.0054   DECnet000E14 DECnet000214   NSP ACK  Data
                                            D=3D02 S=20A4
                                            DACK=1158
10   0.0057   DECnet000E14 DECnet000214   NSP ACK  Data
                                            D=3D02 S=20A4
                                            DACK=1159
17   0.0503   DECnet000214 DECnet000E14   NSP DATA Begin
                                            D=20A4 S=3D02
                                            DSEG=1160 LEN=558
18   0.0037   DECnet000214 DECnet000E14   NSP DATA Middle
                                            D=20A4 S=3D02
                                            DSEG=1161 LEN=558
19   0.0022   DECnet000E14 DECnet000214   NSP ACK  Data
                                            D=3D02 S=20A4
                                            ACK=1160
20   0.0015   DECnet000214 DECnet000E14   NSP DATA Middle
                                            D=20A4 S=3D02
                                            DSEG=1162 LEN=558
22   0.0036   DECnet000214 DECnet000E14   NSP DATA End
                                            D=20A4 S=3D02
                                            DSEG=1163 LEN=384
```

Trace 7-2. Details of DECnet data transfer and acknowledgment packets

Sniffer Network Analyzer data 20-Jun-91 at 08:07:04, file TRIG.ENC, Pg 1

```
- - - - - - - - - - - - - - Frame 1 - - - - - - - - - - - - - - -

DLC:  —- DLC Header —-
DLC:
DLC:  Frame 1 arrived at  08:00:15.78; frame size is
          602 (025A hex) bytes
DLC:  This frame is dated 1 day(s) after capture started.
DLC:  Destination = Station DECnet000214
DLC:  Source      = Station DECnet000E14
DLC:  Ethertype  = 6003 (DECNET)
DLC:
DRP:  —- DECNET Routing Protocol —-
DRP:
DRP:  Data length = 586
DRP:  Data Packet Format = 26
DRP:              0... .... = no padding
DRP:              .0.. .... = version
DRP:              ..1. .... = Intra-Ethernet packet
DRP:              ...0 .... = not return packet
DRP:              .... 0... = do not return to sender
DRP:              .... .110 = Long Data Packet Format
DRP:  Data Packet Type = 6
DRP:  Destination Area    = 00
DRP:  Destination Subarea = 00
DRP:  Destination ID      = 5.2
DRP:  Source Area         = 00
DRP:  Source Subarea      = 00
DRP:  Source ID           = 5.14
DRP:  Next Level 2 Router = 00
DRP:  Visit Count         = 0
DRP:  Service Class       = 00
DRP:  Protocol Type       = 00
DRP:
NSP:  —- Network Services Protocol —-
NSP:
NSP:  Message Identifier = 20
```

```
NSP:             0... .... = Non-extensible field
NSP:             .010 .... = Begin Data Message
NSP:             .... 00.. = Data Message
NSP:             .... ..00 = always zero
NSP:  Type    = 0  (Data Message)
NSP:  Sub-type = 2  (Begin Data Message)
NSP:  Logical Link Destination = 20A4
NSP:  Logical Link Source      = 3D02
NSP:  Data Segment Number = 1156  (normal ACK expected)
NSP:        558 data bytes
NSP:
NSP:  No Process Type Recognized
NSP:
```

- - - - - - - - - - - - - Frame 2 - - - - - - - - - - - - - -

```
DLC:  —- DLC Header —-
DLC:
DLC:  Frame 2 arrived at  08:00:15.78; frame size is
          602 (025A hex) bytes
DLC:  This frame is dated 1 day(s) after capture started.
DLC:  Destination = Station DECnet000214
DLC:  Source      = Station DECnet000E14
DLC:  Ethertype  = 6003 (DECNET)
DLC:
DRP:  —- DECNET Routing Protocol —-
DRP:
DRP:  Data length = 586
DRP:  Data Packet Format = 26
DRP:             0... .... = no padding
DRP:             .0.. .... = version
DRP:             ..1. .... = Intra-Ethernet packet
DRP:             ...0 .... = not return packet
DRP:             .... 0... = do not return to sender
DRP:             .... .110 = Long Data Packet Format
DRP:  Data Packet Type = 6
DRP:  Destination Area    = 00
DRP:  Destination Subarea = 00
```

```
DRP:  Destination ID      = 5.2
DRP:  Source Area         = 00
DRP:  Source Subarea      = 00
DRP:  Source ID           = 5.14
DRP:  Next Level 2 Router = 00
DRP:  Visit Count         = 0
DRP:  Service Class       = 00
DRP:  Protocol Type       = 00
DRP:
NSP:  —- Network Services Protocol —-
NSP:
NSP:  Message Identifier = 00
NSP:          0... .... = Non-extensible field
NSP:          .000 .... = Middle Data Message
NSP:          .... 00.. = Data Message
NSP:          .... ..00 = always zero
NSP:  Type    = 0  (Data Message)
NSP:  Sub-type = 0  (Middle Data Message)
NSP:  Logical Link Destination = 20A4
NSP:  Logical Link Source      = 3D02
NSP:  Data Segment Number = 1157  (normal ACK expected)
NSP:   [558 data bytes]
NSP:
NSP:  No Process Type Recognized
NSP:
```

- - - - - - - - - - - - - - Frame 4 - - - - - - - - - - - - - - -

```
DLC:  —- DLC Header —-
DLC:
DLC:  Frame 4 arrived at  08:00:15.78; frame size is
         60 (003C hex) bytes
DLC:  This frame is dated 1 day(s) after capture started.
DLC:  Destination = Station DECnet000E14
DLC:  Source      = Station DECnet000214
DLC:  Ethertype = 6003 (DECNET)
DLC:
```

```
DRP:  —- DECNET Routing Protocol —-
DRP:
DRP:  Data Length = 29,  Optional Padding Length = 1
DRP:  Data Packet Format = 26
DRP:          0... .... = no padding
DRP:          .0.. .... = version
DRP:          ..1. .... = Intra-Ethernet packet
DRP:          ...0 .... = not return packet
DRP:          .... 0... = do not return to sender
DRP:          .... .110 = Long Data Packet Format
DRP:  Data Packet Type = 6
DRP:  Destination Area     = 00
DRP:  Destination Subarea  = 00
DRP:  Destination ID       = 5.14
DRP:  Source Area          = 00
DRP:  Source Subarea       = 00
DRP:  Source ID            = 5.2
DRP:  Next Level 2 Router  = 00
DRP:  Visit Count          = 0
DRP:  Service Class        = 00
DRP:  Protocol Type        = 00
DRP:
NSP:  —- Network Services Protocol —-
NSP:
NSP:  Message Identifier = 04
NSP:          0... .... = Non-extensible field
NSP:          .000 .... = Data Acknowledgment Message
NSP:          .... 01.. = Acknowledgment Message
NSP:          .... ..00 = always zero
NSP:  Type    = 1 (Acknowledgment Message)
NSP:  Sub-type = 0 (Data Acknowledgment Message)
NSP:  Logical Link Destination = 3D02
NSP:  Logical Link Source      = 20A4
NSP:  Data Acknowledgment Number
NSP:     Acknowledge Qualifier      = ACK
NSP:     Message Number Acknowledged = 1156
NSP:
```

7.7. Coaxial Ethernet Troubleshooting Summary

To summarize, here's a checklist to assist with diagnosing coaxial cable Ethernet and 802.3 failures:

1. Clean the gold fingers and reseat the NIC in the workstation bus.
2. If present, check the board jumper that selects the thin coaxial (BNC) or thick coaxial (DB-15) cable connection.
3. Run the NIC board diagnostics, if available. If you use loop-around testing, use the appropriate cable terminator.
4. Check IRQ, DMA, Shared Memory, and I/O base addresses for conflicts with other boards. If in doubt, remove all boards but the NIC and then reinsert one at a time.

   Visually inspect the NIC for any detached jumpers or loose DIP switches. Activate the DIP switches (forward and then back to the original position) to confirm good contact. If more than one NIC resides in a workstation or server, verify that the shared memory buffers have unique addresses.
5. Confirm the order of CONFIG.SYS and AUTOEXEC.BAT files and any device drivers in use.
6. Verify that the transceiver, transceiver cable, and any applicable option (for example, "heartbeat" or SQE Test) are set consistently for Ethernet version 2.0 or IEEE 802.3 operation.
7. Verify that power and transceiver or AUI cables to any repeaters are properly connected and that SQE Test signals to repeaters are properly administered.
8. Use a TDR to test for any shorted transceivers or other cable faults, such as crimps, kinks, or opens.
9. Verify that you have not violated the minimum distance for transceiver placement (such as 2.5 meters for thick cable) and that you've placed the transceivers at multiples of 2.5 meters (for example, at the 2.5, 5.0, 7.5, and 10.0-meter markings on the cable).

10. Verify that you've followed the network configuration rules (for example, no more than three coax segments plus two IRLs, and so on).

11. Check for any unterminated cable ends.

12. Test terminators with an ohmmeter for a resistance between 48 and 52 ohms.

13. Check for any disconnected or poorly assembled T connectors used with a thin segment.

14. Verify that you've used RG-58A/U (50-ohm thin cable) and not RG-59A/U (75-ohm thin cable).

15. Use the NIC diagnostic disk or protocol analyzer to check for duplicate node addresses.

In 1993 Ethernet celebrated its 20th anniversary. Considering the number of proprietary LANs that have followed their manufacturers into obscurity (or bankruptcy), Ethernet's longevity is a testimony to the support of DEC, Intel, and Xerox. All have worked diligently to make Ethernet an open networking technology. Those efforts remain ongoing, and Ethernet continues to receive significant interest within the trade and technical press, as References 7-12 and 7-13 attest.

The next chapter looks at new versions of Ethernet designed to operate over unshielded twisted-pair cable instead of coax. Clearly Ethernet will remain a networking mainstay for many years to come.

7.8. References

7-1. Some of the material in this chapter first appeared in "Troubleshooting Ethernet," by Mark A. Miller, *LAN Technology Magazine* (August 1989): 50-55.

7-2. DEC, INTEL and XEROX. *The Ethernet, A Local Area Network-Data Link Layer and Physical Layer Specification, Version 2.0.* Document number AA-K759B-TK, November 1982.

7-3. Institute of Electrical and Electronics Engineers. *Carrier Sense Multiple Access with Collision Detection (CSMA/CD), ISO/IEC 8802-3.* ANSI/IEEE Std 802.3, 1990.

7-4. Institute of Electrical and Electronics Engineers. *Supplements to Carrier Sense Multiple Access with Collision Detection.* ANSI/IEEE Std 802.3a, b, c, and e, 1988.

7-5. Standard Microsystems Corporation. *EtherCard PLUS 16 Elite Installation Guide.* 1992.

7-6. 3COM Corporation. *EtherLink III Adapter Guide.* 1992.

7-7. Cabletron Systems, Inc. *Intelligent Repeater Module (IRM-2) Installation Guide.* 1991.

7-8. Digital Equipment Corporation. *DECnet Digital Network Architecture (Phase IV) General Description.* Order number AA-N149A-TC, May 1982.

7-9. Digital Equipment Corporation. *DECnet Digital Network Architecture (Phase V).* Order number EK-DNAPV-GD, September 1987.

7-10. Network General Corporation. *Sniffer Network and Protocol Reference.* Publication 20026-002, July 1990.

7-11. Network General Corporation. *Sniffer Network Analyzer Operations Manual.* Publication 20028-001, May 1990.

7-12. Charles Spurgean. "Guide to Networking Resources Part III: Ethernet." *LAN Technology* (March 1991): 77-87.

7-13. Melanie McMullen. "Hubs Get Carded—Ethernet Adapter Cards." *LAN Magazine* (May 1992): 113-146.

CHAPTER 8

Troubleshooting StarLAN and 10BASE-T Networks

The last chapter examined coaxial Ethernet, including the original DIX Ethernet, 10BASE2, and 10BASE5. This chapter explores the problems and solutions inherent to the twisted-pair Ethernet networks: StarLAN (1BASE5) and twisted-pair Ethernet (10BASE-T).

In the first version of this book, StarLAN, with its 1 Mbps transmission rate was the dominant Ethernet-based twisted-pair network, and 10BASE-T, with its 10 Mbps transmission rate, was just emerging in the market. Since then 10BASE-T has become the dominant technology. Now the market is poised for another major advance that will increase transmission speeds by an order of magnitude. A number of vendors have proposed a 100 Mbps version of IEEE 802.3 networks, called fast Ethernet. Many fast Ethernet characteristics are consistent with 10BASE-T, including a 100-meter distance from workstation to concentrator and the use of unshielded or shielded twisted-pair cable. Other issues, such as the MAC layer protocol, are still under consideration.

As with the early twisted-pair Ethernet products, however, the lack of an accepted standard has not precluded vendors from introducing potentially incompatible products. Network designers considering one of these fast Ethernet products should investigate the status of the new standard to identify potential interoperability problems.

This chapter begins by examining StarLAN (see Reference 8-1).

8.1. StarLAN Topology

When AT&T introduced StarLAN in 1985, it was a cost-effective, twisted-pair alternative to the coaxial-cable-based LANs that dominated the industry. StarLAN adheres to the IEEE 802.3 1BASE5 specification, which a wide variety of companies support, including AT&T, Racal-Datacom, Hewlett-Packard, and others. However, many vendors have migrated their 1 Mbps products to the faster 10BASE-T standard.

StarLAN is a logical bus that can have two physical topologies. Some vendors have implemented a daisy-chained bus that connects up to 10 workstations but is not part of the 1BASE5 standard (see Figure 8-1a). A star-wired arrangement connects 10, 11, or 12 workstations (depending on the manufacturer) to a central hub, as shown in Figure 8-1b. You can also daisy-chain workstations from workstations attached to the central hub.

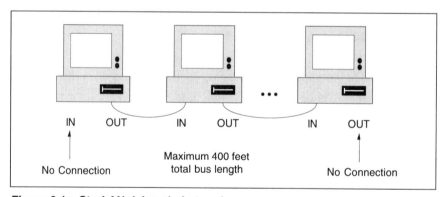

Figure 8-1a. StarLAN daisy-chain topology

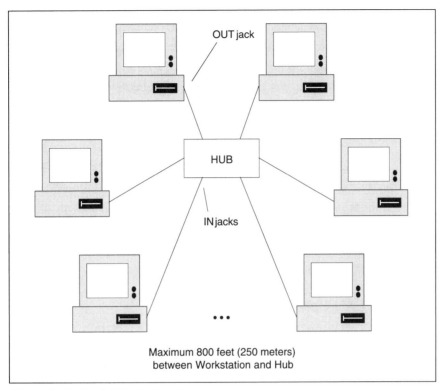

Figure 8-1b. StarLAN star topology

8.2. The StarLAN Physical Layer

StarLAN adheres to the IEEE 802.3 1BASE5 standard and has the following characteristics (for more information see Reference 8-2):

- It uses a signaling rate of 1 Mbps with Manchester encoding. Figure 7-3 illustrates the Manchester-encoded signal.
- The maximum workstation-to-workstation distance is 500 meters via a single hub. Longer distances are possible when hubs are connected in a hierarchical topology.
- StarLAN transmits over standard unshielded telephone wiring, which is typically 22, 24, or 26 gauge.

- It uses two transmission channels: one twisted pair for the upward link, another for the downward link. Most manufacturers designate the pairs transmit and receive, respectively.
- The data pairs can coexist on the same cable as audio and telephone.
- Hubs function as repeaters and propagate the signals they receive from workstations to higher-level hubs. The highest-level header hub loops signals around and sends them down the link to lower-level hubs and workstations. The hubs also perform collision detection. Specially coded collision presence signals inform stations of collisions.
- 1BASE5 allows you to cascade up to five levels of hubs, although some vendor implementations allow more.

8.3. StarLAN Hardware Components

StarLAN's hardware elements include the NIC, wiring hub, and cabling.

8.3.1. StarLAN NICs

StarLAN NICs resemble coaxial Ethernet NICs in that they contain the usual switches, jumpers, and network controller ICs. (The Intel 82588 and the National Semiconductor DP83900 are two examples of StarLAN controllers.) One distinguishing characteristic of StarLAN NICs is their output ports. The in and out ports are used for network cabling, and the phone port is for telephone connections. However, not all vendors support the phone port for integrated voice/data wiring.

8.3.2. StarLAN wiring hubs

The StarLAN hub includes multiple in ports for connections to single or daisy-chained workstations, one out port for connection to a higher-level (uplink) hub, a power connector, and diagnostic LEDs. Hubs require external power. If the entire network (or one star of a multistar configuration) fails, check for a power outage at the hub.

8.3.3. StarLAN cabling

Figures 8-2a and 8-2b and Reference 8-3 detail the 8-pin modular connector (specified as ISO 8877 and usually called an RJ-45) and the cable
pair assignments used with StarLAN. Note that the definitions for transmit
and receive depend on the orientation of the user. Figure 8-2b describes the
NIC. In this case the out port uses Pins 1 and 2 for transmit, and the in port
uses Pins 1 and 2 for receive. The RJ-45 cable itself must have pin-to-pin
continuity. In other words, Pin 1 must connect to Pin 1, Pin 2 to Pin 2, and
so on.

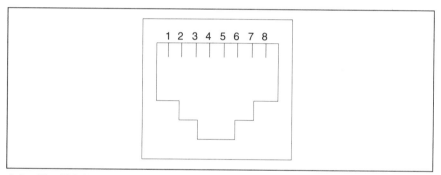

8-2a. The RJ-45 modular jack (front view)

Pin	In Port	Out Port	Phone Port
1	Receive +	Transmit +	NC
2	Receive −	Transmit −	NC
3	Transmit +	Receive +	NC
4	NC	Ring	Ring
5	NC	Tip	Tip
6	Transmit −	Receive −	NC
7	NC	Power	Power
8	NC	Power	Power
NC = No Connection			
Tip/Ring = Analog Telephone Connections			
Power = Power feed for telephone (as required)			

8-2b. StarLAN NIC port assignments

231

8.3.4. Telephone connections

The IEEE 802.3 1BASE5 standard (Reference 8-2, page 143) specifies that 1BASE5 does not use Pins 4 and 5, and Pins 7 and 8 are reserved for future use. Notice from Figure 8-2b that some NICs, such as AT&T/NCR and Western Digital, allow for analog telephone wiring on Pins 4 and 5 and power for telephone accessories, such as a speakerphone, on Pins 7 and 8.

Although you can set up StarLAN to coexist with analog telephone cabling, be careful when doing so. Modular phone connectors allow smaller plugs, such as 4-pin or RJ-11, to fit into larger jacks, such as 8-pin or RJ-45. In addition, the two center pins (Pins 2 and 3 on the 4-pin connector, 3 and 4 on the 6-pin connector, or 4 and 5 on the 8-pin connector) carry the contact for the tip and the ring of the analog telephone circuit. Some phone systems, however, such as PBX and Key System, carry signals for power or station signaling on pins other than the center two, such as 3 and 6. If you plug a StarLAN system into such a system, you may get interference between the StarLAN transmit and receive signals (Pins 1 and 2, 3 and 6) and the telephone or power signals, which can damage both systems.

8.4. StarLAN Hardware Troubleshooting

The NIC is one of the most common sources of network failure. Another is the cabling, despite the fact that the typical 24-gauge unshielded telephone cable terminated with RJ-45 modular connectors seems relatively straightforward.

8.4.1. StarLAN NIC problems

One common NIC problem is incorrect cable connections. You also must be careful to set options correctly for the IRQ, the I/O base address, and the DMA channel. A NIC can have a RAM buffer or ROM BIOS that shares your PC's address space. Be careful to avoid memory conflicts with other devices in your PC. The System Sleuth software program described in Section 3.6 is a valuable tool for this task.

Most StarLAN NICs come with a diagnostic disk to facilitate troubleshooting. Probably the most useful test is the internal loopback, which tests both the transmitter and receiver. Since the transmitter and receiver sections are independent, one can fail while the other operates properly. If a workstation can transmit but not receive, run a loop-around test for confirmation.

8.4.2. StarLAN daisy-chain difficulties

Daisy-chain cabling is the simplest connection scheme for StarLAN networks. One caution, however: Different manufacturers place different limits on the length of the daisy chain, ranging from 400 to 800 feet. Check your NIC installation guide for details.

Several characteristics of StarLAN NICs are also relevant to StarLAN daisy chains. First, the daisy chain must begin with a connection from one out connector to the next in connector. If a dangling cable is attached to the first in or the last out, network problems will result. All buses must terminate with the characteristic impedance of the cable (for example, a 52-ohm cable must terminate with a 52-ohm resistor) to prevent signal reflections. The AT&T and Western Digital StarLAN NICs do this automatically; when a modular cord is not plugged into the in port, a bus terminator automatically inserts at both transmit and receive pairs, shorting the pairs together to complete the bus. Plugging a dangling cord into the first workstation's in port would disrupt the bus termination. Other manufacturers take a different approach, requiring a terminator resistor in any unused in connector and a loop-back plug in any unused out connector. Check the NIC documentation for details on your network.

Workstations connecting to a hub must have a cable running from the out port on the NIC to the in port of the hub. For networks with multiple layers of hubs, the out port on one hub connects to an in port of the higher-layer hub. For example, using AT&T products, a StarLAN network can have several in ports with no modular cords attached but only one unused out port. Violating this rule crashes the network. See Figure 8-3 and Reference 8-3, Section 4, for further details.

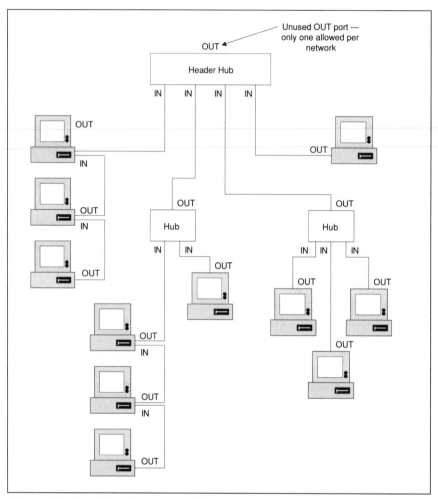

Figure 8-3. StarLAN daisy-chain wiring

8.4.3. Other hardware considerations

The first step in identifying any network failure is to isolate the problem to one section of the network. With StarLAN's modular architecture, this is relatively easy. LEDs indicate power and traffic conditions at the hub, so any abnormal condition should be readily apparent.

To segment a StarLAN network, start at the central hub and isolate the problem to a particular hub and hub port, and finally to a NIC and workstation. Thorough network documentation is essential for this step. As you disconnect individual segments of the network, make sure that no configuration rules are violated (for instance, no more than one unused out port). If you can isolate a failure to one hub, check the power connection and observe any diagnostic LEDs that indicate abnormal network traffic conditions. Beyond that, go to the individual ports and workstations to troubleshoot as discussed previously.

8.5. 10BASE-T Topology

The 1BASE5 standard allows for 1Mpbs transmissions of 250 meters between a workstation and the hub and a maximum of 500 meters between any two workstations. An AT&T study presented to the 1BASE5 Committee, however, concluded that the vast majority of workstations are within 100 meters of a wiring closet. At this distance signals can be transmitted at 10 Mbps. This study is widely cited as the impetus behind the twisted-pair Ethernet IEEE 802.3 10BASE-T project (see Reference 8-4). The 10BASE-T topology resembles that of 1BASE5 in that it is a star-based topology using cables to connect the workstations to a concentrator or hub. This ring also allows you to add daisy-chained offshoot segments. The major difference is 10BASE-T's faster transmission speed.

Many vendors, including SynOptics, Standard Microsystems, AT&T, Hewlett-Packard, and Racal-Datacom, market 10BASE-T products as alternatives to conventional coaxial-cable-based Ethernet and 802.3 networks. These products share several characteristics: a maximum distance of 100 meters between workstations and the wiring closet, the ability to easily connect and cascade wiring closets, and the continued use of 802.3 10BASE5 or 10BASE2 NICs. Figure 8-4 shows a typical 10BASE-T network topology.

8.6. The 10BASE-T Physical Layer

The 10BASE-T standard defines a twisted-pair MAU that allows you to attach AUI-compatible devices to twisted-pair media, instead of the usual coaxial media. Thus 10BASE-T networks can work with existing 802.3 NICs that meet the current specification at the AUI interface.

The maximum distance between the AUI interface (called a twisted-pair MAU, or TPMAU) and a central wiring closet is 100 meters. At the wiring closet a multiport repeater (MPR) connects all workstations on the floor. You can also interconnect multiple wiring closets on different floors. The resulting network topology is a distributed star, which can also have off-shoots. Since the standard assures compatibility at the 802.3 AUI, 10BASE-T networks can connect with existing thin or thick coaxial networks.

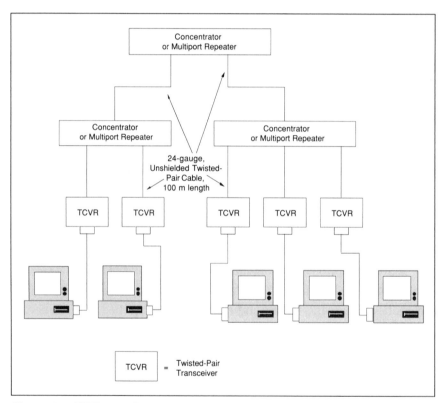

Figure 8-4. IEEE 10BASE-T topology

The distance limitations for the transmission media are governed primarily by the minimum propagation velocity of the cable, expressed as a percentage of the speed of light (c = 300,000 km/sec). For twisted-pair cable, the factor is 0.59c; for fiber-optics, 0.66c; for the 10BASE2 (thin) coaxial,

0.65c; and for 10BASE5 (thick) coaxial, 0.77c. The maximum round-trip signal propagation time for a 10 Mbps 802.3 network is another factor in the distance calculation. One of the primary factors in the proper operation of a CSMA/CD network is that the transmitting station must receive collision information from the most remote station before it stops transmitting even the shortest permissible frame (64 octets, or 512 bits). Because 802.3 networks allow a great deal of flexibility in their choice of transmission media, you must be careful not to exceed the propagation delay specifications (and the resulting cable length limits).

8.7. 10BASE-T Hardware Components

10BASE-T hardware components include interface ICs, NICs, transceivers, concentrators, and cabling.

8.7.1. 10BASE-T interface ICs

Several manufacturers currently produce integrated circuits that support 10BASE-T networks. These integrated circuits provide protocol handling and an interface to the twisted-pair wiring.

AT&T Microelectronics has developed three devices: the T7202 multiport repeater unit, the T7231 station interface, and the T7213 twisted-pair MAU—an interface between the twisted-pair cable and AUI functions. National Semiconductor has developed the DP83902 serial network interface controller for twisted pair (ST-NIC). Intel manufactures the 82503 dual serial transceiver (DST) and the 82506TC twisted-pair MAU (TP MAU). Intel's 82504TA device is identical to the AT&T T7210. The NCR Microelectronics 92C02 requires external analog drivers to the outside world. SynOptics Communication's IC supports the LattisNet product line and is used by a variety of manufacturers, including Racal-Interlan, Western Digital, and Tiara.

All of these manufacturers support the proposed 10BASE-T standard to varying degrees. Thus, by purchasing NICs that are compatible at the chip level, you can avoid interoperability problems.

8.7.2. 10BASE-T NICs

10BASE-T networks can use existing 802.3 10BASE5 or 10BASE2 NICs. To connect these NICs to 10BASE-T networks, you need a transceiver, as discussed in Section 8.7.3. The Racal-Datacom Interlan AT-3M, shown in Figure 8-5, is an example of an Ethernet NIC that directly supports 10BASE-T connections. The NIC has connectors for thick and thin Ethernet and a modular connector (and built-in transceiver) for 10BASE-T. The advantage of this NIC is that you can use it in mixed-media environments, such as a network with a thick Ethernet backbone connecting a number of 10BASE-T concentrators. You can also use these boards to reduce your spare parts inventory, since you need to stock only one type of spare board. One caution, however: NICs with multiple output ports require you to set a switch or jumper to select the proper port. Make sure that this switch or jumper is properly set, or your transmissions will go nowhere. If in doubt, consult the NIC installation guide, such as Reference 8-5.

Figure 8-5. Thick/thin/10BASE-T compatible NIC

(Photo courtesy of Racal-Datacom)

8.7.3. 10BASE-T transceivers

When you use conventional 802.3 NICs with 10BASE-T networks, you need a way to convert between the unshielded twisted-pair, shielded twisted-pair, or fiber-optic media and the conventional DB-15 (AUI) interface. This is the function of the transceivers shown in Figure 8-6.

Network troubleshooters should note that there are two LEDs on these transceivers. The link status LED indicates that the transceiver is connected to a powered host (such as a workstation) and that the connection is operating. A second LED indicates the state of the SQE Test signal selector. (Recall from Chapter 7 that the SQE Test signal, sometimes called heartbeat, must be disabled if you use the transceiver with an IEEE 802.3 repeater.) Use these LEDs to quickly check the status of the link between the workstation and the concentrator.

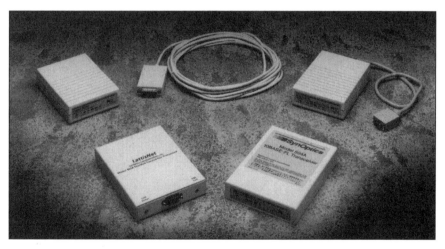

Figure 8-6. Ethernet transceivers
(Photo courtesy of SynOptics)

8.7.4. 10BASE-T concentrators

Concentrators are intelligent devices that function as hubs for multiple network connections. In 10BASE-T networks, the concentrator acts as a multiport repeater, effectively providing a backbone to connect the workstations. Most vendors include status LEDs that indicate the presence of traffic, collisions, link integrity, or a jabber signal. Remote administrative features, such the Simple Network Management Protocol (SNMP), are also becoming more common.

Many vendors also have added special features to their concentrators, such as connectivity to other networks. One example of such an intelligent concentrator is the SynOptics LattisNet System 3000 concentrator (see Figure 8-7 and Reference 8-6). This concentrator allows you to integrate multiple Ethernet, token-ring, and FDDI networks within the same platform. It supports integrated Ethernet switching, bridging, and routing functions. It also allows you to use a variety of cable options, including shielded and unshielded twisted pairs and fiber optics.

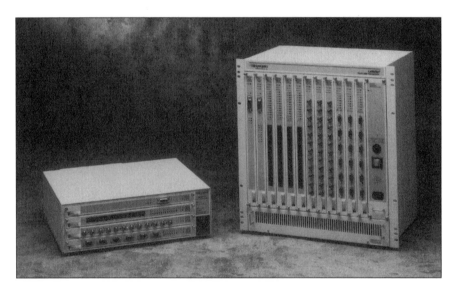

Figure 8-7. LattisNet System 3000 concentrator
(Photo courtesy of SynOptics)

AT&T/NCR's StarLAN 10 SmartHUB offers several other features that are notable from a troubleshooting point of view (see Figures 8-8a and 8-8b and Reference 8-7). The StarLAN 10 SmartHUB has a built-in power supply (see the right side of Figure 8-8a). By checking the LEDs on the power supply, you can determine the concentrator's operational status. Several interface modules are also available for these systems, such as repeaters (see Figure 8-8b). When you insert these modules into the concentrator chassis, be sure to push them in all the way in order to seat the backplane connectors firmly. Also, be sure to use the correct module for the intended application.

Figure 8-8a. StarLAN 10 Network SmartHUB XE
(Photo courtesy of NCR Corp.)

All these items are key elements in the troubleshooting process. Learn about the specifics of your vendor's concentrator for more effective network management.

Figure 8-8b. StarLAN 10 Network SmartHUB XE modules
(Photo courtesy of NCR Corp.)

8.7.5. 10BASE-T cabling

If a cable break or disconnection occurs in star-wired topologies, such as 10BASE-T, the workstation at the end of the cable becomes disconnected from the rest of the network. The IEEE 802.3 10BASE-T standard provides a link integrity test to indicate such a failure. This test applies to both the transmit and receive pairs. At the transmit end it sends either data or an idle signal (called TP-IDL). The receiver listens for these signals and, if they are not present, provides a visual (LED) indication to alert the end user or administrator.

The cable configurations and pinouts for typical 10BASE-T configurations are shown in Figures 8-9a and 8-9b. Since many network difficulties involve cables, a few comments are in order.

First, note the pinouts of the 8-pin modular connectors used between the concentrator and twisted-pair transceiver. There is only one port (unlike Star-

LAN's in and out). The transmit signal goes from the transceiver to the concentrator, or from the concentrator to the next highest concentrator. The receive signal goes in the opposite direction. The 10BASE-T standard uses the term *medium dependent interface* (MDI) to define the interface at the modular connector (see Figure 8-9b). A crossover function, MDI-X, reverses the functions of the transmit and receive signals.

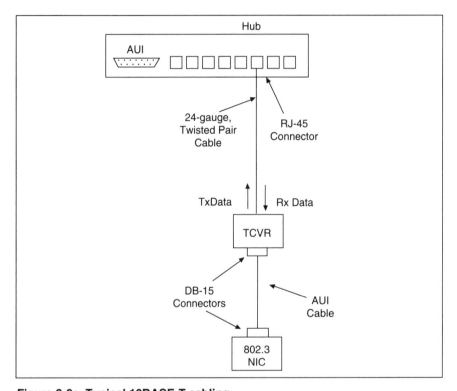

Figure 8-9a. Typical 10BASE-T cabling

The connectors for the cables (24-gauge cables are typically used) must be wired for pin-to-pin continuity; for example, Pin 1 must connect to Pin 1 for proper network operation. In addition, both the transmit and receive pairs must be twisted flat wire, and silver satin cabling is not allowed.

The SynOptics LattisNet products and other intelligent wiring hubs provide a function that automatically detects and corrects wiring polarity problems. For example, if a wire pair is reversed inadvertently at the cross-connect field, the port on the LattisNet concentrator automatically corrects for the miswiring so data is received correctly. In addition, the twisted-pair transceiver output is the DB-15 connector used with other 802.3 devices connecting to the AUI cable. LattisNet complies with 802.3 at this interface, so any 802.3-compliant NIC can attach to the output of the LattisNet transceiver.

Pin	Color	Signal
1	White/Orange	TD +
2	Orange/White	TD -
3	White/Green	RD +
4	Blue/White	NA
5	White/Blue	NA
6	Green/White	RD -
7	White/Brown	NA
8	Brown/White	NA

NA = Not Assigned

Figure 8-9b. 10BASE-T circuit assignments at the Medium Dependent Interface (MDI) port

8.7.6. Using twisted pairs

A detailed discussion of the reuse of the existing twisted-pair cables within a building is beyond the scope of this book. However, if you're interested in this, you should be aware that the standard offers no discussion of how to use the existing cabling in your building for a twisted-pair LAN. The standard (see Reference 8-4) does define a number of electrical parameters to which the cable adheres. These include specifications for insertion loss, characteristic impedance, timing jitter, delay, and crosstalk. You can use a TDR, such as the MicroTest scanners discussed in Chapter 3, to test existing cable for compliance with the 10BASE-T specifications.

8.8. 10BASE-T Hardware Troubleshooting

The intelligent wiring hubs and concentrators commonly used today offer automated network management functions, such as the Simple Network Management Protocol (SNMP). If an automated network management system is not available, manual troubleshooting is required.

10BASE-T's distributed star topology makes network failures straightforward to diagnose. The first step in the manual process is to segment the network, much as we did with ARCNET, and isolate the failure to a particular concentrator, cable section, or transceiver. To do that in an orderly fashion, obtain the network documentation to determine which concentrator is the central (or highest) point in the multitiered star architecture. Many vendors make the fault-isolation task easier by providing diagnostic LEDs on the concentrators and transceivers for a visual indication of network status.

For example, consider the LattisNet network shown in Figure 8-10, and suppose that the 10BASE-T segment is connected to a coaxial backbone. Begin by disconnecting the two segments at point A to isolate the failure to either the coaxial or twisted-pair segment. If the network recovers, the failure exists on the coaxial cable section, so proceed to troubleshoot the coax segment, as discussed in Chapter 7.

If the network remains inoperable, go to the central concentrator (point B) and begin disconnecting the host modules one at a time. When the network recovers, you have identified the faulty downstream concentrator or device.

Let's assume that the unshielded twisted-pair module (point C) looks like the culprit. Reinsert the module into the concentrator chassis to recreate the failure, and then proceed to disconnect the downward links (point D) one at a time. If other concentrators are downward of point D, disconnect their attached workstations (point E) individually as well. When the network recovers the problem has been identified. Only three possible causes remain: the concentrator port, the cable (and possibly the transceiver), or the workstation and its NIC. Replace each of these individually until you've eliminated the failure.

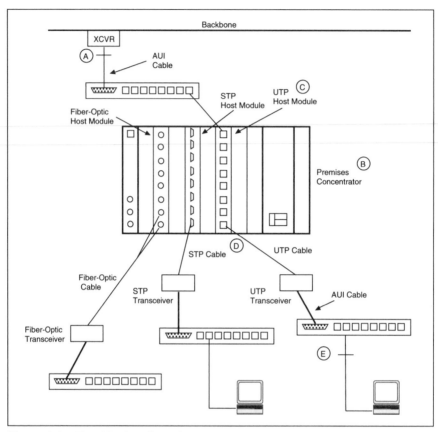

Figure 8-10. Troubleshooting with LattisNet
(Courtesy of SynOptics Communication)

Should you encounter a failing section, unplug it to see if the network failure goes away. If the problem clears, you have isolated the defective section. Continue to segment the network in this fashion until you identify the failing part. If the failure is at the NIC, use the diagnostic disk that came with the board for further troubleshooting.

8.9. StarLAN and 10BASE-T Software Considerations

Both StarLAN and 10BASE-T are physical layer specifications. The data-link layer frame format can be either IEEE 802.3/802.2 or Ethernet. As a result, you can use a protocol analyzer for data-link and higher layer protocol analysis for StarLAN and 10BASE-T architectures.

246

There is one caution at the data-link layer, however. Some NICs come with diagnostic disks that allow you to change the 48-bit source address burned into ROM. If you do this, use extreme caution because other workstations and hosts in the network depend on the consistency of that address and do not react favorably to a sudden change. Should an unusual failure occur, ask whether any software parameters have changed and proceed as discussed previously.

8.10. Protocol Analysis with TCP/IP

ARPANET, sponsored by the Advanced Research Projects Agency of the Department of Defense (DoD), was the first network in the United States to demonstrate the viability of packet switching. ARPANET began operating in 1969 with four nodes and still exists today. To connect the ARPANET to the major research universities and defense contractors, many of which had dissimilar computer hardware and operating systems, the DoD also developed the Transmission Control Protocol/Internet Protocol (TCP/IP) suite (see Reference 8-8). Ethernet was developed and the Ethernet-TCP/IP alliance formed at about the same time. With more of the Ethernet networks converting to the 802.3 family, it makes sense to consider software analysis of TCP/IP over 802.3 network transmission.

Figure 8-11 shows how the TCP/IP suite fits into the OSI model. ARCNET, IEEE 802, and Ethernet networks operate at the data-link layer and can use the TCP/IP protocol for higher-layer functions (see References 8-9, 8-10, and 8-11).

OSI Layer	Protocol Implementation
Application	Application-specific protocols, e.g., Virtual Terminal, Electronic Mail, File Transfer
Presentation	
Session	
Transport	Transmission Control Protocol (TCP)
Network	Internet Protocol (IP)
Data-Link	Network Interface Cards: Ethernet, StarLAN, Token Ring, ARCNET
Physical	Transmission Media, Twisted Pair, Coax, or Fiber-Optics

Figure 8-11. TCP/IP and the ISO/OSI model

At the network layer, the internet protocol (IP) provides datagram service between hosts (or LANs) and network nodes. The IP routes packets from one network to another and contains 32-bit addresses for the source and destination network and host.

The transmission control protocol (TCP) provides transport layer service, supporting process-to-process communication between the two hosts. TCP provides circuit-oriented service (called ports), to assure a reliable, byte-streamed connection. (Connection-oriented service establishes the logical and physical connection between the communicating entities before transmitting data.) TCP/IP uses higher-layer protocols, such as the File Transfer Protocol (FTP), Simple Mail Transfer Protocol (SMTP), and a virtual terminal protocol (TELNET); plus NetBIOS and Server Message Block (SMB) protocols for LANs (see Reference 8-12).

As mentioned previously, TCP/IP is closely associated with Ethernet and 802.3 LANs. Figure 8-12 shows how the 802.3 frame encapsulates the IP and TCP headers and the TCP data (from higher-layer protocols, such as FTP, SMTP, or TELNET).

248

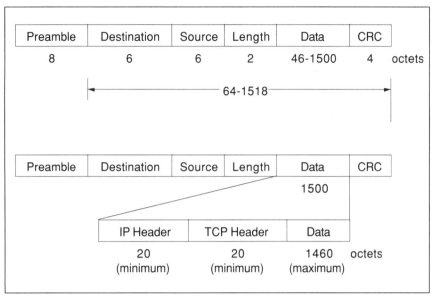

Figure 8-12. Encapsulating a TCP/IP datagram within an IEEE 802.3 frame

The IP header contains at least 20 octets and consists of fields describing the IP version Internet header length; the type of service requested; the total length of the IP datagram; identification, flags, and fragment offset controlling the fragmentation and reassembly of the datagrams; a time to live; the protocol used within the IP data field; a header checksum; source and destination addresses specifying the network and host IDs; and various options, padding, and data from the higher layers, such as TCP (see Reference 8-13).

The TCP header also contains a minimum of 20 octets, and consists of fields defining the source and destination ports (application programs); the sequence and acknowledgment numbers; a data offset; six flags controlling the setup and termination of the session; the receiver window size; a checksum; a pointer to urgent data; and finally options, padding, and data from the higher layers (see Reference 8-14).

The Network General Sniffer protocol analyzer captures the address through data fields of the 802.3 frame (see Figure 8-13). Trace 8-1 shows an example of this captured data, an 802.3 frame with TCP/IP headers and 256 bytes of data. The left margin identifies each layer of protocol, DLC,

LLC, IP, and TCP. The advantages of using a protocol analyzer are obvious when you consider the number of fields and options associated with the TCP/IP protocols. Reference 8-15 provides more information about the operation of the Sniffer analyzer.

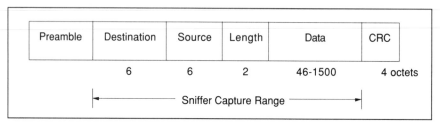

Figure 8-13. Capture range of the Network General Sniffer protocol analyzer for 802.3 Networks

Trace 8-1. A TCP/IP Datagram transmitted over an IEEE 802.3 network and captured by the Network General Sniffer protocol analyzer

Sniffer Network Analyzer data 04-Apr-90 at 01:27:04, file TCP.ENC Pg 1

```
DLC:  —- DLC Header —-
DLC:
DLC:  Frame 2 arrived at  14:30:33.0340 ; frame size is
         313 (0139 hex) bytes.
DLC:  Destination: Station 3Com  138372
DLC:  Source     : Station 3Com  138162
DLC:  802.2 LLC length = 299
DLC:
LLC:  —- LLC Header —-
LLC:
LLC:  DSAP = 06, SSAP = 06, Command, Unnumbered frame: UI
LLC:
IP:   —- IP Header —-
IP:
IP:   Version = 4, header length = 20 bytes
IP:   Type of service = 00
IP:        000. .... = routine
IP:        ...0 .... = normal delay
```

```
IP:          .... 0... = normal throughput
IP:          .... .0.. = normal reliability
IP:     Total length = 296 bytes
IP:     Identification = 0
IP:     Flags = 4X
IP:     .1.. .... = don't fragment
IP:     ..0. .... = last fragment
IP:     Fragment offset = 0 bytes
IP:     Time to live = 60
IP:     Protocol = 6 (TCP)
IP:     Header checksum = 8D4E (correct)
IP:     Source address = [15.6.73.68]
IP:     Destination address = [15.6.73.50]
IP:     No options
IP:
TCP:  —- TCP header —-
TCP:
TCP:  Source port = 46586
TCP:  Destination port = 5696
TCP:  Sequence number = 1108921
TCP:  Acknowledgment number = 346879454
TCP:  Data offset = 20
TCP:  Flags = 18
TCP:  ..0. .... = (No urgent pointer)
TCP:  ...1 .... = Acknowledgment
TCP:  .... 1... = Push
TCP:  .... .0.. = (No reset)
TCP:  .... ..0. = (No SYN)
TCP:  .... ...0 = (No FIN)
TCP:  Window = 1424
TCP:  Checksum = 0 (No checksum sent)
TCP:  No TCP options
TCP:  [256 byte(s) of data]
TCP:
```

8.11. StarLAN and 10BASE-T Networks Troubleshooting Summary

To summarize, here is a checklist to assist with diagnosing StarLAN and 10BASE-T network failures:

1. Clean the gold fingers and reseat the NIC in the PC bus.

2. Run the NIC board diagnostics, if available.

3. Check IRQ, DMA shared memory, and I/O base address for conflicts with other boards. If in doubt, remove all boards but the NIC and reinsert one board at a time. Visually inspect the NIC for any jumpers that may have fallen off or any DIP switches not firmly set.

4. Confirm the order of CONFIG.SYS and AUTOEXEC.BAT files and any device drivers in use.

5. Use the advantage of the star topology to isolate a failure to one hub, concentrator, or multiport repeater, and further to an individual port.

6. Check activity on diagnostic LEDs (if present) on the NIC, hub, or concentrator for proper condition.

7. Check for an unterminated (dangling) cable at the out port of the header hub or the last workstation in a StarLAN daisy-chain configuration. Unplug the cable from the out port to correct.

8. Look for a break in any StarLAN daisy-chain cabling.

9. Verify pin-to-pin continuity (Pin 1 to Pin 1, Pin 2 to Pin 2, and so on) on all cables, and check for any loose crimp connections at the RJ-45 connector.

10. Check for correct power to any hub, concentrator, or multiport repeater; also check fuses.

11. Check for duplicate node addresses with the NIC diagnostic disk or protocol analyzer if you've used software-configurable node addressing.

8.12. References

8-1.   Some of the material in this chapter first appeared in "Troubleshooting StarLAN and Twisted-pair Ethernet," by Mark A. Miller. *LAN Technology Magazine,* (September 1989): 62-66.

8-2.   Institute of Electrical and Electronics Engineers. *Supplements to Carrier Sense Multiple Access with Collision Detection, ISO 8802-3.* ANSI IEEE Std 802.3a, b, c, and e, 1989.

8-3.   AT&T. *StarLAN Network Technical Reference Manual.* Publication 999-300-208, 1986.

8-4.   Institute of Electrical and Electronics Engineers. *Twisted-pair Medium Attachment Unit and Baseband Medium,* Type 10BASE-T. IEEE Std 802.3i, 1990.

8-5.   Racal-Datacom. *InterLan AT Series Installation Manual.* Document 950-1377-00, February 1992.

8-6.   SynOptics Communications, Inc. *LattisNet System 3000 Concentrator Installation and Maintenance Guide.* Document 893-071-C, October 1992.

8-7.   AT&T. *StarLAN 10 Network SmartHUB Installation and Operation Guide.* Document 999-120-771, 1991.

8-8.   Most documentation on TCP/IP and the related Internet protocols are contained in *Request for Comment (RFC)* papers available from the DDN Network Information Center, Government Systems, Inc. (Chantilly, VA) (703) 802-4535 or (800) 365-3642.

8-9.   DDN Network Information Center. *A Standard for the Transmission of IP Datagrams and ARP Packets over ARCNET Networks.* RFC 1201, February 1991.

8-10. DDN Network Information Center. *A Standard for the Transmission of IP Datagrams over IEEE 802 Networks*. RFC 948, February 1988.

8-11. DDN Network Information Center. *A Standard for the Transmission of IP Datagrams over Ethernet Networks*. RFC 894, April 1984.

8-12. DDN Network Information Center. *Protocol Standard for a NetBIOS Service on a TCP/UDP Transport: Concepts and Methods (RFC 1001), and Detailed Specifications (RFC 1002)*. March 1987.

8-13. DDN Network Information Center. *Internet Protocol (IP)*. RFC 791, September 1981.

8-14. DDN Network Information Center. *Transmission Control Protocol*. RFC 793, September 1981.

8-15. Network General Corp. *Sniffer Network Analyzer Operations Manual*. Document 20028-001, May 1990.

CHAPTER 9

Troubleshooting FDDI Networks

With high-resolution graphics, CAD/CAM, multimedia, and other high-bandwidth applications becoming more popular, many desktop applications require higher transmission capacities than those available from any of the LANs discussed so far. Many internetworks also require high capacities for LAN-to-LAN or LAN-to-WAN interconnections. For these and other applications, the Fiber Distributed Data Interface (FDDI) may be an ideal solution.

FDDI is an ANSI standard developed by the ANSI Accredited Standards Committee (ASC) X3, and the ASC X3T9.5 Task Group. Although FDDI is not an IEEE standard, it incorporates elements of the IEEE 802 project. For example, FDDI uses frame formats similar to those found in the IEEE 802.5 frame format, and the FDDI data-link layer uses the IEEE 802.2 LLC.

9.1. FDDI Architecture

FDDI defines a counter-rotating, redundant, dual-ring topology network that transmits at 100 Mbps. One ring operates normally and the second functions as a backup in the event of workstation or cable failure. A token passing protocol grants access to the ring. Attached workstations can be between 2 and 60 kilometers apart, depending on the type of fiber-optic cable used. The total length for the dual ring may not exceed 100 kilometers (or 200 kilometers when wrapped or connected during a fault condition), with a maximum of 500 attached stations. With its high transmission capacity and large geographical coverage, FDDI is ideally suited for campuswide or metropolitan area network (MAN) applications.

9.1.1. FDDI Station attachments

Figure 9-1 illustrates the topology of the architecture. As you can see, FDDI networks consist of trunk rings from which tree topology networks can extend.

Station attachments to rings are of two types: Dual Attachment Stations (DASs) and Single Attachment Stations (SASs). A DAS physically connects to both the primary and secondary rings. If a fault occurs in a DAS, an optical bypass switch reroutes the data traffic around it. If a cable fault occurs, the adjacent DAS uses the secondary ring to wrap the data, bypassing the faulty link. The SAS has a single attachment to the ring. Thus the SAS connects to a concentrator in a star topology and can access only the primary ring.

FDDI defines two types of concentrators: The Dual Attachment Concentrator (DAC) connects to both rings and offers reliability and redundancy capabilities similar to those of the DAS. The Single Attachment Concentrator (SAC) attaches to a DAC or another SAC. You can use SAC connections to extend tree topology networks from the main trunk ring (review Figure 9-1).

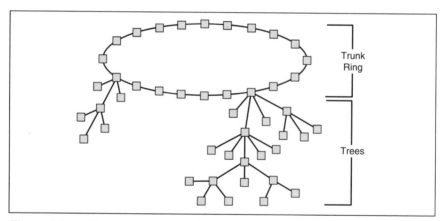

Figure 9-1. FDDI ring of trees topology
(Courtesy of ANSI)

9.1.2. FDDI Port definitions

With all of its topology options, including SAS, DAS, concentrators, and so on, FDDI needs provisions to prevent incorrect configurations. The standard, therefore, defines four port types and specifies a mechanical key for the fiber-optic connector to assure that cables are plugged into the proper port (see Section 9.2.1 for further details on the connector itself). The ports are as follows:

- Port A is a main ring trunk connection with an input from the primary ring and an output to the secondary ring (Port B). This port is used on a DAS or a concentrator.
- Port B is a main ring trunk connection with an input from the secondary ring and an output to a primary ring (Port A). This port is used on a DAS or a concentrator.
- Port M is the master connection for a concentrator and is found only on a concentrator. This port connects an SAS or DAS to a concentrator or provides connections within a concentrator tree.
- Port S is a single attachment station connection and is found only on an SAS or SAC. This port connects to a Port M within a concentrator tree.

9.1.3. FDDI Ring reconfiguration

The dual-ring topology allows you to reconfigure the network if a cable segment, DAS, or DAC fails. Suppose that an FDDI network consists of one concentrator (shown as DAS2 in Figure 9-2a), three SASs (shown as SAS3, 4, and 5), and three DASs (DAS1, 6, and 7). The DASs and the DAC connect to both the primary and secondary rings, while the SASs connect only to the primary ring. Further assume that cable faults occur between DAS2 and SAS3, and between DAS1 and DAS6 (see Figure 9-2b). No automatic cure is available for the first link (DAS2 to SAS3), since only the primary ring is available and it has failed. Thus the concentrator internally reroutes (or wraps) the primary ring connection from the DAS1 port to the SAS4 port, bypassing the failed SAS3 link. Because both primary and secondary rings are available, the cable fault between DAS1 and DAS6 can be automatically bypassed. Internal algorithms within DAS1 and DAS6 reroute the data in the opposite direction and maintain the transmission integrity of the ring. If a DAS failure occurs, two solutions are possible: If the station contains an optical bypass switch, the switch activates automatically and allows the ring to bypass the station. If the bypass switch is not included (as shown in Figure 9-2b), the stations on either side of the failure reconfigure, restoring ring operation.

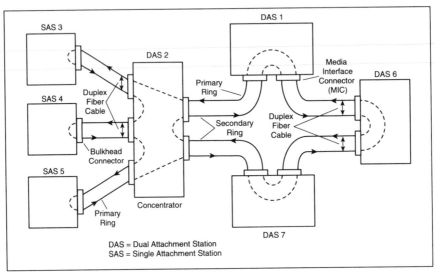

Figure 9-2a. FDDI ring structure

(Courtesy of Advanced Micro Devices, Inc.)

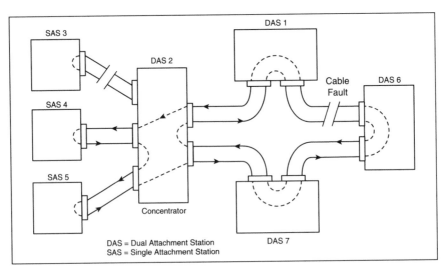

Figure 9-2b. FDDI ring reconfiguration

(Courtesy of Advanced Micro Devices, Inc.)

9.1.4. FDDI Station and concentrator architecture

Figures 9-3a, 9-3b, and 9-3c illustrate the architecture of the SAS, DAS, and concentrator. As you can see in these figures, the SAS, DAS, and concentrators include a number of logical and physical protocol entities, including the port, Configuration Control Elements (CCEs), the Media Access Control (MAC) entity, and Station Management (SMT) algorithms.

Before I describe these entities, you need two definitions. Unlike other types of networks, which use the terms *node* and *station* interchangeably, FDDI networks define these terms somewhat differently. Both nodes and stations are defined as active devices on the FDDI network. Stations, however, are addressable logical and physical nodes, which are capable of transmitting, receiving, and repeating information. Workstations, SASs, DASs, and concentrators are all stations.

Both nodes and stations use a port to access the FDDI ring. The port contains Physical Layer (PHY) and Physical Layer Medium Dependent (PMD) processes that provide the physical connection and data transmission on the ring. Note that the SAS contains port S (Figure 9-3a), the DAS contains ports A and B (Figure 9-3b), and the concentrator contains ports

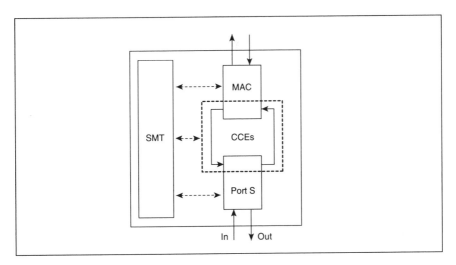

Figure 9-3a. FDDI SAS architecture

(Courtesy of ANSI)

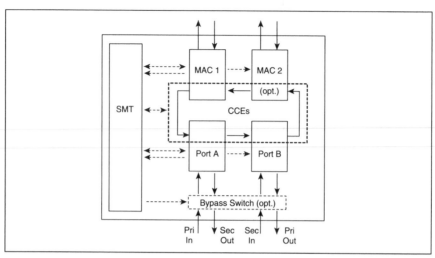

Figure 9-3b. FDDI DAS architecture

(Courtesy of ANSI)

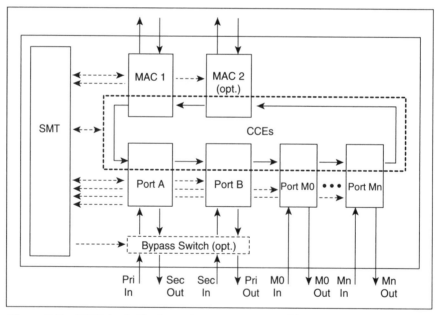

Figure 9-3c. FDDI dual attachment concentrator architecture

(Courtesy of ANSI)

A, B, and M (Figure 9-3c). The DAS and concentrator may also contain an optical bypass switch that takes the signal from the upstream station and passes it directly to the downstream station. This switch can be activated in three ways: internally, from a power failure, or through the intervention of an external operator.

Both nodes and stations use the CCE to manage the port. Should a failure occur, the CCE determines the data path, which can be through a port or in a wrapped configuration.

An FDDI station must contain at least one MAC. The MAC provides the rules for access to the cable, defines the frame and token formats, and so on. Each station also contains a set of SMT algorithms that control its connections to the physical transmission media. The SMT entity interacts with the port, the CCE, and the MAC entities.

For additional information on FDDI architecture, see References 9-1 through 9-5.

9.2. The FDDI Standards

Like the IEEE standards for Ethernet and token-ring networks, the ANSI standards for FDDI address specific aspects of the architecture (see Figure 9-4). ANSI PMD and PHY standards handle the ISO/OSI model's physical layer functions; the MAC standard and the IEEE 802.2 LLC standard discussed in Section 1.4.2 handle the ISO/OSI model's data-link layer functions.

9.2.1. The FDDI PMD layer

The PMD layer occupies the lowest portion of the ISO/OSI model's physical layer (see Reference 9-6). This layer provides the physical connection to the network, specifies cables and connectors, and defines the communication between nodes (see Figure 9-5). It includes specifications for the optical transmitter and receiver and characteristics of the optical signal, such as power levels and acceptable bit error rates.

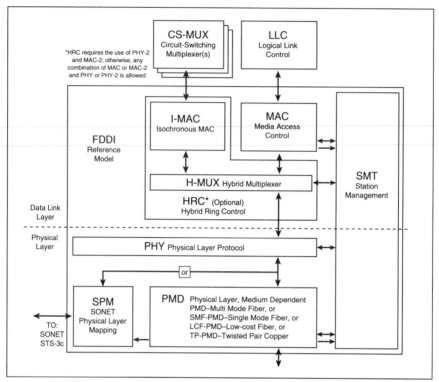

Figure 9-4. FDDI standards
(Courtesy of ConneXions)

The PMD layer also specifies the mode characteristics of the fiber-optic cable. The mode defines how light traverses the cable. In a multimode cable, multiple rays of light of differing wavelengths exist within the cable at the same time. In a single-mode cable, only one mode (or wavelength) is propagated at a time. Generally, multimode fiber is less expensive; single-mode fiber can transmit farther.

As the FDDI standard has evolved, several PMD options have emerged. These include Physical Layer Medium Dependent, using 62.5/125 micron fiber (X3.166-1990 or ISO 9314-3, see Reference 9-6) and Single-Mode Fiber Physical Layer Medium Dependent (X3.194-1991 or ISO 9314-4, see Reference 9-7). Two additional proposals currently under consideration are the low-cost fiber physical layer medium dependent and the twisted-pair physical layer medium dependent.

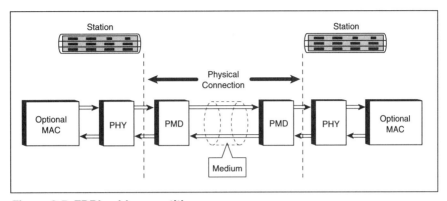

Figure 9-5. FDDI sublayer entities
(Courtesy of Digital Equipment Corp.)

9.2.1.1. Fiber-optic PMD standards. The two currently approved
PMD standards—X3.166 and X3.194—specify different types of fiber-optic
cable. X3.166, sometimes referred to as MMF-PMD, uses multimode fiber-
optic cable. Multimode fiber allows cable lengths between FDDI stations
to extend to 2 kilometers. The cable is manufactured with a 62.5-micron
core, and a 125-micron cladding (written 62.5/125). Alternatives, such as
50/125, 85/125, and 100/140 micron fiber are also allowed. The light sources
are LEDs with a center wavelength of between 1,270 and 1,380 nanometers. The maximum attenuation (end-to-end between FDDI stations) is 11
dB (review Section 4.6). The attenuation, known as the power budget, includes
the cable attenuation and losses from other fiber-optic components, such as
connectors, splices, and so on. With the specifications for MMF-PMD discussed here, the FDDI attachment has a bit error rate (BER) of $1 * 10^{-12}$.

The X3.194 standard, sometimes referred to as the SMF-PMD, uses single-mode fiber. This standard is intended for use in campus environments,
which require longer transmission distances. The SMF-PMD supports links
between FDDI stations of up to 60 kilometers and uses lasers as sources for
the optical signal. Depending on the components used, an SMF-PMD FDDI
network may have a power budget ranging from 10 to 32 dB.

9.2.1.2. Copper PMD proposals. Other PMD layer specifications, including shielded and unshielded twisted-pair alternatives, are in various stages of development.

FDDI over STP (SDDI) is one shielded twisted-pair (STP) proposal jointly developed by 11 computer and silicon manufacturers, including AMD, IBM, Madge Networks, Motorola, National Semiconductor, SynOptics Communication, and others (see Reference 9-8). The objective of SDDI is to allow organizations with an investment in STP cabling to benefit from FDDI's higher transmission rates. SDDI supports cable lengths of up to 100 meters. IBM has developed and currently markets workstation and PS/2 adapter cards that support both the SAS and DAS attachments and a concentrator, the IBM 8240, with a plug-in module for SDDI.

The Copper Distributed Data Interface (CDDI) (tm) is an unshielded twisted-pair (UTP) solution from Crescendo Communications (Sunnyvale, Calif.). CDDI operates over either UTP or STP, at link distances of up to 100 meters. One challenge to UTP implementations at high data rates is to provide enough power for the transmitted signal without exceeding EMI limits. Crescendo's product scrambles the transmitted data into a pseudorandom sequence, which reduces the EMI problem. In addition, a multilevel data encoding scheme, known as MLT-3, encodes the data for transmission on the UTP. This scheme provides the noise immunity necessary to assure reliable data reception, and ANSI has adopted it for the TP-PMD standard (see Reference 9-9). Crescendo has implemented the CDDI designs into workgroup concentrators; EISA, MCA, and SBus (for Sun Microsystems, Inc.'s SPARC Station) adapters; and an FDDI-to-CDDI translator that converts the signals from one format to another.

9.2.2. The FDDI PHY layer

Reviewing Figure 9-4, the PHY layer is the second layer in the FDDI architecture (see Reference 9-10). Together with the PMD layer, it provides the functions of the ISO/OSI model's physical layer. The PHY layer makes the logical connection between the PMD and the data-link layer, providing functions, such as defining, encoding, and decoding symbols, and clock synchronization.

9.2.2.1. FDDI Symbol encoding. A symbol is a specific bit pattern that conveys data or control information. In the transmitting direction, the symbol originates in the higher layers of the protocol, and the MAC layer passes it to the PHY layer. One of the PHY layer processes then encodes the symbol for transmission on the fiber-optic link. In the receiving direction the process is reversed. The encoding conveys the data and clock information in the transmitted stream.

Symbol encoding is a two-step process. The first step converts the symbols coming from the MAC layer into a 5-bit nonreturn-to-zero (NRZ) signal. In the NRZ signal, a signal of high polarity represents a binary 1, and a signal of low polarity represents a binary 0. The second step converts the 5-bit NRZ signals to a nonreturn-to-zero-invert-on-ones (NRZI) signal. In the NRZI signal, a signal transition represents a binary 1, and the absence of a polarity transition represents a binary 0.

The symbol coding chart shown in Table 9-1 defines the conversion process. This encoding scheme is referred to as 4B/5B and stands for 4-bit to 5-bit conversion. The conversion guarantees that each transmitted code group contains at least one bit and thus at least one polarity transition every five bits. This transition maintains the synchronization of the receive clock at the other end of the link and assures proper decoding of the received data. The transmitter and receiver clocks operate at 125 MHz, sending 5 bits per symbol, which results in an effective data rate of 100 Mbps for the 4 bits that the higher (MAC) layer passed down for communication.

Table 9-1. FDDI symbol coding

Decimal	Code Group	Symbol	Assignment	
Line State Symbols				
00	00000	Q	QUIET	
31	11111	I	IDLE	
04	00100	H	HALT	
Starting Delimiter				
24	11000	J	1st. of Sequential SD Pair	
17	10001	K	2nd. of Sequential SD Pair	
Data Symbols				
			Hex	Binary
30	11110	0	0	0000
09	01001	1	1	0001
20	10100	2	2	0010
21	10101	3	3	0011
10	01010	4	4	0100
11	01011	5	5	0101
14	01110	6	6	0110
15	01111	7	7	0111
18	10010	8	8	1000
19	10011	9	9	1001
22	10110	A	A	1010
23	10111	B	B	1011
26	11010	C	C	1100
27	11011	D	D	1101
28	11100	E	E	1110
29	11101	F	F	1111

Table 9-1. *Continued*

Decimal	Code Group	Symbol	Assignment
Ending Delimiter			
13	01101	T	Used to terminate the data stream
Control Indicators			
07	00111	R	Denoting logical ZERO (reset)
25	11001	S	Denoting logical ONE (set)
Invalid Code Assignments			
01	00001	V or H	These code patterns shall not be
02	00010	V or H	transmitted because they violate
03	00011	V	consecutive code-bit zeros or duty
05	00101	V	cycle requirements. Codes 01, 02,
06	00110	V	08, and 16 shall however be
08	01000	V or H	interpreted as Halt when
12	01100	V	received.
16	10000	V or H	

(12345) = sequential order of code-bit transmission.

(Courtesy of ANSI)

9.2.2.2. FDDI Symbol categories. Note from Table 9-1 that the symbols are divided into six categories: line state symbols, starting delimiter, data symbols, ending delimiter, control indicators, and invalid code assignments. Their functions are as follows:

1. Line state symbols are used on the medium between transmissions and include quiet (Q), the absence of transitions on the medium; idle (I), the normal condition between transmissions; and halt (H), control sequences (in the form of line states) or the removal of code violation symbols.

2. The starting delimiter marks the beginning of a data transmission sequence.

3. Data symbols convey arbitrary data (hexidecimal 0-F) within a transmission sequence.

4. The ending delimiter terminates normal data transmission.

5. Control indicators specify logical conditions associated with a data transmission sequence: Reset (R) represents a logical 0 condition; Set (S) represents a logical 1 condition.

6. Invalid code assignments indicate a condition on the medium that does not conform to the symbol set.

9.2.2.3. FDDI Ring latency. Another PHY layer parameter is the ring latency, or the time required for the token to circulate the ring. The ring latency consists of the cumulative effect of the station and cable delays as a particular data transmission circulates the ring. The MAC and SMT layers contain timers that depend on the latency value. The PHY layer defines the algorithms used to calculate the range of latency values that these higher layers will incorporate into their functions.

9.2.3. The FDDI MAC layer

The FDDI MAC layer performs functions similar to those of the IEEE 802 MAC layers. It defines the addressing scheme used on the network, the frame format, and error control techniques (see Reference 9-11). Section 9.5 discusses these functions further. The MAC layer determines the FDDI transmission modes, ring timers and counters, and algorithms for ring initialization and proper operation, as discussed in the following three sections.

9.2.3.1. FDDI transmission modes. One difference between FDDI and other LANs is its ability to transmit in both synchronous and asynchronous modes. In synchronous transmission the SMT process preallocates a maximum bandwidth for a requesting station and assumes a response time (maximum delay). In asynchronous transmission all stations contend for the ring bandwidth, and response times are allocated dynamically. A priority, from 0-7 (000-111 binary), may be optionally assigned to asynchronous transmissions. The MAC layer's Frame Control field indicates the type of transmission, synchronous or asynchronous, and is discussed in Section 9.5.

9.2.3.2. FDDI Ring timers and counters. The FDDI MAC layer also governs the operational relationships between various stations on the ring. To do so, the MAC layer defines three timers and one counter. These four entities are closely associated with token and frame transmission, as discussed in Section 9.5.

The token-holding timer (THT) controls the length of time a particular station may transmit asynchronous frames. The valid-transmission timer (TVX) is used to recover from transient ring error conditions. If this timer expires, it means that the station has seen no valid transmissions (that is, no ring activity) and that ring initialization procedures are necessary to activate the ring. The token-rotation timer (TRT) schedules transmissions on the ring. The late counter (Late_Ct) counts the number of TRT time periods since the MAC layer was reset or a token was received. Since the timers determine proper MAC operation, FDDI analysts should become familiar with these functions.

9.2.3.3. FDDI Ring initialization, operation, and recovery. The third, and perhaps most fundamental, type of FDDI MAC layer functions govern ring initialization, operation, and error recovery.

When the MAC is first initialized, each station uses the claim token process to bid for the right to initialize the ring using its preferred token-rotation timer (TRT) value. To complete the claim token process, each station sends MAC claim frames containing its bid for the target token-rotation time (TTRT) within the Information field. These claim frames circulate the ring. The station needing the shortest response time (having the lowest TTRT) wins the bid and gains the right to issue the first nonrestricted token, initiating operation of the ring.

If the claim token process fails or the ring's physical operation is impaired, the ring begins the Beacon process. For example, say there's a physical break in the cable. Upon detecting the problem, any station can enter the Beacon process, continuously transmitting MAC Beacon frames. Should the station receive a Beacon frame from any of its upstream neighbors (having a different source address), it will repeat the received beacon rather than transmit its own beacon. The process isolates the problem to the location immediately upstream from the station sending the beacons. The transmitting station continues to send Beacon frames until it receives its own transmitted beacon, signaling that the ring has been restored. At this point, the claim token process begins, and ring initialization proceeds. Section 9.5.2.2 examines the details of the MAC claim and Beacon frames.

9.2.4. The FDDI LLC layer

The LLC layer resides at the upper portion of the data-link layer and conveys user information. FDDI networks use the IEEE 802.2 protocol for this function (see Reference 1-7). Section 9.5.2.1 details the LLC frame.

9.2.5. The FDDI SMT function

The Station Management (SMT) function provides the station-level control processes necessary to assure proper operation of the various FDDI layers. Figure 9-4 shows how SMT operates on the PMD, PHY, and MAC layers in the FDDI architecture. The ASC X3 has defined SMT, and it is currently in draft form (X3T9.5/84-49, see Reference 9-12).

SMT defines three areas of FDDI management (see Figure 9-6): Frame-based management gathers information about current FDDI network operation. Connection Management (CMT) handles the physical connections and network topology at the PMD and PHY layers. Ring Management (RMT) deals with the MAC layer's logical ring operation, such as the proper circulation of the token. Section 9.6 discusses further details.

These three books provide more information on FDDI standards: DEC's *A Primer on FDDI* (Reference 9-13) presents an overview of FDDI architectures and shows how the various layers relate to those architectures. Kessler and Train's *Metropolitan Area Networks* (Reference 9-14) discusses each FDDI layer in detail. Codenoll's *Fiber-Optic LAN Handbook* (Reference 9-15) is a collection of various journal articles relating to fiber-optic use within LAN environments.

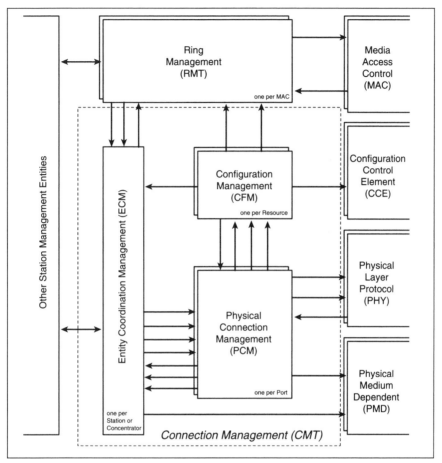

Figure 9-6. FDDI SMT
(Courtesy of ANSI)

9.3. FDDI Hardware Components

FDDI networks resemble other LANs in that their hardware components include controller chips, NICs, hubs (called FDDI concentrators), and cable plant. However, the high cost of fiber-optic components and FDDI equipment means that network managers are less likely to stock large numbers of spare components and extra test equipment.

9.3.1. FDDI controller chips

Three companies make FDDI controller chips: Advanced Micro Devices (AMD, Sunnyvale, Calif.), Motorola (Phoenix, Ariz.), and National Semiconductor Corp. (Santa Clara, Calif.). Databooks from any of these firms (see References 9-16 through 9-18) provide a great deal of technical insight into FDDI architecture and operation.

Most vendors currently use the SUPERNET 2 chip set, the second-generation AMD FDDI controller. The SUPERNET 2 chip set consists of five devices. It uses buffer memory (static RAM) for intermediate frame storage. The fiber-optic ring media access controller (FOMAC, part Am79C830) performs MAC layer functions. The physical layer controller (PLC, part Am79C864), physical data transmitter (PDT, part Am79865), and physical data receiver (PDR, part Am79866) provide PHY and some SMT functions.

Motorola's FDDI chip set contains four elements: the FDDI clock generator (FCG), MC68836; the elasticity and link management (ELM) physical layer interface, MC68837; a MAC circuit, MC68838; and an FDDI system interface (FSI), MC68839. The FSI provides the interface to the host system; the FCG, in conjunction with external driver circuits, attaches to the fiber-optic cable.

National Semiconductor Corp.'s chip set contains five devices: the clock recovery device (CRD), DP83231, and clock distribution device (CDD), DP83241, provide recovery capabilities and distribute the 125-MHz clock extracted from the incoming data stream. The DP83251/55 physical layer controller, DP83261 MAC controller, and the DP83265 device system interface complete the chip set. The host system interface and physical media interface are separate devices.

The data books that accompany these devices provide useful FDDI application information (see References 9-16 through 9-18).

9.3.2. FDDI NICs and Concentrators

A number of companies have joined the FDDI hardware race, including Ascom Timeplex (Woodcliff Lake, N.J.), Crescendo Communications Inc. (Sunnyvale, Calif.), Digital Equipment Corp., Hewlett-Packard Co.,

IBM, Network Peripherals (Milpitas, Calif.), Optical Data Systems (Richardson, Tex.), and SysKonnect (Saratoga, Calif.).

Figure 9-7 shows examples of FDDI and CDDI NICs from Crescendo Communications Inc. The FDDI controller chip, an AMD SUPERNET chip set, is visible in the top center of each board. The NIC at the top of the figure contains a fiber-optic connector (a Media Interface Connection, or MIC, for FDDI use), and the NIC in the lower portion contains a modular connector for unshielded twisted-pair cabling.

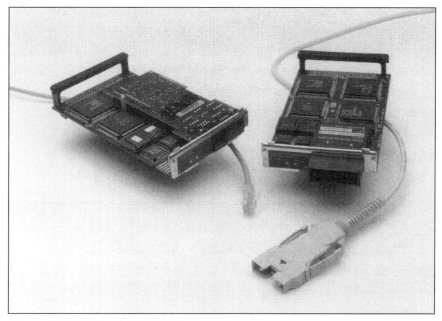

Figure 9-7. FDDI and CDDI NICs
(Photo courtesy of Crescendo Communications Inc.)

Many concentrators offer network management functions, such as support for the Simple Network Management Protocol (SNMP) or a vendor-proprietary management console. Network analysts should become familiar with these functions to minimize network downtime when failures occur. (Remember that as the transmission speed of the network increases, the severity of a network failure increases proportionally. In other words, when the data is expected to move fast, users feel a LAN failure more acutely.) Mike Hurwicz's article "The Fastest Gun in the LAN World" (Reference 9-19) is an excellent summary of the features and capabilities of FDDI NICs and concentrators.

9.3.3. FDDI Cabling systems

As a result of the critical manufacturing tolerances necessary for fiber-optic components, FDDI stations require special connectors to hook up to the fiber-optic cable. This connection is known as the Media Interface Connection (MIC), shown in Figure 9-8. The MIC terminates two fiber-optic cables, one for transmit and one for receive. The MIC receptacle contains a key, or groove, that assures proper connection, as shown in Figure 9-9. (Although the MIC plug is not always keyed, it should be labeled to prevent improper connections.) The MMF-PMD standard specifies four keying arrangements designed for different applications:

- MIC A: Primary In/Secondary Out (DAS to FDDI ring)
- MIC B: Secondary In/Primary Out (DAS to FDDI ring)
- MIC M: Master concentrator
- MIC S: SAS to concentrator

The SMF-PMD defines similar but not geometrically identical keying patterns designated SA, SB, SS, and SM. Since MMF and SMF equipment is incompatible, the connectors are designed to prevent unintentional mis-connection.

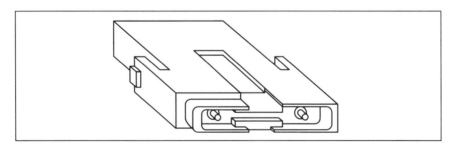

Figure 9-8. FDDI MIC plug
(Courtesy of ANSI)

Specifying FDDI fiber-optic cable may be a new responsibility for some readers. If so, Stoute and Swanson's article (Reference 9-20) may be useful.

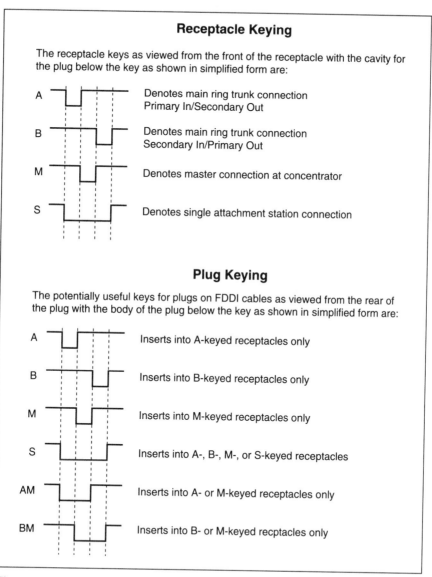

Receptacle Keying

The receptacle keys as viewed from the front of the receptacle with the cavity for the plug below the key as shown in simplified form are:

A — Denotes main ring trunk connection
Primary In/Secondary Out

B — Denotes main ring trunk connection
Secondary In/Primary Out

M — Denotes master connection at concentrator

S — Denotes single attachment station connection

Plug Keying

The potentially useful keys for plugs on FDDI cables as viewed from the rear of the plug with the body of the plug below the key as shown in simplified form are:

A — Inserts into A-keyed receptacles only

B — Inserts into B-keyed receptacles only

M — Inserts into M-keyed receptacles only

S — Inserts into A-, B-, M-, or S-keyed receptacles

AM — Inserts into A- or M-keyed receptacles only

BM — Inserts into B- or M-keyed recptacles only

Figure 9-9. FDDI MIC receptacle and plug keying
(Courtesy of ANSI)

275

9.4. FDDI Hardware Troubleshooting

Because FDDI uses fiber-optic cable, hardware troubleshooting is not as straightforward as testing a copper-based network, such as Ethernet. Fortunately, FDDI-specific tools are available to assist in the process. One example is the FDDI Link Confidence Tester from Fotec, Inc. (Boston, Mass.), shown in Figure 9-10. This tool helps with installation and diagnostics, performing a number of tests specific to FDDI networks. It performs the Link Confidence Test (LCT, defined by the FDDI Station Management standard), identifies the proper port type, and verifies the fiber-optic cable. FDDI network analysis toolkits should include a tool having these or similar capabilities.

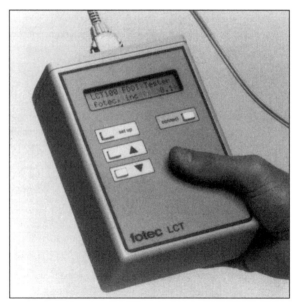

Figure 9-10. The FDDI Link Confidence Tester
(Photo courtesy of Fotec, Inc.)

9.5. FDDI Frames

FDDI uses two frame formats, a token and a frame, to control data transmission on the network. There are two types of tokens, and eight types of frames.

9.5.1. The FDDI token format

The token grants transmission rights to a particular station. The token format contains four fields (see Figure 9-11a). The preamble, transmitted by the originator of the token, contains at least 16 idle symbols. As stations on the ring repeat the preamble, they may add idle symbols to adjust for minor clock discrepancies between stations. Thus stations downstream from the token originator always see at least 16 idle symbols, and possibly more.

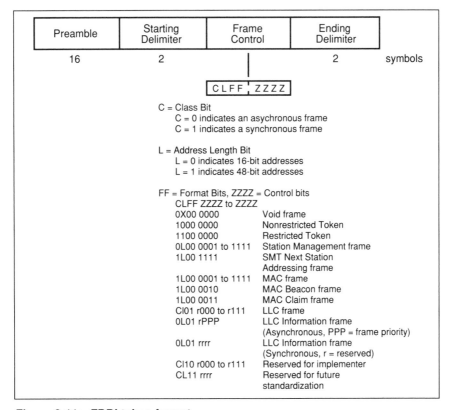

Figure 9-11a. FDDI token format

(Courtesy of ANSI)

The Starting Delimiter (SD) field contains one J-K symbol pair (see Table 9-1). The Frame Control (FC) field defines the frame type and the functions associated with it. These functions include frame Class (C), denoting asynchronous (C=0) or synchronous (C=1) operation; address Length (L), indicating the use of 16-bit addresses (L=0) or 48-bit addresses (L=1); frame Format (F); and Control (Z) bits. Together the C, L, F, and Z bits indicate the frame type:

CLFF ZZZZ to ZZZZ	**Frame Type**
0X00 0000	Void frame
1000 0000	Nonrestricted token
1100 0000	Restricted token
0L00 0001 to 1111	Station Management frame
1L00 1111	SMT Next Station Addressing frame
1L00 0001 to 1111	MAC frame
1L00 0010	MAC Beacon frame
CL01 r000 to r111	LLC frame
0L01 rPPP	LLC Information frame—Asychronous, PPP = frame priority
0L01 rrrr	LLC Information frame—Synchronous, r = reserved
CL10 r000 to r111	Reserved for implementer
CL11 rrrr	Reserved for future standardization

Two frame types specify tokens: nonrestricted tokens and restricted tokens. Any station can have a nonrestricted token to use an available asynchronous bandwidth. A pair of stations can use a restricted token to reserve all of the asynchronous bandwidth temporarily. The other eight frame types define various types of SMT, MAC, or LLC transmission frames. Note that when the frame type (F) bits indicate an LLC frame, the contents of the control (C) bits have meaning for the station or stations identified by the destination address.

9.5.2. The FDDI frame format

The FDDI frame (see Figure 9-11b) contains nine fields, which are divided into three sections: the Start of Frame Sequence (SFS), the Frame Check Sequence (FCS), and the End of Frame Sequence (EFS). The SFS contains the preamble and starting delimiter, which are identical to their counterparts in the token. The FCS coverage section (the portion of the frame over which the FCS operates) contains the frame control, destination and source addresses, information, and the Frame Check Sequence. The frame control field is identical to its counterpart in the token, and the address fields are identical to those used with IEEE 802 LANs. The Information field may contain an LLC, MAC, or SMT frame. For an LLC frame the IEEE 802.2 LLC header precedes the LLC information within the frame. The FCS coverage area may contain up to 9,000 symbols (4,500 octets) of data. Note that the field lengths are given in symbols, where a symbol equals four bits (one-half an octet).

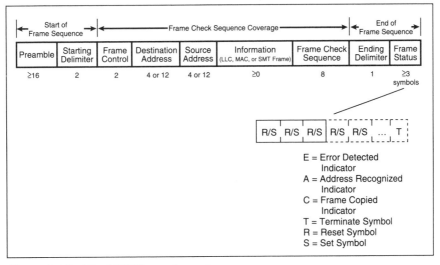

Figure 9-11b. The FDDI frame format
(Courtesy of ANSI)

The EFS contains the Ending Delimiter (ED) and the Frame Status (FS) field. The FS field contains an arbitrary number of control indicator symbols (reset-R or set-S) and may conclude with the terminate (T) symbol. The first three R/S symbols convey special meanings: error detected (E), address recognized (A), and frame copied (C). The station that originates the frame transmits all three indicators in the reset (R) condition. Any station on the ring can set the error detected indicator, indicating that it has detected an error in that frame. The Address Recognized (A) indicator is set when a station recognizes its own individual or group address. The destination station sets the Frame Copied (C) indicator when it copies the frame into its receive buffer.

9.5.2.1. FDDI LLC frames. LLC frames convey user information on an FDDI network as they do on IEEE 802 networks, such as token ring. As you can see in Figure 9-12a, the CL01 in the first symbol of the Frame Control field identifies the FDDI LLC frame. (Recall that C defines the class, either asynchronous or synchronous, and L defines the length of the Address field, either 16 bits or 48 bits.) Asynchronous frames also contain a frame priority within the Frame Control field, identified by the PPP bits. PPP = 000 indicates the lowest priority, PPP = 111 the highest. Reserved (r) bits are set to zero for asynchronous and synchronous frames.

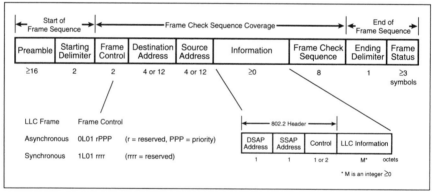

Figure 9-12a. FDDI frame with LLC information
(Courtesy of ANSI)

9.5.2.2. FDDI MAC frames. Section 9.2.3 discussed the MAC claim and Beacon frames used to initiate ring operation and recover from ring failures, respectively. A 1L00 used as the first symbol of the Frame Control field identifies MAC frames. The MAC frame's Information field carries details pertinent to that frame (see Figure 9-12b).

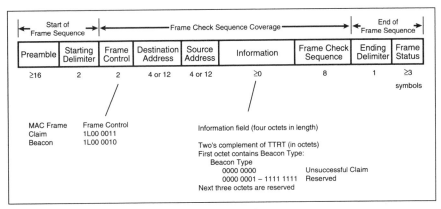

Figure 9-12b. FDDI frame with MAC information
(Courtesy of ANSI)

A Frame Control field of 1L00 0011 identifies the MAC claim frame. The Information field is four octets long and contains the two's complement in octets that the transmitting station is bidding. (The two's complement is an encoding scheme used to represent both positive and negative numbers in binary.) Recall that the lowest TTRT is declared the winner and proceeds to initialize the ring.

A Frame Control field of 1L00 0010 identifies the MAC Beacon frame. The Information field is also four octets long and contains a Beacon-type field (one octet) and three reserved octets. Currently only one Beacon type is defined: Unsuccessful Claim, which is designated 0000 0000.

9.5.2.3. FDDI SMT frames. SMT frames provide control for the FDDI network to assure that the network operates properly. The Frame Control field contains two symbols that identify SMT frames: The SMT Information frame contains 0L00 0001, and the SMT Next Station Addressing (NSA) frame contains 0L00 1111. The FDDI Information field contains the SMT PDU, which consists of an SMT header containing control information and an SMT Information field containing the actual management data (see Figure 9-12c). The next section discusses the details of these frames.

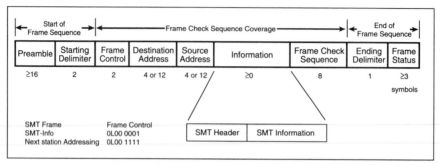

Figure 9-12c. FDDI frame with SMT information
(Courtesy of ANSI)

9.6. Station Management

So far I've discussed the FDDI physical and data-link layers, specifically the PMD, PHY, and MAC layer protocols. As you can see in Figure 9-4, the architecture also includes SMT, which interacts with each layer to provide network control and management. These functions resemble the logical elements (the configuration report server, error monitor, and ring parameter server) of the token-ring architecture. As you can see in Figure 9-6, SMT contains three parts: frame-based management, connection management (CMT), and ring management (RMT).

The SMT model includes four managed object classes. The SMT object provides a model for the management information within an FDDI station and interacts with the other three classes of objects. The MAC object class manages the MAC entities within a station. The path object class manages the configuration path within a station. The port object class deals with the PHY/PMD layers within a station. Figure 9-13 details the SMT frames that carry this information.

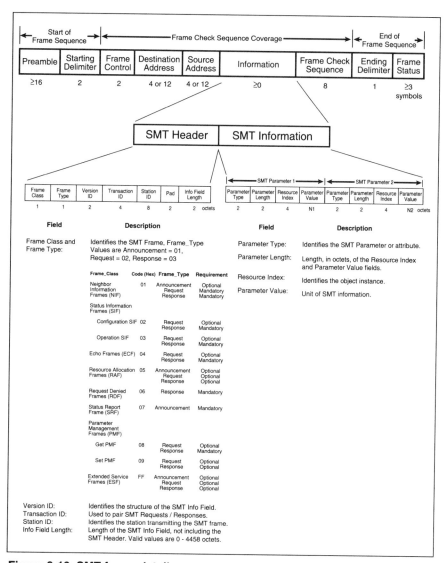

Figure 9-13. SMT frame details

9.6.1. FDDI Frame-based management

SMT's frame-based management is used in two situations: It can communicate FDDI management information between FDDI stations on a peer-to-peer basis, and it can be used for a specific protocol layer (for n-layer communication).

The FDDI Information field carries SMT frames, which are designated by a Frame Control (FC) field ranging from 0L00 0001 to 0L00 1111. There are three types of SMT frames (announcement, request, and response); and two categories of SMT frames (SMT-info and next station addressing, or NSA). The SMT-info frame has FC = 0L00 0001. It is used in all response frames and can also be used for request and announcement frames. An NSA frame has FC = 0L00 1111 and is used with the neighbor notification protocol, as a neighbor information request or announcement.

The FDDI frame's Information field also transports the SMT data, which consists of an SMT header and SMT information (see Figure 9-13). The SMT header contains seven fields that describe the information to follow. The first two fields, frame class and frame type, define one of 10 classes of frames to be sent and the type of function (announcement, request, or response) to be performed. These frames are

- Neighbor information (NIF) frames transmit station address and description information and is used with the neighbor notification protocol.
- Configuration status information frames (Configuration SIF) request or provide station connection and configuration parameters and is used with the status information frame protocol.
- Operation status information frames (Operation SIF) request or provide operational statistics and is used with the status information frame protocol.
- Echo frames (ECF) perform SMT-to-SMT loopback testing on an FDDI ring and is used with the Echo protocol.
- Resource allocation frames (RAF) allocate network resources. The only currently identified resource is synchronous bandwidth.
- Request denied frames (RDF) provide notification of SMT request frame format and protocol errors.
- Status report frames (SRF) announce station status that may be of interest to the FDDI manager and is used with the status report protocol.

- Get parameter management (Get PMF) provides remote access to station attributes and is used with the parameter management protocol.
- Set parameter management (Set PMF) provides for the remote modification of the station attributes and is used with the parameter management protocol.
- Extended service (ESF) extends and exercises new SMT services.

The rest of the header includes five fields. The version ID field identifies the structure of the SMT Information field. The transaction ID field pairs SMT requests and responses. The station ID field is a 64-bit field that identifies the station transmitting the SMT frame. The pad and info field length fields complete the header, identifying the length of the SMT information. With a maximum FDDI frame size of 4,500 octets, the MAC Information field may contain 4,478 octets (4,500 minus the 16-octet MAC header and the 6-octet MAC trailer). Of that 4,478 octets, the SMT header uses 20 octets, leaving 4,458 octets for the SMT Information field.

The SMT Information field (shown in the right side of Figure 9-13) contains the SMT parameters, which are expressed using four subfields. The parameter type field identifies the SMT parameter or attribute. The parameter length field provides the length, in octets, of the parameter value and resource index fields. The resource index identifies management information and further delineates whether a port, path, or MAC-related value is being communicated. The parameter value is a unit of SMT information. This SMT information is encoded for transmission on the network using the Basic Encoding Rules (BER) for Abstract Syntax Notation One (ASN.1), defined by the ISO standard 8825.

9.6.2. Network analysis with SMT frames

Of the 10 frames described in the previous section, the NIF frames are the most useful for network analysis. The NIF Information field contains the following information: the upstream neighbor address; a station description that indicates a concentrator; the number of master (M) ports on the concentrator; a station state, which indicates whether the station is wrapped, twisted, connecting ports A to A or B to B rather than A to B, or rooted on a dual ring; and the existence of any duplicate addresses (either the station's or its upstream neighbor). You can use NIFs to build a ring map detailing stations currently active on the ring.

The ECF is similar to the TCP/IP Ping command. It allows the analyst to determine whether a station is active on the ring, and whether the path to that station is operational. RAFs are not very common, since synchronous applications are not as common as asynchronous ones. An RDF normally occurs as a response to an SMT request that is not supported by the receiving station. For example, suppose a station that supports SMT version 7.2 makes a request to another station that supports SMT version 6.2. The protocol incompatibility that results from the SMT version 7.2 request would trigger an RDF transmission.

The SRF (and its underlying status report protocol) conveys information regarding station events, frame errors, duplicate addresses, wrapped conditions, and other significant events. The Get and Set PMFs perform network management. Since support for the network management functions is optional, an error condition (that is, PMF) may result. For example, if a station sends a Get PMF to a station that doesn't support PMF, an RDF frame would be returned, indicating the incompatibility. Because vendors use ESFs to define product-specific parameters and values, they are not as useful to the analyst as the NIF, SIF, and RDF. Become familiar with the use and display of these frames on your network analyzer to maximize your knowledge of network operation.

9.6.3. Connection Management

Figure 9-6 shows Connection Management (CMT) within the FDDI station management architecture. CMT deals with the physical connections to the FDDI ring. One example is the port operations that insert a station into, or remove a station from, the ring. As such, CMT works primarily with the PMD and PHY layers. Other examples include control of the (optional) optical bypass switch, fault detection, and link testing.

CMT is subdivided into three areas. Entity Coordination Management (ECM) coordinates the activity of the ports and controls the bypass relay. Physical Connection Management (PCM) manages the physical connection between a port on the station and another station on the ring. Configuration Management (CFM) manages the configuration of the MAC and port entities within a station or concentrator. The CFM communicates with a Configuration Control Element (CCE) defined for each type of port (A, B, or S) within the device. The CCE, in turn, interacts with the PHY and MAC layers to specify the connections to be formed for a given implementation.

The Link Confidence Test (LCT) algorithms are useful CMT functions. These tests determine whether the link quality is adequate for proper operation, and whether the claim, Beacon, and token processes are working properly. When shopping for FDDI test equipment, look for tools that support the LCT functions.

9.6.4. Ring Management

Ring Management (RMT) assures the operational status of the ring. RMT receives status information from both the MAC and CMT and uses that information to report the status of the MAC to SMT. RMT functions include identifying a stuck Beacon and initiating a trace function to recover from the stuck Beacon; detecting duplicate MAC addresses; and limiting the duration of station dialogs that use restricted tokens.

9.7. FDDI Protocol Analysis with the Sniffer

To summarize the FDDI protocols and processes discussed in this chapter, I will examine a trace file captured by the Network General Sniffer FDDI analyzer. In this example, the ring consists of three devices, a Cisco Systems, Inc., router, a Sniffer, and a Novell NetWare workstation. The Sniffer captures and decodes frame information beginning with the Frame Control field (see Figure 9-14).

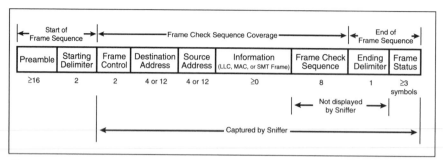

Figure 9-14. Capture range of the Network General Sniffer protocol analyzer for FDDI networks

(Courtesy of Network General)

The trace summary shows the frames transmitted by the three stations on the ring (see Trace 9-1). The summary column shows all the protocols present in a particular frame, including the data-link control (DLC), Station Management (SMT), Logical Link Control (LLC), Subnetwork Access Protocol (SNAP), Xerox Network System (XNS), and NetBIOS (NET) protocols. The frames containing XNS information (frames 3, 4, 9, and 10) are NetWare broadcasts from the router onto the FDDI ring. The destination and source addresses for those frames are NetWare addresses. Frames 1, 2, 5, 6, 7, and 8 are transmitting SMT information. These transmissions are SMT Neighbor Information (NIF) frames, communicated between adjacent nodes on the ring. Frames 1 and 2 are between the router and the Sniffer; frames 5 and 6 between the Sniffer and the NetWare workstation; and frames 7 and 8 between the NetWare workstation and router. From this communication sequence, you can determine the physical order of the stations on the ring: router to Sniffer to NetWare workstation to router, and so on.

Trace 2 details the first two SMT frames. Frame 1 is an NIF request (Class = 1, Type = 2), with a transaction ID of 3CDFF00H. Note that the NIF response in frame 2 (Class = 1, Type = 3) uses the same transaction ID. The station ID fields for each frame identify the transmitting device (Sniffer or Cisco Router). The SMT Information fields contain four parameters in the request/response: the upstream neighbor address, station descriptor, station state descriptor, and frame status capability. From these fields you can determine details of the station's node and topology parameters.

The station descriptor determines whether the node is a station or concentrator, the number of MAC entities present, the number of nonmaster (A, B, or S) ports present, and the number of master (M) ports present. The station state descriptor indicates whether any topology problems have been detected, such as a wrapped station or a twisted ring (A-A or B-B connection), and whether a duplicate MAC address has been detected. The frame status capabilities define how the address recognized and frame copied (A and C) flags within the frame status field will be handled for bridged FDDI environments.

Looking at the details of frame 1 in Trace 9-2, the station descriptor indicates a station (not a concentrator), having one MAC entity and two A, B, or S ports (a DAS). (Note that in Frame 2 the nonmaster count = 1, indicating a SAS.) The station state descriptor indicates a wrapped condition, in other words, one A or B connection is broken. The rooted station indication means that it is on a dual ring; that is no A, B, or S ports are active in tree mode. Finally, the frame status capability indicates the handling of the A and C bits within the frame status field.

Section 7.3.1.3 of the SMT standard details these four parameters. When analyzing FDDI networks look for these NIF frames; they are transmitted on a periodic basis and contain valuable ring status details. Consult Reference 9-21 for further details on the use of the FDDI Sniffer Analyzer.

Trace 9-1. Summary of SMT and NetWare traffic transmitted on an FDDI ring and captured by the Network General Sniffer Protocol Analyzer

Sniffer Network Analyzer data 15-Apr-92 at 10:56:12 file FINDSRVR.FDC Pg 1

```
SUMMARY Delta T   Destination    Source      Summary

M 1               Broadcast      Router      DLC FC = 4F (SMT Frame)
                                             SMT NIF Request from DAS
        2 0.0006  Router         Sniffer     DLC FC = 41 (SMT Frame)
                                             SMT NIF Response
                                             from SAS
```

```
3 1.3897  00000104.FF...  00000105.10...  DLC FC = 50 (LLC Frame)
                                           LLC C D=AA S=AA UI
                                           SNAP Ethernet Type=8137
                                             (Novell)
                                           XNS NetWare IPX
                                             WAN Broadcast
                                           NET Find name NGCUNKNOWN
4 0.0352  00000104.FF..   00000105.10...  DLC FC = 50 (LLC Frame)
                                           LLC C D=AA S=AA UI
                                           SNAP Ethernet type=8137
                                             (Novell)
                                           XNS NetWare IPX
                                             WAN Broadcast
                                           NET Find name NGCUNKNOWN
5 0.8558  Broadcast       Sniffer         DLC FC = 4F (SMT Frame)
                                           SMT NIF Request from SAS
6 0.0007  Sniffer         NetWare Stn     DLC FC = 41 (SMT Frame)
                                           SMT NIF Response
                                             from DAS
7 0.1255  Broadcast       NetWare Stn     DLC FC = 4F (SMT Frame)
                                           SMT NIF Request from DAS
8 0.0005  NetWare Stn     Router          DLC FC = 41 (SMT Frame)
                                           SMT NIF Response
                                             from DAS
9 0.9588  00000104.FF...  00000105.10...  DLC FC = 50 (LLC Frame)
                                           LLC C D=AA S=AA UI
                                           SNAP Ethernet Type=8137
                                             (Novell)
                                           XNS NetWare IPX
                                             WAN Broadcast
                                           NET Find name NGCUNKNOWN
10  0.0353 00000104.FF...  00000105.10...  DLC FC = 50 (LLC Frame)
                                           LLC C D=AA S=AA UI
                                           SNAP Ethernet Type=8137
                                             (Novell)
                                           XNS NetWare IPX
                                             WAN Broadcast
                                           NET Find name NGCUNKNOWN
   .
   .
   .
```

Trace 9-2. SMT Neighbor Information frame details transmitted on an FDDI ring and captured by the Network General Sniffer Protocol Analyzer

Sniffer Network Analyzer data 15-Apr-92 at 10:56:12 file FINDSRVR.FDC Pg 1

```
- - - - - - - - - - - - - - Frame 1 - - - - - - - - - - - - - - - - - -


SMT: —- FDDI Station Management —-
SMT:
SMT: Frame class = 1 (Neighbor info)   Frame type = 2 (Request)
SMT: Version ID = 1, transaction ID = 3CDFF00
SMT: This Station ID = 0000 cisco 01ABCE , length = 40
SMT: Upstream neighbor address =  NwkGnl0A000E
SMT: Station descriptor:
SMT:    Node class      = Station
SMT:    MAC count       = 1
SMT:    Non-master count = 2
SMT:    Master count    = 0
SMT: Station state descriptor
SMT:    Pad = 00 00
SMT:    Topology = 11
SMT:        .... ...1 = Station wrapped
SMT:        ...1 .... = Rooted station
SMT:    Duplicate Address = 00
SMT:        .... .... = (none)
SMT: Frame status capabilities for MAC 3
SMT:    .... .... .... .1.. = FSC-Type 2 (reset C and set A on C
                               set and A reset if not copied)


- - - - - - - - - - - - - - Frame 2 - - - - - - - - - - - - - - - - -


SMT: —- FDDI Station Management —-
SMT:
SMT: Frame class = 1 (Neighbor info)   Frame type = 3 (Response)
SMT: Version ID = 1, transaction ID = 3CDFF00
SMT: This Station ID = 0000 NwkGnl0A000B , length = 40
SMT: Upstream neighbor address =  cisco 01ABCE
SMT: Station descriptor:
SMT:    Node class      = Station
SMT:    MAC count       = 1
```

```
SMT:      Non-master count = 1
SMT:      Master count    = 0
SMT: Station state descriptor
SMT:      Pad = 00 00
SMT:      Topology = 11
SMT:          .... ...1 = Station wrapped
SMT:          ...1 .... = Rooted station
SMT:      Duplicate Address = 00
SMT:          .... .... = (none)
SMT: Frame status capabilities for MAC 1
SMT:          .... ....  .... ...1 = FSC-Type 0 (repeats A/C indicators
                                          on copy with intent to
                                          forward)
```

9.8. Future FDDI Standards

Since end users seem to have an insatiable need for bandwidth, FDDI's prospects look promising. The ANSI X.3 committee has been working on FDDI enhancements for some time. Figure 9-4 shows two general classes of enhancements. The first includes PMD options, such as FDDI over twisted pairs (see Section 9.2.1), and options that map FDDI to synchronous optical network (SONET) transmission links.

A second category of enhancements, known as FDDI-II, adds circuit-switched capabilities to the basic packet-switched services. These capabilities are often referred to as isochronous communication and are intended for voice and video applications. Only one commercial product currently supports FDDI-II, an NIC from MultiMedia LANs, Inc. (Charlotte, N.C.). This dearth of products has led some analysts to speculate that other technologies, such as asynchronous transfer mode (ATM), a broadband integrated services digital network (ISDN) technology, may emerge as the preferred high-bandwidth transport medium. See References 9-22 through 9-24 for further information on FDDI-II.

9.9. FDDI Troubleshooting Summary

To summarize, here's a checklist to assist with diagnosing FDDI network failures:

- Verify NIC options that relate to the host processor and its bus, such as IRQ lines, DMA channels, and so on.
- Verify the integrity of the fiber-optic backbone cable before connecting NICs, concentrators, or other devices. After installation, use the NICs link integrity indicator (LED), if available, to determine the usability of the fiber link.
- If the fiber plant is in question, check and clean the connectors. A speck of dust can impair the optical signal.
- If the ring is not operating at all, look for twists in the duplex fiber-optic cables, for example port A to port A (or B to B), instead of port A to port B. (The A-A or B-B configuration may not work in all configurations.) To correct, swap the connectors on one end and retest.
- Double-check the connectors used with the fiber-optic cable to be sure you're using the correct keyed MIC plugs and receptacles for that cabling application (that is, an A to B cable, not an M to S cable, and so on).
- If a portion of the network is not operating, check to see whether an M port on a concentrator has been connected to the FDDI ring (instead of to an SAS).
- If as SAS is not operating, check the network elements local to the station, such as the concentrator port, the cable, or the NIC.
- If a DAS can no longer communicate with its server, check to see whether a link failure has segmented the ring into two smaller rings. The DAS could now be on one ring and the server on another. If so, isolate the problem that caused the ring segmentation and restore operation to that of a single ring.
- If two nonadjacent DAS stations have gone down in the trunk ring, you'll have two segmented rings. Look at the details of the NIFs for wrapped stations to isolate the failure.

- Look for periodic NIFs transmitted between workstations. Analyze the content of those frames to determine whether the network topology is appropriate for the application and whether it matches the last known state of the ring.
- An existing ring that periodically starts to enter the claim process and then to beacon may indicate a number of problems, including a faulty fiber-optic link. To diagnose the problem, determine the source of the beacons; the fault may be located in the source station's upstream link. This condition could indicate excessive delay in the ring, which would require a physical reconfiguration. This condition could also mean that a station on the ring has an excessively low (out-of-spec) value for the TTRT. Recall that the lowest TTRT wins the bid and initiates the claim process. If the TTRT value is too low, the other stations may be unable to operate. To correct, remove the faulty station.
- If the operation of the ring is suspect, use the link confidence test to determine whether the quality of the line is adequate.
- Become familiar with the 10 types of SMT frames and the diagnostic capabilities they provide.

FDDI analysis has been a popular topic in the trade press lately. References 9-25 through 9-27 are examples of good articles about FDDI analysis.

9.10. References

9-1.   Floyd E. Ross, et. al. "FDDI—A LAN Among MANs." *Computer Communication Review* (July 1990):16-31.

9-2.   Bradford T. Harrison. "On the Way to FDDI." *DEC Professional* (March 1992): 36-46.

9-3.   Steven T. Ough, et. al. "Analyzing FDDI as a Backbone." *LAN Technology* (May 1992):41-56.

9-4.   Carol Rosaire. "FDDI: The Promised LAN." *Infoworld* (August 10, 1992): 42-43.

9-5.   Doug Sherman. "Understanding FDDI: Standards, Features, and Applications." *3TECH, the 3Com Technical Journal* (Winter 1992): 18-32.

9-6.   American National Standards Institute. *Fiber Distributed Data Interface (FDDI)—Token Ring Physical Layer Medium Dependent (PMD).* ANSI X3.166, 1990.

9-7.   American National Standards Institute. *Fiber Distributed Data Interface (FDDI)—Single-Mode Fiber Physical Layer Medium Dependent (SMF-PMD).* ANSI X3-184, 1991.

9-8.   Lee C. Haas, et. al. "FDDI to the Desk Using Today's Shielded Twisted-Pair Cabling." *INTEROP Spring-Conference Proceedings.* 1992.

9-9.   Noel Lindsay. "Improving Network Performance with Twisted-Pair FDDI." *Telecommunications* (July 1992).

9-10. American National Standards Institute. *Fiber Distributed Data Interface (FDDI)—Token Ring Physical Layer Protocol (PHY).* ANSI X3.148, 1988.

9-11. American National Standards Institute. *Fiber Distributed Data Interface (FDDI)—Token Ring Media Access Control (MAC).* ANSI X3.139, 1987.

9-12. Accredited Standards Committee X3. "FDDI Station Management (SMT)." Draft Proposed American National Standard X3T9.5/84-49. June 25, 1992.

9-13. Digital Equipment Corporation. *A Primer on FDDI: Fiber Distributed Data Interface, Version 2.0.* Document EC-H1580-42/92, June 1992.

9-14. Gary C. Kessler and David A. Train. *Metropolitan Area Networks— Concepts, Standards and Services.* New York: McGraw-Hill, 1992.

9-15. Codenoll Technology Corp. *The LAN Handbook, 3d ed.* Document 05-0050-00-0318, January 1991.

9-16. Advanced Micro Devices, Inc. *The SUPERNET 2 (tm) Family for FDDI—Data Book and Technical Manual.* 1989-1992.

9-17. Motorola, Inc. MC68836, MC68837, MC68838, and MC68839 *User's Manuals*, 1991.

9-18. National Semiconductor Corp. *Fiber Distributed Data Interface (FDDI) Databook.* 1991.

9-19. Mike Hurwicz. "The Fastest Gun in the LAN World." *Network World* (December 14, 1992): 49-59.

9-20. Garfield D Stoute and Steven E. Swanson. "How to Specify the Right FDDI Optical Fiber." *LAN Times* (February 4, 1991): 46-48.

9-21. Network General Corp. *Sniffer Network Analyzer Operations Manual.* Document 20072-002, June 1992.

9-22. Gary C. Kessler. "Inside FDDI-II." *LAN Magazine* (March 1991): 117-125.

9-23. Mark S Wolter. "ANSI X3T9.5 Update: Future FDDI Standards." *ConneXions, the Interoperability Report* (October 1991):21-23.

9-24. Ross Halgren. "FDDI-II to Provide Multimedia Pipe to the Desktop." *Lightwave* (September 1992): 40-43.

9-25. Jim Umphrey. "FDDI Networks—Technology and Testing." *Hewlett-Packard Communications Test Symposium.* 1992.

9-26. George Shinopoulos and David Rankin. "FDDI Testing Simplified." *Lightwave* (October 1992): 26-44.

9-27. Bahaa Moukadam. "Analysis of FDDI Internetworking Issues." *Lightwave* (November 1992): 49-51.

CHAPTER 10

Keeping the Net Working

This book has described the ISO/OSI model, LAN documentation, test equipment, cabling, and information you need to troubleshoot the major types of LANs, such as Ethernet, ARCNET, token ring, and FDDI. But how do you put this all together into a coherent plan? This chapter offers you some practical, hands-on tips for keeping your net working (see Reference 10-1).

10.1. Don't Push Network Design Limits

Each network architecture has variety of fixed design parameters. For example, IEEE 802.3 10BASE5 networks have a maximum segment length of 500 meters before a repeater; ARCNET networks can have a maximum of 255 nodes. Exceeding these design limitations almost always causes problems. For example, an overly long Ethernet bus cable can cause excessive collisions. Duplicate addresses on an ARCNET network can cause the reconfiguration algorithm to fail.

If you find you're pushing your network architecture to the limit, you may be using the wrong technology, or you may need to add components such as a repeater or bridge. Design limits exist for a reason—don't try to get around them.

10.2. Install with Care

By some estimates between 70 and 90 percent of all network failures are hardware related. If these estimates are indicative, you can prevent many network failures by installing hardware components—cables, NICs, jacks, cross connectors, and so on—carefully.

When installing hardware be aware of the details. For example, consider where your cables go. Do they run close to the fluorescent lights? Could someone plug a floor polisher or portable arc welder into the same power circuit that feeds the server? What happens when a user moves his or her workstation? Have you considered other issues that might impact users, such as printer or plotter locations?

Because of the many options available for topology, cabling, hardware and software components, and operating systems, each network is unique. Therefore, it's also a good idea to develop an installation action plan unique to your network. Such a plan should cover the following four areas:

1. Verify the electrical or optical continuity of all wiring, cables, and connectors. Also make sure that each plug goes to the appropriate receptacle. For example, double-check that FDDI cables are plugged into the correct port.
2. Identify the network's functional requirements from a user's point of view. In other words, make sure the applications and peripherals a user is likely to use work properly on the network.
3. Check the operation of all peripherals, including network printers, and servers.
4. Verify that redundant systems, such as the UPS on the server or the power-fail transfer equipment on communication circuits, are operational. Don't wait for the power utility to test these for you during a power outage!

Install your network with care. Be patient and do it right the first time.

10.3. Document Your Network

People commonly tend to procrastinate when it comes to completing the finishing touches on your LAN. But it's important to make sure your network documentation doesn't fall by the wayside. Thoroughly document the workstation configuration, network connections, cabling, and servers.

To document the workstation configuration, record node names and addresses, which are either set by DIP switches or burned into a ROM. Also consider software addresses, such as an Internet protocol (IP) address that a terminal emulation program may contain. Document the CPU type, amount of memory, and so on. Track other devices (for example, graphics, or terminal emulation cards) installed in the workstation. Keep specific details about each PC add-in card, such as the DMA channel, IRQ line, shared memory address, and so on.

Network connection information should include the hub port or jack number and the type of connection, that is, thin or thick Ethernet, 10BASE-T hub, and so on. A convenient way to document these parameters is to stick an adhesive label to the rear or bottom panel of the PC. Remember to update the label when you change these add-ins.

The moment of crisis is no time to wonder where that orange/yellow pair really goes. Know what workstation, server, printer, or peripheral is at the end of each cable. This is especially important if you've run multiple coaxial cables in a common cable tray, or if you've used twisted-pair wiring with 66-type punch-down blocks.

If a user on your network claims that he or she can't access the server, you need to know which server to troubleshoot. Having a network map that details the users and peripherals attached to each server will simplify fault isolation. Many network operating systems provide utilities that can help document these details. For a quick test of the server, go to another workstation attached to it and try to communicate with it by sending an electronic mail message or accessing a file. If this is successful, the fault probably lies in the workstation.

You can isolate many failures to a particular section of the network, such as the cable segment beyond a given repeater, or a gateway to the host computer. Since devices such as bridges, routers, repeaters, and gateways are often very complex, develop a plan for testing and verifying the operation of those devices.

10.4. Understand Your LAN and Its Relationship to the OSI Model

Although the ISO/OSI model provides a theoretical framework for computer communication, it can also help you determine whether a network failure has occurred in hardware or software.

Most network failures are hardware related and thus correspond to the ISO/OSI model's physical and data-link layers. Helpful tools for troubleshooting these problems include VOMs, TDRs, optical power meters, break-out boxes, and so on. The most important tool, however, is the diagnostic disk that comes with most NICs. These disks can do loop-around tests, read the value of the address ROM, and perform other internal diagnostics for the board. Make sure that you're familiar with the operation of this disk.

Software causes problems at the network and higher layers. You'll need a protocol analyzer, such as the Network General Sniffer, Novell's LANalyzer, and Hewlett-Packard's Network Advisor, to diagnose software problems. Again, don't wait for a failure to learn how to use these tools. Experiment on a live network to obtain benchmark measurements for traffic patterns and network utilization for comparison when a failure occurs.

Understanding your LAN also includes familiarizing yourself with your LAN's unique advantages, disadvantages, and potential sources of failure. For example, ARCNET and ARCNETPLUS are quite flexible in allowing you to mix various transmission media, such as twisted pairs, coaxial, or fiber optics. But because these networks require you to use DIP switches to set the node address manually, they also have a greater potential for failures due to human error.

The sophistication of the IEEE 802.5 standard gives token-ring networks many built-in failure recovery attributes. However, some users may have difficulty assembling the hermaphroditic (genderless) connectors.

Because Ethernet and coaxial IEEE 802.3 networks have the longest histories in the LAN marketplace, they offer you a wider choice of vendors. But compatibility problems can arise due to small differences between the DIX Ethernet standard and the IEEE 802.3 10BASE5 standard. These include differences in cable and connector pinouts. Be sure that you understand these technical differences.

The star topologies of StarLAN and twisted-pair IEEE 802.3 networks simplify failure isolation. However, it may be difficult to reuse existing twisted-pair cabling. In some cases you may be better off installing new twisted pairs to eliminate questions of cable length or integrity.

FDDI networks bring the advantages of high-speed data transport and a fault-tolerant, dual-ring topology. However, since FDDI is based on fiber optics, analysts must stock their toolkit with optical test equipment, in addition to the more common copper-based tools.

All LAN architectures have their unique characteristics; make sure that you understand the distinctions of your network.

10.5. Predict Network Failures

You can apply three failure measurements, or metrics, to the network and its components to get an early fix on potential problems: mean time between failures (MTBF), mean time to repair (MTTR), and network availability.

MTBF is the measure, in tens of thousands of hours, of the average (or mean) time a device should operate properly before a failure occurs. For example, a workstation's motherboard might be rated for an MTBF of 45,000 hours, meaning that you should expect a failure about every five years (one year equals 8,760 hours). Factors that influence MTBF include the network topology, whether the various elements are connected in serial or parallel, and the reliability of components.

MTTR is a measurement, usually less than 10 hours, of the average time required to identify and repair or replace the failed component. For example, if a system has an MTTR of 8 hours, one business day is sufficient for fault diagnosis, repair, and retesting. Two factors that affect the MTTR are the complexity of the network and the availability of spare parts. If your organization does its own network maintenance, you can significantly improve the MTTR by keeping service manuals and spare parts readily available. This foresight will eliminate the time needed to obtain a replacement when a failure occurs.

Network availability is a measurement, expressed as a percentage, of the ratio between MTBF and the total time (MTBF plus MTTR):

$$\text{Availability} = \frac{\text{MTBF}}{(\text{MTBF} + \text{MTTR})}$$

Obviously a very high MTBF and a very low MTTR is optimum.

To determine the most vulnerable parts of your network, obtain the MTBF and MTTR estimates from the vendors and consider the effect that the failure of any one component will have on the entire network. You may need to stock additional spare parts, get training in repair procedures, or add design redundancy (such as dial backup for communication circuits or disk duplexing on a server). Reference 10-2 provides further mathematical details that impact on network design.

10.6. Don't Overlook Power Protection

Many mysterious network problems, such as servers rebooting and work-stations failing, are often power problems in disguise. Because of their intermittent occurrence, power and grounding problems are among the most difficult problems to track down, often requiring expensive test equipment. Since many firms do not have the in-house expertise for this work, it may be helpful to call the local power company or an electrical contractor.

One way to eliminate problems is to add a separate power feed (115 VAC, 15 A, or as required) and ground circuit from the breaker panel to the server. Separate other appliances, such as fans or copy machines, from this circuit. References 10-3 through 10-5 provide further information on this vital subject.

10.7. Develop a Troubleshooting Plan

Any troubleshooting plan should concentrate on identifying the failed network component. Here are some guidelines for developing your plan:

1. If a user calls with a network problem, ask these questions: What do you see on the workstation's screen? Have you made any recent changes to the workstation's hardware or software? What were you doing when the problem occurred? What's different this time from the last time you tried the same procedure?

2. Isolate the failure to a single device using the network-specific techniques discussed in the previous chapters. For example, isolate an ARCNET failure to a specific hub by disconnecting the individual cable sections, and then use a similar procedure to isolate the problem to a particular workstation. Many connectivity hubs, such as 10BASE-T multiport repeaters or token ring MSAUs, include diagnostic LEDs to aid with the troubleshooting process. Become familiar with these diagnostic aids before a failure occurs.

3. Once you've pinpointed the cause of the problem, make sure you have the tools necessary for further diagnosis and repair. These might include the NIC diagnostic disk, diagnostic software for the workstation, cable testing equipment, or a protocol analyzer for suspected software problems.

4. Become familiar with diagnostic procedures for each device. You can glean many good troubleshooting hints from the hardware installation and operation guides. If the manual contains no information, ask the vendor for additional information, such as a maintenance guide, or design your own troubleshooting plan. Reference 10-6 offers an excellent example of a methodical process for diagnosing phone-line problems, and you can adapt this to many LAN difficulties.

5. Consider developing a fault-isolation flowchart unique to your network using reference material from the hardware and software vendors. Use the model flowcharts in Figures 10-1a–e as a starting point.

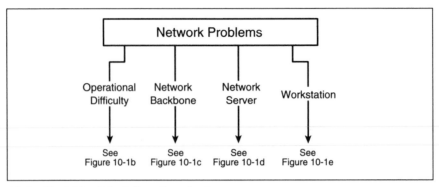

10-1a. Model fault isolation flowchart

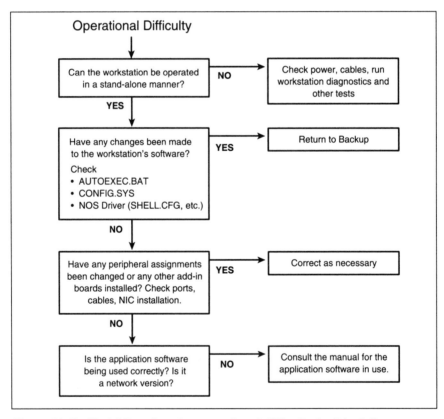

Figure 10-1b. Model flowchart for operational difficulty fault isolation

306

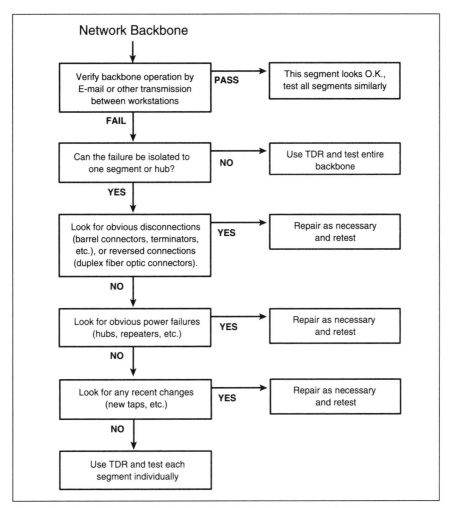

Figure 10-1c. Model flowchart for network backbone fault isolation

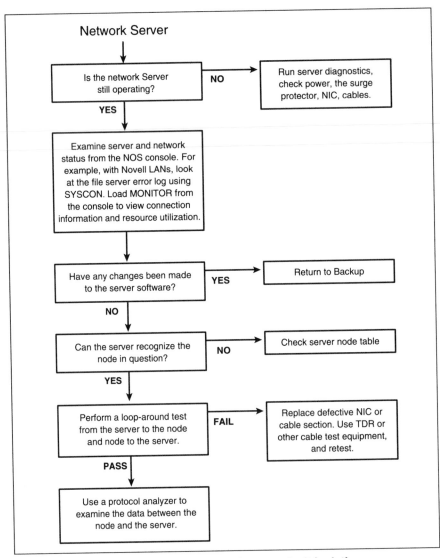

Figure 10-1d. Model flowchart for network server fault isolation

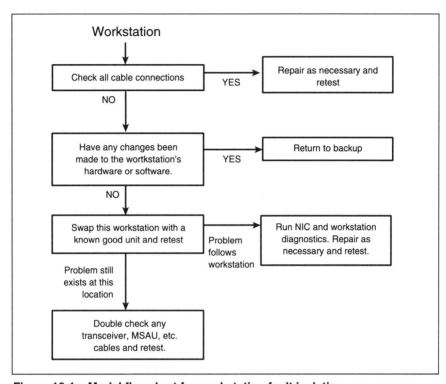

Figure 10-1e. Model flowchart for workstation fault isolation

During the troubleshooting process be sure to change only one hardware or software parameter at a time. Rarely does a network failure result from a combination of two or more failures, so making random changes (the "shotgun technique") only makes the situation worse. Also, take notes during the process; after trying many solutions, it's easy to forget what you've already tried.

Once you've solved the problem, you should document the symptoms and identify problems and final solutions. Network problems tend to recur, and it's helpful to know what solutions have worked in the past.

10.8. Don't Miss the Obvious

When the smoke finally clears, you may find your network problems end up being "operational difficulties" or "cockpit errors." Look for the simple failures: an unplugged power cord, a turned-off power strip, a BNC T connector disconnected at the wrong end, a mysteriously revised config.sys file, or a CRT whose brightness has been turned down. Make a list of the typical failures that plague your network and distribute it to the network users. By enlisting their help in the troubleshooting process, everyone wins.

10.9. Understand Your Protocols

Even though 70 to 90 percent of network problems can be attributed to hardware failures, software causes some faults. To solve these problems, you need a protocol analyzer. Unfortunately, these expensive ($5,000 to $40,000) tools are only as effective as their human operators. You must educate yourself about network protocols, such as TCP/IP, DECnet, SDLC, X.25, NetBIOS, or the network operating system.

10.10. Look Beyond Your LAN

Most LAN installations are a subset of your firm's total voice and data communications network. Be sure to understand the big picture. Consider the impact that a failure of the communication lines (for which you might not be responsible) can have on your network. What would happen if the gateway to the host or the public data network failed? If there was a fire in your office, would your backups be destroyed (along with your data), or have you stored backup disks or tapes in another location? Do your network components have adequate air circulation? Consider these and other areas, and do a little network "managing by wandering around."

Finally, remember that there's no substitute for a thorough, working knowledge of the network. The best person to troubleshoot the network is the person who installed it and who administers it on a daily basis.

10.11. References

10-1. Some of the material in this chapter originally appeared in "The Well-Tended Network," by Mark A. Miller, *LAN Technology Magazine*, (October 1989): 60-65.

10-2. Peter M. Haverlock. "The Formula for Network Immortality," *Data Communications*, (August 1988): 112-116.

10-3. Mark Waller. *PC Power Protection.* Indianapolis, Ind.: Howard W. Sams, 1989.

10-4. Frank Leeds and Jim Chorey. "Charge of the Power Brigade." *LAN Technology* (April 1992): 83-98.

10-5. Laurel Howe. "What's Up With UPSs?" *Data Communications* (November 21, 1992): 89-98.

10-6. Jack Douglas. "How to Find Phone-Line Faults and What to Do About Them." *Data Communications,* (September 1988): 179-197.

Addresses of Standards Organizations

CCITT Recommendations and Federal Information Processing Standards (FIPS)
U.S. Department of Commerce
National Technical Information Service
5285 Port Royal Road
Springfield, Va. 22161
703-487-4650

ISO and ANSI Standards
American National Standards Institute
11 W. 42nd St.
New York, N.Y. 10036
212-642-4900

ISO Standards
International Organization for Standardization
1, Rue de Varembe
CH-1211
Geneva 20, Switzerland
41 22 749 0111

ECMA Standards
European Computer Manufacturers Association
114, Rue de Rhone CH-1204
Geneva, Switzerland
41 22 735 3634

EIA Standards
Electronics Industries Association
Standards Sales
2001 Pennsylvania Ave.
Washington, D.C. 20006
202-457-4966
800-854-7179

Federal Telecommunication Standards-U.S.A.
General Services Administration
Federal Supply Service Bureau Specification Section
470 E. L'Enfant Plaza S.W., Ste. 8100
Washington, D.C. 20407
202-755-0325

IEEE Standards
Institute of Electrical and Electronics Engineers
445 Hoes Lane
Piscataway, N.J. 08855
908-981-0060
800-678-4333

AT&T Publications
AT&T Technologies Commercial Sales
P.O. Box 19901
Indianapolis, Ind. 46219
317-322-6557
800-432-6600

IBM Cabling System Worksheets and Forms

Building _____ Floor _____	Cable Schedule		Wiring Closet Location _____ Date of Last Update _____	
Cable Number	Cable Routing Information		Cable Length	Distribution Panel Jumpers	Additional Information
	Cable Runs From	Cable Runs To			

Note: When you update this cable schedule you should also update the System Configuration Worksheet found in *Using the IBM Cabling System with Communication Products.*

Form 1

Work Area Worksheet

Worksheet Number _____

Cable Requirements

Wiring Closet Location Number _____

Work Area Location	Faceplates/Devices							Cable Drop Length	Cable Requirements						
	1	1S	1W	2*	2S*	UM	WB**		1	1 Plenum	2	2 Plenum	8	9	
1															
2															
3															
4															
5															
6															
7															
8															
9															
10															
11															
12															
13															
14															
15															
16															
17															
18															
19															
Totals															

Total drops on this worksheet

Form 2

317

Wiring Closet Worksheet

Worksheet Number _____

Totals from Work Area Worksheet

Wiring Closet Location Number	Faceplates/Devices						Total Drops	Cable Requirements						
Work-sheet Number	1	1S	1W	2	2S	UM	WB		1 Plenum	2	2 Plenum	5	8	9
1														
2														
3														
4														
5														
6														
7														
8														
9														
10														
11														
12														
13														
14														
15														
16														
17														
Totals for this Wiring Closet														

Data Connectors — Standard / Undercarpet

Telephone Jack Connectors

Cables from Wiring Closet/Controller Room Worksheet

Total Drops for this Wiring Closet

Optical Fiber Connector

Dual Socket Clips

Two data connectors are required for each faceplate (any type).

One telephone jack connector is required for each type 2 and 2S faceplate.
* Record the port number for the type 2 and 2S faceplates.

** Record the port number for the Wall box used.

Distribution Panels

Equipment Racks

Rack Grounding Kits

Cable Label Packages

Form 3

Wiring Closet/Controller Room Worksheet

Building _____
Floor _____
Worksheet_____

Cable Routes within a Single Building

	Wiring Closet Location/ Floor	Wiring Closet or Controller Room Location/ Floor	Number of Cables	Cable Length	Cable Requirements					
					Type 1	Type 1 P	Type 5	Faceplate Devices 1 / 1S / 1W		
1										
2										
3										
4										
5										
6										
7										
8										
9										
10										
11										
12										
13										
14										
15										
Totals										

Cable Routes Between Buildings

	Wiring Closet Location/ Floor	Surge Surpressor Location/ Floor	Wiring Closet or Controller Room Location/ Floor/ Building	Length of Indoor Cable in this Building	Cable Requirements						
					Type 1 No./Total Feet	Type 1P No./Total Feet	Length of Outdoor Cable	Type 1 Outdoor No./Total Feet	Surge Suppressors
1									
2									
3									
4									
Totals									

Data Connectors _____

Distribution Panels_____
Distribution Rocks _____

Rock Grounding Kit _____
Cable Label Packages _____

Form 4

IBM Token Ring Network Planning Forms

Rack Inventory Chart

Wiring Closet Number _____
Rack Number _____
Date _____
Planner's Initials _____

Instructions

Fill out a Rack Inventory Chart for each equipment rack.

1. Enter the wiring closet location number, the equipment rack identification number, and the planner's initials.

2. Using the template for the Rack Inventory Chart that came with this manual, draw an outline of each component that will be installed in the rack.

3. The slots at the bottom of the distribution panel template are used only for the lowermost distribution panel in a rack. The slots indicate that there are 38.1 mm (1-1/2 in.) between that panel and the next unit in the rack.

4. Write the unit identification number on each component on the chart.

Example:

Form 1

IBM 8228 Cabling Chart

Date _____ _____

Section 1 Identification

Unit	Building _____	Rack-mounted ☐
Number _____	Location _____	Wall-mounted ☐ Ring _____

Section 2 Receptacle Connections

Receptacle	1	2	3	4	5	6	7	8
Connect to:								

Device								

Section 3 Ring Connections

A. Connect RI of this 8228 to: _____

B. Connect RO of this 8228 to: _____

Form 2

IBM 8230 Cabling Chart

Section 1 Identification   Unit Number [＿＿＿＿]   Date [＿＿＿＿]

Check Appropriate Box

Ring Data Rate	☐ 4 Mbps	☐ 16 Mbps
Lobe Cable Type	☐ Unshielded Twisted Pair	☐ Data Grade Media
Voltage Setting	☐ 115 v	☐ 230 v
RI Module	☐ Copper	☐ Optical Fiber
RO Module	☐ Copper	☐ Optical Fiber
	☐ Wrap Plug	☐ 16/4 Media Filter

Physical Location

Building Number [＿＿＿＿]

Wiring Closet [＿＿＿＿]

Rack Number [＿＿＿＿]

Ring Number [＿＿＿＿]

Addresses

PO Address [＿＿＿＿]

PI Address [＿＿＿＿]

S Address [＿＿＿＿]

Section 2 Ring Connections

(Copper RI) [＿＿＿＿]

A. Connect RI of this 8230 to:
☐ DMG-to-Type 3 Filter
☐ 16/4 Repeater Filter

(Optical Fiber RI)

Orange [＿＿＿＿]

Black [＿＿＿＿]

(Copper RO) [＿＿＿＿]

B. Connect RO of this 8230 to:
☐ DMG-to-Type 3 Filter
   16/4 Repeater Filter

(Optical Fiber RO)

Orange [＿＿＿＿]

Black [＿＿＿＿]

Section 1 Lobe Attachment Module Connections

Number of Lobe Attachment Modules connected
to this 8230   [＿＿＿＿]

Form 3

LAM 1

Receptacle	1	2	3	4	5	6	7	8	9	10
Connect to:										
Device:										

Receptacle	11	12	13	14	15	16	17	18	19	20
Connect to:										
Device:										

LAM 2

Receptacle	1	2	3	4	5	6	7	8	9	10
Connect to:										
Device:										

Receptacle	11	12	13	14	15	16	17	18	19	20
Connect to:										
Device:										

LAM 3

Receptacle	1	2	3	4	5	6	7	8	9	10
Connect to:										
Device:										

Receptacle	11	12	13	14	15	16	17	18	19	20
Connect to:										
Device:										

LAM 4

Receptacle	1	2	3	4	5	6	7	8	9	10
Connect to:										
Device:										

Receptacle	11	12	13	14	15	16	17	18	19	20
Connect to:										
Device:										

Form 3 *Continued*

IBM 8218 Cabling Chart

Section 1

Date _____

Ring _____

_____ Unit Number _____

Building _____

Location _____

Rack-Mounted ☐

Wall-Mounted ☐

Section 2

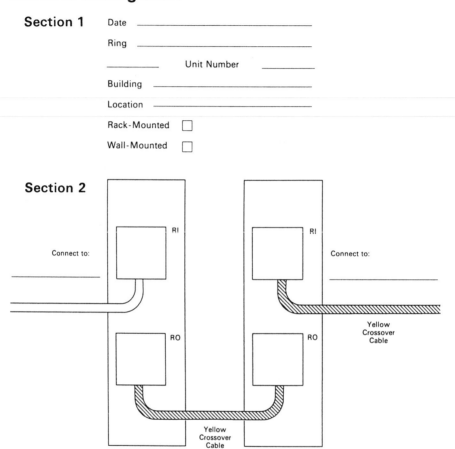

Connect to:
_____

RI

RO

Connect to:
_____

RI

RO

Yellow
Crossover
Cable

Yellow
Crossover
Cable

Form 4

326

IBM 8219 Cabling Chart

Section 1   Date _____

Ring _____

_____   Unit Number   _____

_____   Building   _____

_____   Location   _____

☐   Rack-Mounted   ☐

Section 2   ☐   Wall-Mounted   ☐

O-O   O-O

DP or MB
Connections

B-B   B-B

Receive   Receive
O   B
B   O
Transmit   Transmit

Connect to: Connect to:

_____   _____

Yellow   Yellow
☐ Crossover   Crossover
Cable   B = Black   Cable
or   O = Orange
☐ Patch Cable   MB = Optical Fiber Cable Mounting Bracket
DP = Distribution Panel

Form 5

327

Ring Sequence Chart

Ring Number _____   Date _____   Page ____ of ____

cable from _____

on page _____

(component) _____
(location) _____

(component) _____
(location) _____

(component) _____
(location) _____

(component) _____
(location) _____

(component) _____
(location) _____

(component) _____
(location) _____

(component) _____
(location) _____

cable to _____

on page _____

Suggested Abbreviations:

DP - Distribution Panel
P - Patch Cable
YCP - (Yellow) Crossover Patch Cable
OFP - Optical Fiber Patch Cable

FP - Faceplate
MB - Optical Fiber
     Mounting Bracket
SS - Surge Suppressor

MSAU - IBM 8228 Multistation Access Unit
RPTR - IBM 8218 Copper Repeater
OFRPTR - IBM 8219 Optical Fiber Repeater

Form 6

Physical Location to Adapter Address Locator Chart

Physical Location	Adapter Address	Device Identification	Ring Number	IBM Access Unit No.

Form 7

329

Adapter Address to Physical Location Locator Chart

Adapter Address	Physical Location	Device Identification	Ring Number	IBM Access Unit No.

Form 8

AT&T StarLAN 10 Network Forms

StarLAN 10 Network Wiring Closet Design Form

Organization: _____   **Date** _____

Building: _____   **Sheet** _____ of _____

Network Designer: _____

Building Wiring: _____

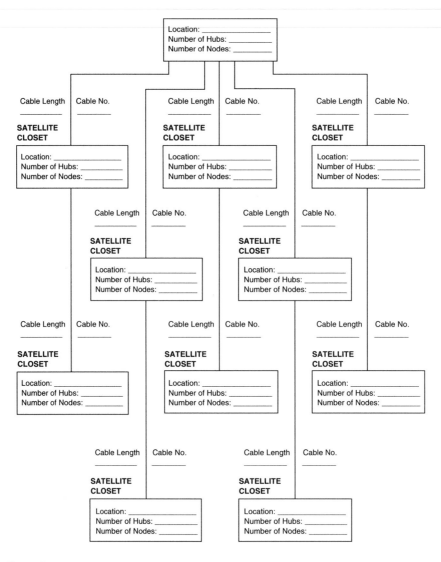

Form 1

StarLAN 10 Network Hub Unit Design Form

Organization: _____   Date: _____
Hub Location: _____   Hub ID: _____
Network Designer: _____   Building: _____
Hub Serial Number: _____   Hub Purchase Date: _____

IN or OUT JACK 1:
Node Name or Hub ID: _____
User: _____
Location: _____ Cord Length: _____

JACK 2:
Node Name: _____
User: _____
Location: _____ Cord Length: _____

JACK 3:
Node Name: _____
User: _____
Location: _____ Cord Length: _____

JACK 4:
Node Name: _____
User: _____
Location: _____ Cord Length: _____

JACK 5:
Node Name: _____
User: _____
Location: _____ Cord Length: _____

JACK 6:
Node Name: _____
User: _____
Location: _____ Cord Length: _____

JACK 7:
Node Name: _____
User: _____
Location: _____ Cord Length: _____

JACK 8:
Node Name: _____
User: _____
Location: _____ Cord Length: _____

JACK 9:
Node Name: _____
User: _____
Location: _____ Cord Length: _____

JACK 10:
Node Name: _____
User: _____
Location: _____ Cord Length: _____

JACK 11:
Node Name: _____
User: _____
Location: _____ Cord Length: _____

AUI PORT:
Node Name: _____
User: _____
Location: _____ Cable Length: _____

NOTES:
_____
_____
_____
_____

Form 2

StarLAN 10 Network Fiber Hub Unit Design Form

Organization: _____ Date: _____
Fiber Hub Location: _____ Fiber Hub ID: _____
Network Designer: _____ Building: _____
Fiber Hub Serial Number: _____ Fiber Hub Purchase Date: _____

IN or OUT Jack
Optical Fiber Port 1 — Optical Fiber Port 2
Optical Fiber Port 3 — Optical Fiber Port 4
Optical Fiber Port 5 — Optical Fiber Port 6
AUI Port

IN or OUT JACK:
Node Name or Hub ID: _____
User: _____
Location: _____ Cord Length: ____

OPTICAL FIBER PORT 1:
Node Name: _____
User: _____
Location: _____ Fiber Length: ____

OPTICAL FIBER PORT 2:
Node Name: _____
User: _____
Location: _____ Fiber Length: ____

OPTICAL FIBER PORT 3:
Node Name: _____
User: _____
Location: _____ Fiber Length: ____

OPTICAL FIBER PORT 4:
Node Name: _____
User: _____
Location: _____ Fiber Length: ____

OPTICAL FIBER PORT 5:
Node Name: _____
User: _____
Location: _____ Fiber Length: ____

OPTICAL FIBER PORT 6:
Node Name: _____
User: _____
Location: _____ Fiber Length: ____

AUI PORT:
Node Name: _____
User: _____
Location: _____ Cable Length: ____

NOTES:
_____
_____
_____
_____

Form 3

StarLAN 10 Network Node Record Form

Name and Location

User: _____

Primary Server: _____Login: _____

Office Location: _____

Phone Number: _____Node Type: _____

Node Function: _____Node Name: _____

NAU Type: _____

NAU Network Physical Address: _____

NAU Serial Number: _____NAU Purchase Date: _____

NAU Diskette Serial Number: _____

Computer

Operating System and Version/Release: _____

Network Software Package(s): _____

_____

Software Serial Number(s): _____

Purchase Date(s) _____

NOTES: _____

_____

_____

_____

_____

Form 4

Data Communication and LAN Interfaces

Interface Connectors

If your equipment has this connector type	For this interface		If your equipment has this connector type	For this interface
DB25 (4-, 12-, or 24-pin)	RS-232(V.24), RS-530 IBM® Parallel		IEEE-488	GPIB, HPIB
DB37	RS-449, 442, 423; Bernoulli®		M/34	V.35
DB50	Dataproducts® Datapoint®, UNIVAC®, and others		M/50	Dataproducts, UNIVAC, DEC™, and others
DB15 / High Density DB15	Texas Instruments®, NCR® POS, Ethernet IBM PS/2™ (High Density)		BNC / BNC and TNC	Coaxial (BNC or TNC), WANG®, Dual Coaxial (BNC and TNC)
DB9	449 Secondary, ATARI®, DAA, and Video Interfaces		Twinaxial	IBM AS/400™, Systems 34, 36, 38, 5520, and others
5-Pin Din / Mini 6-Pin Din	IBM PC Keyboard (5-Pin) PS/2 Keyboard (Mini 6-Pin)		Telco	Telephone (Voice and data)
Mini 8-Pin Din	Apple® Macintosh®		RJ-11 / RJ-45	Voice Telephone (RJ-11) Data Telephone (RJ-45)
36-Pin	Parallel printers: Centronics®, EPSON®, Gemini®, and others		Modified Modular Jack (MMJ)	DEC423 DECconnect™ System
Mate-N-Lok®	Current Loop, Telephone		Barrier Block	Utility current loop, and other 2- or 4-wires

Form 1

(Reprinted by permission, Black Box Corporation, Pittsburgh, PA © Copyright, 1989. All rights reserved.)

RS-449 and RS-232 Interfaces

RS-449 Interface

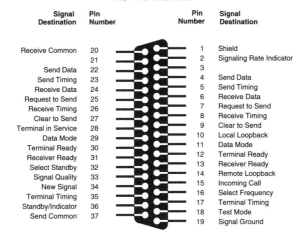

Signal Destination	Pin Number		Pin Number	Signal Destination
Receive Common	20		1	Shield
	21		2	Signaling Rate Indicator
Send Data	22		3	
Send Timing	23		4	Send Data
Receive Data	24		5	Send Timing
Request to Send	25		6	Receive Data
Receive Timing	26		7	Request to Send
Clear to Send	27		8	Receive Timing
Terminal in Service	28		9	Clear to Send
Data Mode	29		10	Local Loopback
Terminal Ready	30		11	Data Mode
Receiver Ready	31		12	Terminal Ready
Select Standby	32		13	Receiver Ready
Signal Quality	33		14	Remote Loopback
New Signal	34		15	Incoming Call
Terminal Timing	35		16	Select Frequency
Standby/Indicator	36		17	Terminal Timing
Send Common	37		18	Test Mode
			19	Signal Ground

RS-232 Interface

Signal Destination	Pin Number		Pin Number	Signal Destination
Secondary Transmitted Data	14		1	Protective Ground
DCE Transmitter Signal Element Timing	15		2	Transmitted Data
Secondary Received Data	16		3	Received Data
Receiver Signal Element Timing	17		4	Request to Send
	18		5	Clear to Send
Secondary Request to Send	19		6	Data Set Ready
Data Terminal Ready	20		7	Signal Ground/Common Return
Signal Quality Detector	21		8	Received Line Signal Detector
Ring Indicator	22		9	+ Voltage
Data Signal Rate Selector	23		10	− Voltage
DTE Transmitter Signal Element Timing	24		11	
	25		12	Secondary Received Line Signal Detector
			13	Secondary Clear to Send

Form 2

339

Pinout Table for EIA RS-449, EIA RS-232/CCITT V.24

9 PIN AUX.	37 PIN A	37 PIN B	RS-449 CIRCUIT	RS-449 DESCRIPTION	25 PIN	EIA-RS-232C CIRCUIT	CCITT-V.24 CIRCUIT	RS-232 DESCRIPTION	GND	DATA From DCE	DATA To DCE	CONTROL From DCE	CONTROL To DCE	TIMI From DCE
1	1			Shield	1	AA	101	Protective Ground	X					
5	19		SG	Signal Ground	7	AB	102	Signal Ground/Common Return	X					
9	37		SC	Send Common			102a	DTE Common	X					
6	20		RC	Receive Common			102b	DCE Common	X					
	4	22	SD	Send Data	2	BA	103	Transmitted Data			X			
	6	24	RD	Receive Data	3	BB	104	Received Data		X				
	7	25	RS	Request to Send	4	CA	105	Request to Send					X	
	9	27	CS	Clear to Send	5	CB	106	Clear to Send				X		
	11	29	DM	Data Mode	6	CC	107	Data Set Ready				X		
	12	30	TR	Terminal Ready	20	CD	108.2	Data Terminal Ready					X	
	15		IC	Incoming Call	22	CE	125	Ring Indicator				X		
	13	31	RR	Receiver Ready	8	CF	109	Received Line Signal Detector				X		
	33		SQ	Signal Quality	21	CG	110	Signal Quality Detector				X		
	16		SR	Signaling Rate Selector	23	CH	111	Data Signal Rate Selector (DTE)					X	
	2		SI	Signaling Rate Indicator	23	CI	112	Data Signal Rate Selector (DCE)				X		
	17	35	TT	Terminal Timing	24	DA	113	Transmitter Signal Element Timing (DTE)						
	5	23	ST	Send Timing	15	DB	114	Transmitter Signal Element Timing (DCE)						X
	8	26	RT	Receive Timing	17	DD	115	Receiver Signal Element Timing (DCE)						X
3			SSD	Secondary Send Data	14	SBA	118	Secondary Transmitted Data			X			
4			SRD	Secondary Receive Data	16	SBB	119	Secondary Received Data		X				
7			SRS	Secondary Request to Send	19	SCA	120	Secondary Request to Send					X	
8			SCS	Secondary Clear to Send	13	SCB	121	Secondary Clear to Send				X		
2			SRR	Secondary Receiver Ready	12	SCF	122	Secondary Received Line Signal Detector				X		
	10		LL	Local Loopback			141	Local Loopback					X	
	14		RL	Remote Loopback			140	Remote Loopback					X	
	18		TM	Test Mode			142	Test Indicator				X		
	32		SS	Select Standby			116	Select Standby					X	
	36		SB	Standby Indicator			117	Standby Indicator				X		
	16		SF	Select Frequency			126	Select Transmit Frequency				X		
	28		IS	Terminal in Service									X	
	34		NS	New Signal									X	

Form 3

340

V.35 Interface

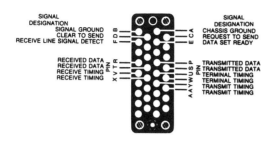

PIN	NAME	To DTE	To DCE	FUNCTION
A	FG			Frame (or protective) ground
B	SG			Signal (or reference) ground
C	RTS		→	Request to send
D	CTS	←		Clear to send
E	DSR	←		Data set ready
F	RLSD	←		Received line signal
H	DTR		→	Data terminal ready
J	RI	←		Ring indicator
K	LT		→	Local test
R				Received data (Sig. A)
	RD	←		
T				Received data (Sig. B)
V				Serial clock receive (Sig. A)
	SCR	←		
X				Serial clock receive (Sig. B)
P				Send data (Sig. A)
	SD		→	
S				Send data (Sig. B)
U				Serial clock xmit ext. (Sig. A)
	SCTE		→	
W				Serial clock xmit ext. (Sig. B)
Y				Serial clock transmit (Sig. A)
	SCT	←		
a				Serial clock transmit (Sig. B)
h, i, j, k, m, n				Unused
L, M, N, Z, b, c, d, f, g				Unused

Form 4

Centronics Parallel Interface

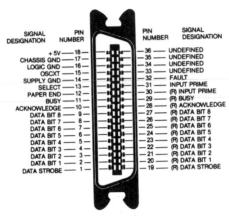

SIGNAL DESIGNATION	PIN NUMBER	PIN NUMBER	SIGNAL DESIGNATION
+ 5V	18	36	UNDEFINED
CHASSIS GND	17	35	UNDEFINED
LOGIC GND	16	34	UNDEFINED
OSCXT	15	33	UNDEFINED
SUPPLY GND	14	32	FAULT
SELECT	13	31	INPUT PRIME
PAPER END	12	30	(R) INPUT PRIME
BUSY	11	29	(R) BUSY
ACKNOWLEDGE	10	28	(R) ACKNOWLEDGE
DATA BIT 8	9	27	(R) DATA BIT 8
DATA BIT 7	8	26	(R) DATA BIT 7
DATA BIT 6	7	25	(R) DATA BIT 6
DATA BIT 5	6	24	(R) DATA BIT 5
DATA BIT 4	5	23	(R) DATA BIT 4
DATA BIT 3	4	22	(R) DATA BIT 3
DATA BIT 2	3	21	(R) DATA BIT 2
DATA BIT 1	2	20	(R) DATA BIT 1
DATA STROBE	1	19	(R) DATA STROBE

(R) INDICATES SIGNAL GROUND RETURN

Signal Pin No.	Return Pin No.	Signal	Direction (with ref. to Printer	Description
1	19	STROBE	In	STROBE pulse (negative going) enables reding data.
2	20	DATA 1	In	1st to 8th bits of parallel data.
3	21	DATA 2	In	Each signal is at HIGH level when data is logical
4	22	DATA 3	In	"1" and LOW when
5	23	DATA 4	In	logical "0."
6	24	DATA 5	In	
7	25	DATA 6	In	
8	26	DATA 7	In	
9	27	DATA 8	In	
10	28	ACKNLG	Out	LOW indicates that data has been received and that the printer is ready to accept other data.
11	29	BUSY	Out	HIGH indicates that the printer cannot receive data.

Note: Pins 12, 13, 14, 15, 18, 31, 32, 34, 35, and 36 vary in function depending upon application; they are commonly used for printer auxiliary controls, and error handling and indication.
Pins 16 and 17 are commonly used for logic ground and chassis ground, respectively.

Form 5

(Reprinted by permission, Black Box Corporation, Pittsburgh, PA © Copyright, 1989. All rights reserved.)

Data Communications, PC, and LAN Diagnostic Software

We have collected a number of programs for your use in diagnosing PC and LAN faults. Please understand that these programs are public domain or shareware—we *do not* offer any license or guarantee regarding any program's performance. Please use these programs with some caution.

Some programs use on-screen documentation, others have documentation files with a .DOC or.TXT extension. You should not attempt to use any program without first printing out and reading the documentation.

The files on the disk are

ARCDIAG:	ARCNET diagnostic program.
BAUDCHG:	Allows user to change baud rate of a program.
BRKBOX:	Displays the RS-232 signals of the COM1 or COM2 ports.
CHIPS:	Benchmark program for CPU MIPS and performance.
CI:	Provides CPU information.
D'SCOPE:	Turns a PC into a data scope or data line monitor.

DIAGS: Serial port, parallel port, video and memory diagnostics. Allows the currently used IRQ lines to be determined.

IRQR: Reports status of 8259 hardware interrupt channels.

EQUIP: Displays the current equipment configuration for the PC.

RS232:   Displays status of COM1 or COM2 signals on the CRT.

SETUP: Sets up printer, CRT, and serial port parameters. Will also redirect printer to a serial port.

SPEED99   Performs CPU speed and relative performance tests.

SWAPCOM: Swaps between COM1 and COM2 ports; executing a second time will swap the ports back.

SWAPPRT   Swaps between LPT1 and LPT2 ports; executing a second time will swap the ports back.

VSI   Visual display of the PC's current configuration.

Index

A Library of Technical References
from M&T Books

LAN Protocol Handbook
by Mark A. Miller, P.E.

This is the extraordinary companion volume to *LAN Troubleshooting Handbook*, a volume that specifically illustrates the techniques of protocol analysis — the step-by-step process of unraveling LAN software failures. You'll get the details of how networks transmit frames of information between workstations and create LAN performance measurements, protocol analysis methods, and protocol analyzer products. Individual chapters discuss the most popular networks including Net-Ware and VINES. Also discusses Token-Ring and AppleTalk. The optional set of six demo disks surveys six protocol analyzers, allowing you to demo them and choose the one that best suits your needs. A valuable reference tool. 324 pp.

Book	$34.95	#0990
6-Disk Set	$39.95	#1148

Level: Advanced

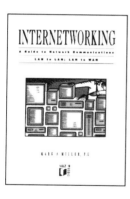

Internetworking
A Guide to Network Communications
LAN to LAN; LAN to WAN
by Mark A. Miller, P.E.

This is how to put it all together — from "big picture" to vital details, from LAN to WAN and back again! Discover the essentials of building communications facilities such as leased lines and T-1 circuits and find out which is most viable for your network. Plus a guide to internetworking standards, designs and applications, as well as in-depth discussions of the function of repeaters, bridges, routers, and gateways. Also examined: x.25, TCP/IP and XNS protocols in addition to the specific internetworking capabilities and inter-operability constraints of the most popular networks. An essential guide for network managers working with internetworks. 425 pp.

Book	$34.95	#1431

Level: Beginning - Advanced

1-800-628-9658

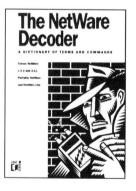

A Library of Technical References from M&T Books

NetWare User's Guide, Version 2.2
by Edward Liebing

Everyone who uses Novell's NetWare needs a little help once in awhile. Now you can get the most from your network by having a complete guide to network operations at your fingertips. Detailed explanations of all utilities and network printing guide you every step of the way. If you're an advanced Netware user you'll appreciate the troubleshooting section that helps you solve and prevent network problems before they become real headaches. Covers versions 2.2. 662 pp.

Book	$29.95	#2357

Level: Beginning – Intermediate

NetWare Programmer's Guide
by John T. McCann

Covers all aspects of programming in the NetWare environment — from basic planning to complex application debugging. This book offers practical tips and tricks for creating and porting applications to NetWare. NetWare programmers developing simple applications for a single LAN or intricate programs for multi-site internetworked systems will find this book a valuable reference to have on hand. All source code is available on disk in MS-PC/DOS format. 425 pp.

Book	$34.95	#1520
Book/Disk	$44.95	#1547

Level: Advanced

1-800-628-9658

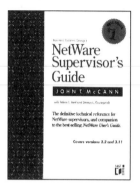

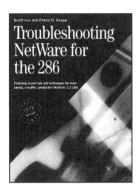

A Library of Technical References
from M&T Books

Delivering Electronic Mail: Installing and Troubleshooting Electronic Mail Systems
by Phillip Robinson

Network administrators: if you're responsible for installing, maintaining, and troubleshooting an electronic mail system, this is the one for you! Addresses concerns of choosing a system and provides a thorough overview of the different types of E-Mail systems available. Helps you select the system most appropriate for your needs. 352 pp.

Book $29.95   #1709

Level: Beginning - Advanced

Printing on NetWare
by Stephen Kalman

Get into this complete guide to the why and how-to of network printing and you'll find out how to successfully set up and maintain a printing environment. Procedures for installing printer servers, configuring printers, and establishing print queues. Case studies. Covers NetWare 2.2, 3.11, and Windows. 381 pp.

Book $26.95   #2578

Level: Beginning-Advanced

ORDER FORM

To Order:

Return this form with your payment to M&T Books, 115 West 18th Street, New York, NY 10011 or **call toll-free 1-800-628-9658.**

ITEM #	DESCRIPTION	DISK	PRICE

Subtotal	
NY residents add sales tax ____%	
Add $4.50 per item for shipping and handling	
TOTAL	

Charge my:

☐ **Visa**
☐ **MasterCard**
☐ **AmExpress**

☐ **Check enclosed, payable to M&T Books.**

CARD NO. _____

SIGNATURE _____ EXP. DATE _____

NAME _____

ADDRESS _____

CITY _____

STATE _____ ZIP _____

M&T GUARANTEE: If your are not satisfied with your order for any reason, return it to us within 25 days of receipt for a full refund. Note: Refunds on disks apply only when returned with book within guarantee period. Disks damaged in transit or defective will be promptly replaced, but cannot be exchanged for a disk from a different title.

Tell us what you think and we'll send you a free M&T Books catalog

It is our goal at M&T Books to produce the best technical books available. But you can help us make our books even better by letting us know what you think about this particular title. Please take a moment to fill out this card and mail it to us. Your opinion is appreciated.

Tell us about yourself
Name_____
Company_____
Address_____
City_____
State/Zip_____

Title of this book?
_____

Where did you purchase this book?
☐ Bookstore
☐ Catalog
☐ Direct Mail
☐ Magazine Ad
☐ Postcard Pack
☐ Other

Why did you choose this book?
☐ Recommended
☐ Read book review
☐ Read ad/catalog copy
☐ Responded to a special offer
☐ M&T Books' reputation
☐ Price
☐ Nice Cover

How would you rate the overall content of this book?
☐ Excellent
☐ Good
☐ Fair
☐ Poor

Why?
_____
_____

What chapters did you find valuable?
_____
_____
_____

What did you find least useful?
_____
_____
_____

What topic(s) would you add to future editions of this book?
_____
_____
_____

What other titles would you like to see M&T Books publish?
_____
_____
_____

Which format do you prefer for the optional disk?
☐ 5.25"   ☐ 3.5"

Any other comments?
_____
_____
_____

☐ Check here for
M&T Books Catalog

M&T ▰▰▰
BOOKS

3109